Regards

R. William Weisberger

SPECULATIVE FREEMASONRY
AND
THE ENLIGHTENMENT

A STUDY OF THE CRAFT IN LONDON,
PARIS, PRAGUE, AND VIENNA

1528624

by

R. WILLIAM WEISBERGER

EAST EUROPEAN MONOGRAPHS, BOULDER
DISTRIBUTED BY COLUMBIA UNIVERSITY PRESS, NEW YORK
1993

EAST EUROPEAN MONOGRAPHS, NO. CCCLXVII

For: Patty, Carolyn, Alice, Sidney, and Phil

Contents

V. CONCLUSION: AN EVALUATION OF EIGHTEENTH CENTURY SPECULATIVE FREEMASONRY IN LONDON, PARIS, PRAGUE, AND VIENNA

III. PARISIAN MASONRY, THE LODGE OF THE NINE SISTERS, AND THE FRENCH ENLIGHTENMENT

IV. PRAGUE AND VIENNESE FREEMASONRY, THE ENLIGHTENMENT, AND THE OPERATIONS OF THE TRUE HARMONY LODGE OF VIENNA

Foreword

I especially am indebted to Dr. Seymour Drescher and Dr. Steven Vardy for their advice in the publication of this study. I also am indebted to the late Dr. James Clarke. Without assistance from other individuals, this work could not have been published. I wish to thank Keith Arrington of the Iowa Masonic Grand Lodge Library and Roy Goodman of the American Philosophical Society. Librarians from Princeton, the University of Pennsylvania, and the University of Pittsburgh gave me invaluable assistance. Finally, my deepest gratitude is extended to my wife, Patricia B. Weisberger, and to Dr. Stephen Fischer-Galati, the editor of the East European Monograph Series.

I. INTRODUCTION

A. The Problem and Thesis

My study is involved with Speculative Freemasonry during the eighteenth century. Speculative Masons significantly differed from their Operative counterparts. Operative Masons traced their origins to the ancient world, were known as skilled artisans and builders, and in European history designed and erected important cathedrals and state buildings. Speculative Masons, on the other hand, operated secretly in bodies known as lodges and staged ceremonies or rituals to dramatize important cultural and moral concepts. Speculative Freemasonry emerged in 1717 in England and between approximately 1725 and 1750 spread to Europe. Masonic lodges appeared in Paris in 1725, in Prague in 1726, and in Vienna in 1742.[1]

My work focuses on Masonry in four European cities and attempts to demonstrate major affinities between the Craft and eighteenth century European culture and society. This study investigates Enlightenment patterns appearing in England, France, and the Habsburg Empire and examines the rites and organization of Masonry in these three states.[2] It also examines the cultural activities of London, Parisian, Prague, and Viennese Masons and assesses them in relation to the Enlightenment.

This cultural and institutional study of Masonry and the Enlightenment emphasizes four facets of the Craft. The first facet pertains to how lodges functioned in London, Paris, Prague, and Vienna. By electing their officers and members, by recognizing the natural liberties of their members, and by enacting laws by majority rule, lodges in these four cities operated according to important Enlightenment political doctrines. These lodges consequently helped their members in many instances to acquire leadership skills.[3] The lodges also performed social functions. These bodies operated as voluntary associations and as clubs and in many respects helped to meet the needs of urban life. Masonic lodges became known as communicative centers and as amiable meeting places. Lodges also provided financial assistance to their members and engaged in philanthropic enterprises.[4]

The second facet of my study pertains to the cultural importance of Masonic degrees. Masonic rites were associated with two important cultural functions. English, French, and Habsburg degrees embodied and offered vivid visual explanations of significant ancient and modern cultural tenets; their degrees thus served as a valuable vehicle for the diffusion of Enlightenment ideologies. It will be argued, as well, that important symbols and teachings conveyed in Masonic rites constituted the basis of a civil religion. The rites of the order helped to imbue Masons with ethical and secular principles, thus influencing their attitudes towards and their behavior in the state.[5] The study will suggest how some Masons viewed ideas connected with the civil religion and with the Enlightenment.

The third aspect of this monograph concerns the activities of London, Parisian, Prague, and Viennese Masons. As will be seen, most Masons from these cities performed valuable cultural functions; they exhibited a compelling interest in and acted to promote Enlightenment ideologies. Numerous Masons participated in learned societies, published works about Enlightenment concepts, and viewed the Craft as a vehicle for the diffusion of eighteenth century culture. Most members of the Craft were minor aristocratic and bourgeois gentlemen who perceived Masonry as an important Enlightenment institution, but a few Masons were eminent Enlightenment thinkers.[6]

The fourth facet of my study relates to important ramifications of belonging to the Masonic order. Masons in Paris and Vienna differed from their counterparts in London who had many cultural institutions with which they could affiliate. As will be seen, Parisian and Viennese Masons thus felt a need to establish Masonic learned societies and utilized these bodies to promote the arts and sciences and to sponsor special cultural activities. Some English, French, and Habsburg lodges and Masons became involved with special projects. They funded schools, libraries, museums, and hospitals. Masonry in several cases became identified with political movements and with other causes.

B. The Historiography of Eighteenth Century Masonry

Two schools of historiography dominate the study of Freemasonry during the eighteenth century. The proponents of the conspiracy theory constitute the first school and, as exemplified in the writings of Barruel and Cochin, argue that the rites of Masonry were associated with and stimulated revolutionary activities. These two writers maintain that the *philosophes* and Masons used Masonic lodges and reading circles as agencies to diffuse the subversive doctrines of the Enlightenment, to undermine conservative institutions in European states, and to wage revolution.[7] The views of the puppet theory of history make entertaining reading and suggest some important insights. Advocates of the conspiracy theory correctly suggest that the study of the social composition of Masonic lodges is required to ascertain the motivations and operations of personnel involved with the order. By arguing that Masonry served as the major vehicle for the launching of the 1789 French Revolution, writers of the conspiracy school indirectly exhibit their respect for the order and tend to distort its importance.

Ritualists, who for the most part are Masons, constitute the second major school of historiography. *Symbolical Masonry* by H. L. Haywood, *The Three Degrees and the Great Symbols of Masonry* by Joseph Newton, and *Morals and Dogma* by Albert Pike are considered classics of Masonic literature. The studies of these three authors are quite reliable, offering detailed explications of the doctrines and symbols of the Craft. These and similar works revolve around the premise that Masonic lodges function explicitly for the purpose of staging rites. Most Masonic ritualists, however, have failed to examine the degrees of the order within the context of the eighteenth century.

Several scholars not affiliated with the Craft correctly suggest the ideological and sociological importance of Masonic rites. To Hobsbawm, Masonry is a ritual movement; the degrees of the Craft are conferred to explain its doctrines and symbols and to enable its members to identify with the Masonic community.[8] Abner Cohen and Georg Simmel agree with Hobsbawm about the concept of community in Masonry. They maintain that the ritualistic teachings of the Craft help to produce cohesion and solidarity within Masonry. These two sociologists also believe that the rites of the order revolve around universal moral doctrines and well explain in symbolical terms the place of man in nature and society.[9] Simmel, who wrote about the sociology of secret societies, and Cohen, who is known for his account of Masonic lodges in Sierre Leone, offer perceptive views applicable to the study of eighteenth century Masonry. The ideas of these two scholars help to suggest how eighteenth century Masonic rites served as a means for diffusing cultural and moral concepts and how Masonic lodges at that time reflected distinctive male bonding patterns.

There are several reasons why eighteenth century English, French, and Habsburg lodges and their members have not been adequately studied. It has been difficult, in many cases, for investigators to obtain evidence about eighteenth century lodges. Although recorded, the minutes and rosters of numerous lodges either were lost or destroyed. The absence of pertinent primary materials is especially apparent in the case of early eighteenth century England. London lodges, for the most part, did not record their minutes, evidently wished to preserve the private and secret character of Masonry, and thus are difficult institutions for researchers to examine. There are, however, some membership lists of London lodges during the Augustan Era. A few articles appearing in *Ars Quatuor Coronatorum* about eighteenth century London members of the Craft, the Masonic histories of Coil, Findel, and Robbins, and the biographical accounts and writings of London Masons provide researchers with information about the activities of Masons in the British capital and suggest some insights about the lodges with which these London Masons were affiliated.

There are only a few works about eighteenth century lodges and Masons in the Habsburg Empire and in France. The voluminous *Geschichte der Freimaurerei in Oesterreich-Ungarn* by Ludwig Abafi, based on the few extant primary sources about Habsburg Masonry, describes in some cases the operations of Prague and Viennese lodges, lists many members of lodges in these two studies, and proved to be indispensable for my study. Three recent scholarly works treat the Craft in eighteenth century France. *Francs-Maçons et Ateliers Parisiens de la Grande Loge de France au XVIIIe Siècle* by Alain Le Bihan offers some insights into the operations of Parisian lodges, and, more importantly, contains numerous biographical accounts of less known Masons in the French capital. *Les Ducs Sous L'Acacia* and *Histoire de la Franc-Maçonnerie Française: École de l'Egalité, 1725–1799* by Pierre Chevallier adequately survey major developments arising in eighteenth century French Masonic History, comment on the operations of some Parisian lodges and on the activities of their members, and allude to the importance of the Parisian Masonic learned society known as the Lodge of the Nine Sisters.[10]

The major problem involving the study of the Nine Sisters concerns the lack of evidence about the structural operations of this lodge. The Lodge of the Nine Sisters, in differing from ordinary Masonic bodies, was established in 1776 to foster the study of the arts and sciences, but regretfully neither kept minutes nor published journals. An examination of the important cultural and organizational operations of this lodge thus requires probing the writings of and secondary sources about its members. An analysis of this Masonic learned society further entails investigating the few accounts written about its history.

Une Loge Maçonnique d'avant 1789 by the nineteenth century French grand lodge administrator Louis Amiable is the most extensive account of the Nine Sisters. This work has several strengths. The study of Amiable is written in light of evidence obtained, for the most part, from eighteenth century memoirs, biographical accounts, and the few Masonic documents available to him. By utilizing these sources for his study, Amiable is able to recount some major developments arising during regular meetings and during banquets of the Nine Sisters. Amiable also provides his readers with illuminating accounts of minor intellectuals affiliated with the Nine Sisters but tends to exaggerate the importance of the accomplishments of lodge members.

There are weaknesses, however, in the study of Amiable. It suffers from the lack of topical arrangement and from that of direction. Moreover, it reveals the anticlerical sentiments of its author. Nor does Amiable satisfactorily explain the relationship of the Nine Sisters to the Grand Orient or to local lodges either in Paris or in France. Amiable does not refer to elites functioning in Masonry or in Paris and does not suggest why Masons from specific cultural groups wished to belong to the Nine Sisters. He mentions some special lodge sessions devoted to lectures about various topics but does not explain well how the Nine Sisters functioned as a learned society.

Several scholars have offered views about the Nine Sisters. An ardent advocate of the conspiracy theory, Bernard Fay perceives the Nine Sisters as having been a significant agency for the dissemination of eighteenth century radical doctrines and for the training of Masonic revolutionaries.[11] The views of Echeverria, Hahn, and Hazard differ from those of Fay. In their terse accounts of the Nine Sisters, these three scholars maintain that this lodge consisted of numerous *philosophes* and was involved with some important cultural activities.[12] In his short article about the Nine Sisters in the *Proceed-*

ings of the American Philosophical Society, Nicholas Hans summarizes rather well major findings of Amiable and briefly remarks about the operations and personnel of this lodge. He mentions that lodge meetings were devoted to cultural, ritualistic, and social activities and claims that the sponsoring of educational institutions in Paris represented the major achievement of the Nine Sisters in its role as a learned society. Hans devotes considerable attention to the Masonic career of Benjamin Franklin, emphasizing his contributions as Master of the Nine Sisters. Hans also lists approximately 100 members of the lodge, but, despite his access to primary sources of the American Philosophical Society, failed to consult works pertaining to the cultural functions of intellectuals associated with the Nine Sisters.[13]

There are numerous primary and secondary sources concerning the cultural functions of personnel affiliated with the Nine Sisters in the American Philosophical Society and in other libraries in the Philadelphia vicinity. As a consequence of the involvement of Franklin in the Nine Sisters, writings, memoirs, and some letters of lodge members are housed in Philadelphia collections. My research indicates that many members of the Nine Sisters participated in salons and learned societies and, for the most part, were affiliated with elites headed by Lalande, Bailly, Fourcroy, Franklin, Court de Gébelin, and Pilâtre de Rozier. My research also suggests that minor intellectuals of the Nine Sisters envisioned themselves as contributors to an international Masonic learned society and to eighteenth century culture.

Problems arise in the investigation of the Viennese True Harmony Lodge and in some cases resemble those encountered in writing about the Lodge of the Nine Sisters.[14] Reconstructing the history of the True Harmony Lodge is difficult, since the writings of and the secondary sources about most lodge members are not numerous. Like its Parisian counterpart, the Viennese True Harmony Lodge was created in 1781 to stimulate the study of the arts and sciences, but did not publish either its minutes or its roster. Proceedings of the True Harmony Lodge, however, were published and in part help the researcher to understand how this body functioned as a learned society.

What is lacking is a comprehensive account about the Masonic activities and the cultural operations of the True Harmony Lodge. The study of Abafi about Habsburg Freemasonry contains several valuable sections devoted to the workings of this lodge. Abafi mentions how the True Harmony functioned as a Masonic lodge; he shows that the True Harmony functioned under the jurisdiction of the Austrian Grand Lodge, conferred rites during its regular meetings, and held several special meetings with other lodges in the city to recruit new members.[15] Abafi lists approximately 150 Masons associated with the True Harmony, mentions some important articles appearing in the two journals sponsored by the lodge, but fails to specify how the True Harmony operated as a learned society.[16]

What is apparent is that the major function of the True Harmony Lodge in its role as a learned society was to publish a literary and a scientific journal. My research indicates that neither Masonic historians nor scholars have investigated the writings appearing in these two journals and that the True Harmony was the first Masonic lodge to publish journals devoted to literature, philosophy, music, and the sciences. As will be seen, contributors to the *Journal für Freymaurer*, edited by Alois Blumauer, wrote essays and poems to vindicate reform legislation instituted by Joseph II. Some lodge members published articles about the doctrines and symbols of Masonry, thus attempting to demonstrate the importance of Masonic philosophy to the intellectual life of the eighteenth century. My investigation of the volumes of the *Physikalische Arbeiten der Einträchtigen Freunde in Wien*, edited by Ignatz von Born, reveals that many scientists affiliated with the True Harmony published in this journal significant findings concerning geology. While encouraging members to contribute to its two journals, the True Harmony Lodge held few sessions devoted either to the presentation of papers or to the staging of special cultural events.

Several works contain accounts about the members of the True Harmony. Biographical portraits about many lodge members are in the volumes of *Biographisches Lexicon des Kaiserthums Oesterreich* by Constantin Wurzbach. *Jesuits and Jacobins* by Paul Bernard and *Mozart and Masonry* by Paul Nettl also provide details about the careers of numerous members of the True Harmony. Bernard and Nettl suggest that as a result of serving as a center of literary, reform, musical, and scientific activities, the True Harmony Lodge performed valuable cultural functions and succeeded in recruiting Masons from Vienna and from other cities in the Habsburg Empire.[17] My research suggests that most active and corresponding members of the True Harmony were associated with elites headed by Born, by Blumauer, or by Sonnenfels.

Similar to topics involved with the study of Masonic learned societies, many facets of eighteenth century European Freemasonry merit investigation but have not received attention from scholars. In some cases it is difficult for scholars not associated with the Craft to secure access to Masonic sources; they frequently meet with resistance from some Masonic librarians who are not permitted to open their files to researchers not holding membership in the order. Scholars who have been allowed to consult materials from Masonic libraries sometimes are disappointed to discover that Masonic sources either do not contain answers to certain questions or are missing. If and when Masonic libraries change their restrictive policies, numerous aspects of Masonry during the eighteenth century can be examined. Ample evidence is available in Masonic and scholarly libraries to show how the rites of Masonry explicated major tenets of eighteenth century culture, to illustrate how lodges functioned in specific states and regions, and to suggest how these institutions filled social, cultural, political, and philanthropic needs in urban centers. Scholarly studies can be written to show what aristocratic and bourgeois groups gravitated to Masonry, to explain how Masons acted and thought, and to suggest how they interacted with each other in specific elite groups in urban centers. Evidence also can be obtained to substantiate the novel view of J. M. Roberts that from 1720 until 1789, anti-Masonic groups failed to thwart the evolution of European Masonry.[18]

As a result of my affiliation with the Masonic order, I became interested in the study of the Craft during the eighteenth century and was able to investigate sources housed in Masonic collections. I belong to several Masonic research societies and have published two books and numerous articles about Masonry. In doing research for this study I obtained permission to use materials belonging to the Grand Lodge Libraries of Iowa and Pennsylvania. Since the Nazis destroyed many important sources in European Masonic Libraries, materials relating to eighteenth century European Freemasonry in these two excellent grand lodge collections are invaluable. The collections of the American Philosophical Society, the Library Company of Philadelphia, the University of Pennsylvania, and Princeton University also contain pertinent primary materials pertaining to eighteenth century English, French, and Habsburg Masonry.

My book is written as a contribution to Masonic and eighteenth century scholarship. What seems fair to say is that few scholarly works have been published about eighteenth century Masonry and that most Masonic historians have not adequately explained how the Craft is related to eighteenth century culture and society. Unlike the few other studies about eighteenth century Masonry, my study shows that Masonic rites embodied cardinal Enlightenment doctrines and served as an effective vehicle for their transmittance. As opposed to other studies about the Craft, this study emphasizes that the institutional operations of Masonic lodges were important to the cultural and social life of major cities in eighteenth century Europe and that the cultural functions of many Masons were involved with the promotion of the ideas of the Enlightenment. I examine Masonry and the Enlightenment in London, Paris, Prague, and Vienna. By focusing on these four cities, I intend to illustrate the patterns and variations of the Craft and the Enlightenment in England, France, and the Habsburg Empire and to explain the relationship of these two movements to each other in each of these states.

C. The Enlightenment

1. Enlightenment Objectives

As Gay, Cassirer, and other eighteenth century scholars show, the Enlightenment revolved around several major aims. Enlighteners shared the belief that reason could be employed to investigate and to classify knowledge. Those involved with the physical sciences devoted their efforts to probing Nature to ascertain her laws; some enlighteners attempted to determine laws governing the social sciences, and others tried to discover principles governing the humanities. Most enlighteners also endorsed the view that the study of ancient and modern knowledge would lead to the achievement of material progress.[19]

Promoting the natural sciences became paramount during the Enlightenment. Many achievements in experimental science were identified with the principles, theories, and models of Sir Isaac Newton and with those of his disciples. Pertinent Newtonian ideas led to noted discoveries in astronomy, physics, and electricity during the first half of the eighteenth century and contributed to the evolution of chemistry and geology during the last half of this century. It also was evident that some Newtonian concepts were fruitfully applied to advance the study of eighteenth century medicine.

The Enlightenment centered on efforts to foster the study of the social sciences and humanities. Some enlighteners postulated political theories. In Augustan England, many political theorists were proponents of Whiggism and attempted to justify the functions of Parliament in light of this philosophy. Most French and Habsburg political writers, on the other hand, were spokesmen of secular reforms. Writers from these two states denounced the status of the Catholic Church and its clergymen, favored the separation of church and state, and like their English counterparts called for the implementation of religious toleration and other natural liberties. Numerous British, French, and Habsburg enlighteners, who were involved with the study of the social sciences and humanities, subscribed to deistic doctrines; what these enlighteners believed was that the tenets of this philosophy helped to explain the place of man in Nature and contained pertinent moral and cultural teachings of the ancients. It also was apparent that concepts and models of antiquity were meaningful to the humanities during the Enlightenment. Many enlighteners pursuing the study of literature, music, and the fine arts helped to revive ancient ideas, rendered modern interpretations of classical tenets, and thus attempted to promote the neoclassical movement.

What the Enlightenment needed for the investigation and diffusion of knowledge were cultural and social institutions. British, French, and Habsburg enlighteners, for the most part, relied upon institutions in urban centers to publicize their ideas. Some enlighteners from these states played an active role in learned societies; salons, taverns, coffeehouses, and Masonic lodges further emerged as significant urban institutions, enabling many enlighteners to disseminate effectively their beliefs. Masonry and club life, especially in London, were important for the spread of Enlightenment ideas.

2. The Enlightenment in Augustan England

Newtonian science was important to the British Enlightenment. As Cohen and Schofield argue, mechanistic principles and theories, postulated by Newton in 1687 in the *Principia*, did constitute the first school of Newtonian science. Newton in the *Principia* used mathematics and inductive techniques to demonstrate that celestial and terrestrial objects function in space and time in accordance with the laws of gravity and motion. He further postulated that matter is endowed with primary and secondary qualities and operates according to the theories of attraction and repulsion.[20] As Schofield explains, many English scientists were advocates of mechanism. These scientists helped to explain principles concerning the Newtonian mechanical cosmology and to repudiate the physical theories of the Cartesians; English mechanists further offered their interpretations about motion and gravity and about the mechanical attributes of matter. A few mechanists performed experiments to describe the properties of electricity and to explain how motion applied to the study of steam engines.[21] As will be seen, Speculative Freemasonry enlisted the support of some mechanists in London. The rites of Modern Masonry embodied explanations of mechanistic concepts, and London lodges provided mechanists with the opportunity to present their ideas.

Although not as numerous as the mechanists, the materialists constituted the second major school of Newtonian science during the Enlightenment in Augustan England. In the *Opticks*, first published in 1704, Newton discusses many findings pertaining to his experiments with light particles and proposes theories about the properties of matter; he develops a corpuscular theory, speculating that corpuscles constitute the smallest particles in light rays and in other forms of matter. Newton further believes that the aether governs the operations of the most minute particles in matter and thus emerges as a proponent of atomism.[22] My research indicates that a few materialists were affiliated with London Masonic lodges. English Masonic materialists performed some experiments with light rays and, more importantly, devoted attention to developing taxonomies of metallic substances.[23]

Similar to Newtonian physical concepts, Whiggish political doctrines were important to the thought of the British Enlightenment. Kramnick, Pocock, and Speck share the belief that during the first half of the eighteenth century, Whigs endorsed balanced constitutions, mixed governments, Parliamentary sovereignty and patronage, and natural liberties. Kramnick and Speck argue that Whigs secured support from the English aristocracy and bourgeoisie and favored expanding the roles of Parliament and the prime minister; Whigs acted to implement the New Industrial Policy of Walpole and maintained their positions against the Tories who accused them of destroying the political and economic foundations of England.[24] Pocock claims that the Whigs, in the Harringtonian sense, constituted the Court Party during the Augustan Era and were fortune hunters, working to increase trade, commerce, and their land holdings. He explains that despite their corrupt practices, Whigs, like the Florentine and Venetian leaders of the Renaissance, envisioned themselves as promoters of civic humanism and virtue.[25] My research reveals that most Masons were Whigs. Some Masons affiliated with the party of Walpole to secure political favors. Others subscribed to Whiggish theories concerning civil liberties, especially endorsed the principle of religious toleration, and in many cases were proponents of deism.

Various tenets of deism were significant to the Enlightenment in Augustan England. Newton, in the Scholia, a document appended to Book III of the *Principia*, advances deistic ideas to explain important scientific concepts. Newton believes that God is the First and the Final Cause and that the mechanical properties of gravity and the operations of the universe and nature are traced to Him. McGuire and Rattansi maintain that to substantiate his mechanistic views, Newton referred to the deistic beliefs of Pythagoras, Plato, and other ancient thinkers.[26] Other ideas, as well, were involved with English deism. As Gay and Stromberg demonstrate, English deists, for the most part, envisioned God as being Benevolent and Omniscient. English deists further believed that as the source of ancient and modern knowledge, the Creator endowed humans with reason to enable them to determine His Grand Design and understand divine, natural, and moral laws.[27]

Enlighteners from numerous groups in Augustan England subscribed to deistic doctrines and, in some cases, affiliated with Masonry. Christian Deists under the leadership of Toland and Tindal arose in Hanoverian London, shared the belief that reason would enable man to reveal the truths of Christianity, but were not involved with Masonic lodges in the British capital.[28] Members of Protestant sects, however, were quite numerous in Masonry and, in many cases, endorsed deistic beliefs. Many members of Protestant dissenting groups advocated the deistic and Masonic doctrine of religious toleration and believed that the Craft could serve as a valuable agency for ameliorating relations among Protestant sects. As Jacob shows, some Anglican Latitudinarians belonged to London lodges and believed that the rites of Masonry vividly explained salient deistic and mechanistic concepts.[29] It was also apparent that members of scientific, literary, and other cultural circles in London considered the deistic tenets of Masonry to be meaningful. By identifying deistic teachings of the Craft with moral, secular, and scientific doctrines of the ancients and the moderns, some prominent and many minor English enlighteners became involved in London lodges.

Literature was also used to diffuse Enlightenment ideologies in Augustan England. Many Augustan writers referred to the beliefs of ancient authors to substantiate modern ethical and political concepts. As Humphreys and others maintain, English writers translated major works of the Greeks and Romans, praising the ancients for the clarity of their models, for their love of Nature, and for their perceptive explanations of the qualities of man.[30] A few English writers published essays about the Roman architect Vitruvius, endorsing his principles based on harmony, order, and coherence.[31] As Marjorie Nicolson shows, English writers, as well, emerged as propagandists of the new science. The Mason, Alexander Pope, and other minor writers, who in some instances affiliated with the Craft, revealed interest in materialistic theories associated with experiments concerning light rays and lauded Newton for discovering mechanical laws to explain the orderly operations of Nature.[32]

Numerous institutions were involved with the promotion of the Enlightenment in early Hanoverian London. The Royal Society of London developed into an important cultural hub; the society was identified with discoveries of Newton and published the experiments and findings of the mechanists and materialists.[33] This institution further consisted of scholars not involved with the sciences and of aristocratic and bourgeois gentlemen interested in learning about Enlightenment ideas. There were, however, other cultural agencies in early eighteenth century London. As Rudé explains, the College of Physicians, the Society of Antiquaries, and the St. Martin's Lane Academy functioned as important centers for the diffusion of Enlightenment ideas.[34] Many Masons participated in these learned societies and frequented London coffeehouses and taverns. As Timbs and Rudé maintain, the many coffeehouses and taverns located in the Covent Garden and in other districts of London performed valuable social and cultural functions. As a result of their involvement in these institutions, London Masons were able to dine and to drink with each other, to discuss political matters, and on occasion to deliver lectures and to perform experiments.[35] Coffeehouses and taverns further served as the aristocratic and bourgeois institutions from which Speculative Freemasonry was to evolve and, in functioning as communicative centers and as "penny universities" in London, helped to spread Enlightenment tenets.[36]

3. French Enlightenment Patterns

As most historians maintain, Newtonian concepts circulated in France between approximately 1720 and 1740 and were important to the development of the French Enlightenment. As Gay shows, Voltaire and other French intellectuals generated interest in the views espoused by Newton and by his disciples. They corresponded with British Newtonians, visited England, were admitted to the Royal Society and other London learned societies, in many cases became Anglophiles, and published translations of important works of Newtonian science.[37]

Many French scientists became mechanists; they campaigned against and succeeded in discrediting the advocates of Cartesian physical theories. French mechanists were especially interested in the study of astronomy and electricity and also wrote treatises about the inertial properties of matter. Baker and Thackray argue that by approximately 1760, French mechanists became positivists, attempting to develop models and a scientific language to explicate rather than to describe Newtonian mechanical laws.[38] My research reveals that a few astronomers, electrical theorists, and physicians were members of the Craft and that most eighteenth century French Masonic scientists were more interested in the ideas posited in the *Opticks* than in those advanced in the *Principia*.

Materialistic concepts were of central significance to the development of science during the French Enlightenment. Materialistic views influenced the taxonomic schemes of Buffon and those of other eighteenth century French geologists.[39] According to Schofield and Thackray, pertinent concepts advanced in the *Opticks* produced their most significant impact in France during the 1770s and 1780s and shaped the development of chemistry. As a result of the studies of Lavoisier, minor French chemists, who in many cases were associated with Masonry, conducted experiments concerning properties, weights, and phlogiston contents of varying forms of matter. These experiments further helped to demonstrate the interest of French enlighteners in the atomistic theory.[40]

The Neoclassical Movement dominated the arts during the French Enlightenment. Lucie-Smith and Levey emphasize the intimate relationship of Neoclassicism to eighteenth century French art and sculpture; an accurate depiction of Nature, the feats of ancient gods and heroes, and the portraits of eminent moderns characterize the paintings of French Neoclassical artists. An accurate portrayal of facial features and an emphasis upon clarity and symmetry appear in the busts and statues of sculptors connected with the French Neoclassical School.[41]

John Lough cogently demonstrates the pervasive influence of Neoclassicism upon eighteenth century French literature; he shows that French writers published translations of important ancient poems and succeeded in having their modernized presentations of Greek and Roman comedies and tragedies staged in Parisian theaters.[42] What is distinctive about French writers was their interest in aesthetics. According to Gay, many French enlighteners held the view that ancient Greek and Roman theories relating to the arts and humanities constituted the basis of aesthetics and could be integrated into a philosophical system to explain the concept of beauty.[43] As will be seen, many French Masons contributed to the fine arts and humanities, and a few members of the order were concerned with aesthetic questions.

Varying philosophies of deism were propounded during the French Enlightenment and in many cases revolved around concepts espoused by the ancients. As Manuel demonstrates, ancient allegories, myths, and teachings of the mystery cults were embodied in the deistic philosophies of Voltaire, d'Holbach, Court de Gébelin, and minor French enlighteners. By investigating the writings of the ancients, many French deists, like their English counterparts, attempted to demonstrate that the ancients had postulated doctrines of a universal morality to explain the relationship of man to God and to Nature. Like Court de Gébelin, some French deists believed that the ancients had evolved principles to explain the Great Order established by the Supreme Creator.[44]

Doctrines of deism in France were also related to those of Newtonianism, Masonry, and state reform. As Gay and others suggest, some French deists, who were Newtonians and in many cases Anglophiles, tried to explain the importance of mechanistic and materialistic concepts in light of major tenets of moral philosophy.[45] As will be seen, Masonic rites conferred in France served as an important source of deism; these rites emphasized the importance of reason for the investigation of Nature and depicted God as the Supreme Creator, as the First and Final Cause, and as the Moral Governor. As a result of embodying deistic tenets, Masonry appealed to Newtonians, to individuals who were falling away from Christianity, and even in some cases to those seeking an understanding of Enlightenment doctrines to reinforce their religious beliefs. Masonic rites in France embodied the deistic philosophy of "secular salvation," stressing that the Moral Governor delegates individuals with natural liberties and encourages Masons to work for the implementation of state reforms.[46]

As Parker and Kors maintain, varying groups supported the cause of state reforms during the French Enlightenment. Parker claims that important and minor *philosophes* were associated with the "Cult of Antiquity," having been educated in the ancient classics and having integrated views of Greek and Roman authors into their arguments concerning state reforms.[47] Kors shows that major and minor proponents of reform were affiliated with different elite groups in Paris during the 1770s and 1780s and that the behavior, thought, and statuses of these writers sharply varied.[48] My research indicates that most Masonic advocates of reform were familiar with the political doctrines of the ancients and were minor writers associated with varying Parisian elites. A few Masonic enlighteners looked to the Bourbon Monarchy and its ministers to initiate needed reforms, but many others were critical of the crown for not instituting them.

Numerous French enlighteners embraced the cause of legal reform. A few enlighteners were aristocrats who served as judges in the parlements. As Ford and Shackleton show, these judges endorsed salient reform proposals of Montesquieu and were advocates of the *thèse nobiliaire*, believing that the parlements should take measures to abolish unjust laws and should serve as the protector of natural liberties.[49] Other enlighteners also wished to introduce legal changes in France. Some minor *philosophes* endorsed legal reforms proposed by Voltaire and by the Milanese aristocrat Beccaria. Most of these *philosophes* were Parisian Masons, advocating the extension of civil liberties to the Huguenots and sweeping reforms of the French criminal code and legal systems.

Under the influence of Voltaire, many of these minor Parisian writers became involved with the issue of religious toleration. Most of these writers were connected with the Masonic circle of Court de Gébelin and favored the granting of this civil liberty to the Huguenots. Their writings have remained important, to some extent influenced the decision of Louis XVI to issue the 1787 Edict of Toleration, but have received minimal attention from historians.

Few studies have been published about educational reform proposals during the French Enlightenment. As Lough explains, after the expulsion of the Jesuits from France in 1764, minor writers in Paris during the 1770s and 1780s called upon the crown to terminate the control of Catholic clergymen over French schools and to secularize educational institutions. As will be seen, many of these writers were Masons, favoring the separation of church and state, and contributing leadership and funds to *lycées* and *musées* established in Paris.[50]

Cultural institutions contributed to the diffusion of Enlightenment ideologies in Paris. As Baker and Hahn show, the Paris Academy of Sciences served as the nucleus of science during the French Enlightenment. This academy functioned as an intensively competitive institution, only recruiting to its ranks professional scientists and thus differing from the Royal Society. The Paris Academy, for the most part, consisted of some mechanists, of many materialists, and of a few Masons.[51] The *Académie de Peinture et de Sculpture*, the *Académie Française*, and Parisian salons also evolved into major agencies for the spread of Enlightenment concepts. As will be seen, a few Parisian Masons belonged to these institutions and, in several instances, held membership in provincial learned societies. Many others participated in the affairs of Parisian salons and were provided with the opportunity to display their artistic works and to deliver lectures concerning state reforms and literature.[52]

Parisian intellectuals also utilized publications to spread Enlightenment ideas. Prominent *philosophes* and some Masonic writers published articles about varying topics relating to the Enlightenment in the *Journal de Paris*, the *Journal des savants*, the *Mercure de France*, and in other Parisian journals. As Hazard and Darnton show, articles of numerous *philosophes* appeared in the *Encyclopédie* and contain significant knowledge about the liberal arts and sciences. Despite the efforts of the censors to prevent its publication and circulation, this work was distributed in Paris and throughout France and served as an important vehicle for the dissemination of Enlightenment beliefs.[53] According to Hazard and Schlegel, Masonic administrators supposedly financed the publication of the *Encyclopédie*, and Masons wrote numerous articles for this work.[54] My research indicates that definitive evidence concerning Masonic sponsorship of the *Encyclopédie* is lacking and that only two Masonic writers contributed articles to this major work. What can be said is that minor Parisian Masonic intellectuals belonged to cultural circles, headed by eminent *philosophes*, and that promoting the arts and sciences was important to Masons and *philosophes*.

4. Enlightenment Patterns in the Habsburg Empire

Unlike those in France, major Enlightenment ideas in the Habsburg Empire were identified with successful state building policies and thus with enlightened despotism. There is, however, some debate about despotism among historians studying the Habsburg Empire during the eighteenth century. Peter Gay and a few historians refuse to recognize enlightened despotism, claiming that this term is too vague to explain political and cultural developments in Central

and Eastern Europe.[55] Gagliardo, Wines, and most historians argue
that enlightened despotism led to the transformation of the Habsburg
Empire and was associated with reforms instituted by Maria Theresa
and by her son Joseph II.[56]

Historians offer varying views about the aims of the reform programs of these two monarchs. Ernst Wangermann and Robert Kann
believe that imperial reform programs were designed to achieve monarchical absolutism and to reduce the powers of the estates.[57] Lhotsky
and Valjavec argue that the centralization and the efficient operations
of imperial institutions were ascribed as major motives for the implementation of reforms.[58] As Bernard and Gagliardo cogently argue,
Maria Theresa and Joseph instituted reforms to secularize the empire
in light of many theories proposed by West European enlighteners.[59]
As will be argued, the centralization, the consolidation, the secularization, and the efficient operation of Habsburg institutions characterized the imperial programs of these two monarchs.

Administrative and legal reforms were enacted to ameliorate the
efficacy of imperial institutions. As Kann and McGill show, Maria
Theresa established the State Council to coordinate administrative
operations and empowered the High Court of Justice to direct legal
activities.[60] Bernard maintains that during the reign of Joseph, imperial councils and commissions were centralized and operated to assure
the implementation of the edicts of the emperor.[61] The emperor as
well established a legal commission under the direction of the natural law theorist Joseph von Sonnenfels; this important commission
was instructed to propose revisions of imperial laws and changes regarding legal proceedings and punishments.[62] Kann and Frankovich
emphasize the importance of recommendations of this commission,
explaining that the proposals of Sonnenfels embodied theories advocated by Italian and French enlighteners.[63]

Economic reforms of Maria Theresa and Joseph were enacted to
increase industrial production. As Bernard and Tapié demonstrate,
economic policies of both monarchs embodied cameralist theories and
thus revealed the influences of West European reform advocates.[64]
Both monarchs took measures to assist businessmen, craftsmen, and
industrialists. As Bernard and Tapié further argue, the granting of religious toleration during the 1780s to Jews and Protestants in imperial
lands marked a distinctive variation of the Habsburg Enlightenment.
According to both historians, these religious groups played a cardinal role in improving banking and business, in increasing industrial

production, and in promoting Enlightenment culture in the Empire.[65]

Educational reforms led to the secularization of imperial schools and thus were important to the Habsburg Enlightenment. As Kann explains, Maria Theresa allocated funds for the operations of primary, secondary, and technical schools; she believed that her subjects should be trained for specific careers.[66] While serving as co-regent, Joseph became involved with educational problems. As Macartney shows, Joseph suspended in 1773 the operations of the Jesuits, thus ending the pervasive influence of this order over imperial education.[67] During the early 1780s, Joseph applied the principle of state intervention to ameliorate imperial educational institutions. As Wangermann explains, the emperor abolished many clerical orders, confiscated their properties, and allocated monies from the sale of these lands for educational improvements. Wangermann emphasizes that the Educational Commission was authorized to fund imperial schools, to hire secular teachers, and to appropriate monies for programs offered in imperial universities.[68] As will be seen, many Masons served as imperial administrators and supported the educational, legal, clerical, and religious reforms instituted by Joseph.

Many Prague and Viennese writer-bureaucrats were enlighteners and Masons involved with the promotion of the humanities. Most Prague intellectuals wrote in German, devoted minimal attention to the study of Czech culture, and displayed astute interest in West European Enlightenment ideas.[69] Prague enlighteners issued German translations of major British and French plays and poems and, like their Viennese counterparts, wrote some essays regarding clerical abuses, deism, and religious toleration for Jews and Protestants. As Bernard shows, many Viennese writer-bureaucrats, who in some instances were former Catholic clergymen, became involved with the literature of reform; they used literature as a vehicle for the vindication of Josephinian reforms. Many Viennese writers were proponents of Neoclassical themes, referring to salient teachings of the ancients to justify their views concerning imperial reforms and also to substantiate their deistic beliefs. As Bernard further argues, Alois Blumauer and minor writers connected with his circle were advocates of Neoclassicism and Josephinian reforms and more importantly worked to establish a distinctive Viennese literary school.[70] As will be argued, Blumauer, his rival Alxinger, and other minor Viennese writers played an active part in Masonry and engaged in literary activities to disseminate Enlightenment and Masonic ideas in the imperial capital.

The development of the fine arts in the eighteenth century Habsburg Empire acutely differed from that of the arts in England and in France. Music—rather than architecture, painting, and sculpture—occupied a central place in the empire and was especially significant to the cultural life of Josephinian Vienna. As Grout, Lang, and other historians of music argue, the evolution of the sonata-symphony, of the piano concerto, and of opera was important to music in the imperial capital. As Grout and Lang explain, the sonata-symphony arose in eighteenth century Austria and stressed intricate modulations and themes; it further emphasized the usage of the chorus, winds, and strings. Popularized by Mozart, the piano concerto centered on the effective interplay between the pianist and the orchestra and provided music with great flexibility and range.[71] Grout and Lang further maintain that after the reforms of Gluck, opera was presented in German and skillfully conveyed human traits and ancient legends.[72] As will be seen, some composers and many musicians affiliated with Viennese and Prague lodges received financial assistance from Habsburg nobles, and used music as a vehicle for the presentation of Masonic and Enlightenment ideas.

Enlightenment concepts, moreover, contributed to the development of the physical sciences and medicine in the Habsburg Empire. As opposed to those in Vienna, scientific and medical activities in Prague were of minimal importance. My research indicates that a few Viennese scientists were mechanists. Their works, which have not been investigated, contain explanations of fundamental concepts concerning gravity, motion, and electricity. In his fine biography of Gerard van Swieten, Frank Brechka explains how this enlightener improved the medical facilities of the University of Vienna Medical School.[73] My research reveals that historians have overlooked the role of Viennese Masonic physicians. These doctors held important positions in the University of Vienna Medical School and wrote about the functions of body organs in light of mechanistic concepts. Geology arose as the major science in Vienna during the Josephinian Enlightenment, revolved around materialistic concepts, and has received minimal attention from historians. Schneer and Thackray allude to the stratigraphic theories of Torbern Bergman concerning the composition of minerals but mention nothing about the impact of his views upon Habsburg geologists.[74] As will be seen, the materialistic theories and classification schemes of this Swedish enlightener influenced the thinking of Masonic geologists in Vienna and in other imperial lands.

Cultural institutions and journals involved with the diffusion of Enlightenment ideas appeared to be lacking in Prague and in Vienna. There were no major scientific academies or publications in either Habsburg city. A few Viennese scientists, however, belonged to scientific societies in Western Europe and published some papers in the journals of these societies. As Kimball shows, the Bohemian Society of Learning was one of the few learned academies in Prague. Members of this society engaged in literary and philosophical studies, issued a journal, and in some cases were associated with Prague Masonry.[75] There seemed to be few academies in Vienna resembling the Bohemian Society. There were, however, two pertinent Viennese publications involved with the promotion of the humanities. As will be seen, the *Wiener Musenalmanach* and the *Wiener Realzeitung* contain poems, plays, and literary essays written by some important Viennese Masonic enlighteners.[76] As a consequence of the paucity of learned societies in Prague and in Vienna, Masonry served as a significant vehicle for the spread of Enlightenment ideas in these two cities. As will be argued, Masons from various cultural circles in Prague and in Vienna were provided with ritualistic explanations of salient Enlightenment concepts and frequently utilized their lodges to promote eighteenth century culture.

Comparative analysis can serve as a useful tool for the examination of the cultural functions and organizational operations of eighteenth century Masonry. Such analysis can reveal the ritualistic, structural, and membership patterns of Masonry in London, Paris, Prague, and Vienna. It also can illustrate how Masonry was related to the Enlightenment in each of these cities. In the next chapter, my purpose is to investigate the origins, organization, and ritualism af Modern Speculative Freemasonry in London and to examine the cultural functions of its members.

II. SPECULATIVE FREEMASONRY IN EARLY HANOVERIAN LONDON

A. The Evolution of the Modern London Grand Lodge

1. From Operative to Speculative Freemasonry

The origins of the Modern Grand Lodge cannot be understood without some reference to Operative Masonry. The London Company of Freemasons and other operative Masonic guilds in the British capital during the first two decades of the eighteenth century performed similar functions. Members of these Masonic organizations were contracted to design and to build churches, palaces, and mansions. Since the London fire of 1666, their services were in great demand.[1] London guilds also provided financial assistance to needy members and their families and conferred rites. The rites of these organizations contained secrets regarding the building craft, explained passwords and signs to their initiates, and embodied oaths based on Christian principles.[2]

Operative Masons in early eighteenth century London met in lodges and had two distinctive kinds of members. It is known that the London Company of Freemasons at this time had several lodges. Known as assemblies, these lodges elected masters and wardens as presiding officers, initiated candidates into the company, and celebrated holidays.[3] What should be noted was that apprentices, who were skilled in the craft of building Masonry, and "accepted" or non-operative Masons were admitted to lodges in London.[4] Prior to 1715, accepted or speculative Masons constituted a small minority within the ranks of operative lodges and were not very active in lodge affairs. Speculative Masons, for the most part, were "gentlemen-scholars," being admitted to Operative Masonry in light of their interest in architecture and mathematics and in some instances hiring operative brothers to build them mansions in the Palladian Style.[5]

The precise connection between Operative and Speculative Freemasonry from 1715 to 1717 is still in dispute. Yet, one thing is clear. With the admittance of more accepted members into Operative lodges between 1715 and 1717, some Speculative Masons evidently wished to create their own Masonic organization and in 1717 realized this aim, establishing the Modern Grand Lodge of London. Most Masonic historians claim that the Modern London Grand Lodge was an outgrowth of Operative Masonry and that its early leaders between 1717 and 1723 gradually modified the organizational structure, rites, and traditions of Operative Masonry to develop and to consolidate their new movement.[6] These historians cogently show the obvious connections between Operative and Speculative Freemasonry. However, they view the evolution of the Modern Grand Lodge solely from the context of the world of Masonry and mention little about the cultural and social environment in which the grand lodge arose.

The Modern Grand Lodge emerged and functioned as an Enlightenment institution in early Hanoverian London. However, this new institution, in some respects, relied upon Operative Masonry for its development. Founding fathers of the Modern Grand Lodge evidently recognized that the rites and architectural symbols of Operative Masonry served as effective teaching vehicles and with some modifications and additions could be used to offer simplified visual explanations of Enlightenment ideas regarding experimental science, philosophy, political thought, and morality. It further was apparent that the fathers of Speculative Freemasonry combined several Operative lodges to establish the governing body of Modern Masonry, but, more importantly, relied upon institutions intimately connected with the Enlightenment in London to develop a workable network of local lodges. Coffeehouses and taverns contributed significantly to the evolution of Modern Masonry in the British capital. As meeting places for the various literary, political, philosophical, and scientific groups, these institutions through club life helped to spread Enlightenment ideas in London and in their role as Masonic lodges capably promoted the cultural and social activities of the Craft. Coffeehouses and taverns also facilitated the recruitment function of Speculative Masonry, enabling modern lodges to attract to their ranks some prominent intellectuals associated with London learned societies and numerous London gentlemen of property who wished to learn about Enlightenment culture.[7]

As suggested by the few sources relating to the inceptive years of the Grand Lodge movement, Modern Masonry in London developed quite gradually. Obscure individuals from the Goose and Gridiron Ale-house in St. Paul's Church Yard, from the Crown Ale-House in Parker's Lane, from the Apple-tree Tavern in Charles Street, and from the Rummer-and-Grapes Tavern in Channel Row met on St. John Baptist's Day, or June 24, 1717, to establish the London Grand Lodge.[8] Several decisions were made during the first grand lodge meeting staged at the Goose and Gridiron Tavern. Founding fathers of Modern Masonry elected a Grand Master and other officers. They also agreed to hold quarterly communications and an annual assembly and to entrust the grand lodge with the power to create and recognize local lodges.[9] Members attending the 1718 Grand Lodge Assembly elected a new Grand Master and proceeded to terminate the session.[10]

The leadership of Modern Masonry during its first two years was not impressive. Minimal information has been discovered about the leaders of the Modern Grand Lodge during its first two years. It consequently has been difficult to determine with certainty how these leaders perceived Modern Masonry and interacted with each other. What can be said, however, was that the Grand Masters of this new organization in 1717 and 1718 were Speculative Masons and that a few Operative Masons also served as officers in it. Anthony Sayer was a patron of the Apple-tree Tavern and became the first Grand Master of Modern Masonry. Sayer was a wealthy bourgeois gentleman, who during the late 1720s lost his fortune, and in 1717 took no action to advance the cause of the Modern Grand Lodge.[11] During the 1718 Grand Lodge Assembly, Thomas Morrice and John Cordwell, two minor Operative Masons, were named as Grand Wardens, and George Payne, a man of means and a Speculative Mason, was elected as Grand Master. Payne, who probably did not know either Morrice or Cordwell prior to 1718, exhibited some interest in Masonry. This gentleman, who was affiliated with the Whig Party and who later became an administrator in the Tax Office, was interested in the study of ancient architecture. Payne and several members of the Grand Lodge in 1718 collected documents and books concerning ancient Masonry. However, Payne that year did not act to establish a grand lodge committee either to examine these works or to promote the study of Masonry.[12] Under the direction of Payne, the Modern Grand Lodge lacked effective governance and distinguished members and well might have been destined to failure.

2. J. T. Desaguliers and the Modern London Grand Lodge

As suggested by his early career, J. T. Desaguliers was intimately involved with Enlightenment activities in London and was well qualified in 1719 to serve as Grand Master of Modern Masonry and to provide this body with needed leadership. Reared in a Huguenot family which in 1685 left France as a result of the revocation of the Edict of Nantes and which settled in London, young John Desaguliers was well educated; at age seventeen, John was privately tutored by a Mr. Sanders and between 1700 and 1705 studied under this man.[13] Desaguliers then attended Oxford, receiving his Bachelors Degree in 1710, his Masters in 1712, and Doctorate of Laws in 1718. He exuded intellectual versatility, expressing interest in the classics, in theology, in mathematics, and in experimental science.[14] Science especially proved to be significant to the career of Desaguliers between 1710 and 1717. By becoming one of the finest students of the Newtonian John Keill and by holding the Chair of Experimental Philosophy in Hart Hall College, Oxford, Desaguliers succeeded in establishing ties to the scientific community in London. Desaguliers developed cordial relations with Newton and became friendly with Samuel Clarke, Francis Hauksbee, Stephen Gray, and many other proponents of mechanism. Like most apostles of the Newtonian creed, Desaguliers was elected in 1714 to the Royal Society of London and assumed an active part in this organization, serving as curator of experiments for the society.[15] He also had other connections with the Enlightenment in London. An Anglican minister, Desaguliers in 1717 was named as chaplain of James Brydges, the First Duke of Chandos and evidently helped the duke to stage cultural activities in his mansion located near Covent Garden. As a result of his affiliation with Chandos, Desaguliers was given the opportunity to meet numerous aristocratic and bourgeois patrons of the Enlightenment, probably delivered an occasional sermon, and more importantly gave frequent scientific demonstrations.[16] It is also known that Desaguliers delivered his scientific lectures in coffeehouses and taverns, was active in the club life of Augustan England, and met administrators involved with Modern Masonry. He undoubtedly was familiar with the ancient teachings of Masonry and believed that the Modern Grand Lodge could be transformed into an effective vehicle for the promotion of Newtonian ideas and other tenets associated with the Enlightenment.

To achieve this objective, the ambitious Desaguliers in 1719 took measures to enable the Grand Lodge to "flourish in Harmony, Reputation, and Numbers."[17] He first "reviv'd the old regular and peculiar Toasts and Healths of the Free Masons," attempting through this tradition to illustrate the importance of the role of the Grand Master.[18] Desaguliers then received approval from the grand lodge to institute changes regarding the duties of the Grand Master; the outgoing Grand Master was to be allowed to appoint a Deputy Grand Master and the Grand Wardens.[19] Strengthening the position of the Grand Master proved to be significant to the development of the Modern Grand Lodge. After 1719, most Grand Masters of Modern Masonry were English nobles exhibiting an interest in Enlightenment ideas and residing in London; these Grand Masters during the early 1720s did not appoint any Operative Masons to administrative positions in the London Grand Lodge, but rather named English aristocrats, bourgeois gentlemen, and enlighteners to these posts. Grand Masters of Modern Masonry during the 1720s also received extensive support from Desaguliers, who during the early 1720s served as Deputy Grand Master and as a member of several important grand lodge committees.

Several friends of Desaguliers between 1721 and 1723 provided the Grand Lodge of London with capable leadership. Upon the recommendation of Desaguliers, John, the Second Duke of Montagu, was elected in 1721 and again in 1722 to serve as Grand Master of Modern Masonry. Like Desaguliers, Montagu developed connections with Enlightenment agencies in London. The duke was admitted to the Royal Society but did not deliver any papers before this organization. Montagu frequently dined with members of the Royal Society Club in the Mitre Tavern, attended cultural events staged in the Cavendish Square mansion of his Whiggish friend, the Duke of Chandos, and consequently was presented with the opportunity of knowing Desaguliers quite well.[20] During his first term as Grand Master, Montagu actively worked to establish several local lodges in the vicinity of Covent Garden and more importantly commissioned a Committee of "Fourteen Learned Brethren" to draft a constitution for Modern Masonry.[21] With Desaguliers, Dr. James Anderson directed the Committee of Fourteen, compiled the materials for, and wrote this significant work. An obscure intellectual who, however, contributed significantly to the London Grand Lodge, Anderson established ties with enlighteners in London. After receiving his doctorate in divinity from the University of Aberdeen, Anderson in 1710 came to London, served as minister of the Scottish Presbyterian Church in Swallow Street in Westminster, and became chaplain for the Masonic enlightener David, Earl of Buchan. Anderson in his *Royal Geneologies* revealed interest in deistic ideas and ancient religions, occasionally lectured about philosophical and religious matters in the Goose and Gridiron Ale-house, and was admitted about 1719 to the lodge connected to this tavern, where he met and became quite friendly with Desaguliers.[22] There was good reason for a friendship to develop between Anderson and Desaguliers. Both individuals were Protestant clergymen and worked for London aristocratic enlighteners. Anderson and Desaguliers also perceived themselves as enlighteners and as the high priests of Speculative Masonry; they evidently wrote the *Constitutions* in 1722 to explain how Masonry functioned as an important cultural institution in the ancient and modern world. After its completion in 1722, the *Constitutions* received approval first from the Committee of Fourteen and then from grand lodge administrators and was published the following year.[23]

This work contains the perceptions of Desaguliers and Anderson concerning the origins and the evolution of Speculative Freemasonry. In the first sections of the *Constitutions*, both men write as enlighteners, constantly referring to ancient architecture and culture and obviously attempting to suggest the importance of ancient ideas to Modern Masonry and the Enlightenment. They first trace the mythical origins of Masonry to Adam. Desaguliers and Anderson then claim that the principles of ancient Masonry enabled the building of the Egyptian pyramids and the Temple of Solomon. Anderson and Desaguliers imply that from a philosophical viewpoint architectural principles seemed to be meaningful to the ancient Egyptians and Jews. These principles were identified with the perfection of a Divine Governor of all civilizations, with the powers of kings, with the strength of states, and with the operations of Nature.

> Great Kings and men practiced the Royal Art. On the River Nile, we find improvement in Geometry, which consequently brought Masonry in great request. The famous Pyramids particularly demonstrate the early taste and genius of the ancient Kingdom. . . .

> The sumptuous Temple of Solomon attracted inquisitive artists of all nations to spend time in Jerusalem and to survey its excellencies. . . . The Temple has exact Dimensions, from the magnificent Porch on the East, to the glorious and reverend *Sanctum Sanctorum* on the West, with most lovely and convenient Apartments for the Kings and Princes, Priests and Levites, Israelites and Gentiles. It was

the House of Prayer for all Nations, and was justly esteemed as the finest piece of Masonry upon the Earth before or since, and the chief Wonder of the World. . . .[24]

Anderson and Desaguliers explain that architecture was significant to Graeco-Roman Civilization. They argue that the Brotherhood of Pythagoras helped to foster the study of geometry and Masonry in the ancient world and that Greek and Roman Masons erected "Civil and sacred edifices" in light of Doric, Ionic, and Corinthian principles.[25] Anderson and Desaguliers suggest that these principles reflected the symmetrical designs of ancient buildings and the harmonies within Nature. They further believe that classical architecture reached its zenith during the reign of Augustus Caesar and was advanced by "the great Vitruvius," an architect known for designing temples and villas.[26]

Anderson and Desaguliers devote attention to the development of modern architecture and Speculative Freemasonry. Ancient rather than medieval architecture was of particular importance to the moderns. According to Desaguliers and Anderson, the "Augustan Stile" was revived first by Palladio during the Renaissance and then by the Englishman Ingio Jones during the seventeenth century. The authors of the *Constitutions* explain that Jones, who made frequent trips to Italy to study the models of Palladio and Serglio, served at the court of James I and designed for the first Stuart king the White-Hall Palace and the Banqueting-House in the Palladian style. They maintain that since the Civil War, the Augustan style has been prevalent in the British capital and that in its role as an Enlightenment institution, the Modern Grand Lodge of London would attempt to promote the study of ancient and modern knowledge relating to architecture, science, morality, and the liberal arts.[27]

> After the Civil War was over, Masonry was restor'd, especially upon the unhappy Occasion of the Burning of London, *Anno* 1666. Then the City-Houses were rebuilt after the Roman Stile. . . . Charles II founded also his royal palace at Greenwich, according to Mr. Jones's Design. . . . But in the Reign of his brother King James II, though some Roman Buildings were carried on, the Lodges of Free-Masons in London much dwindled into Ignorance. . . . But after the Revolution, *Anno* 1688, King William, having a good Taste of Architecture, carried on two famous Hospitals of

Greenwich and Chelsea, and built the fine part of his royal
Palace of Hampton Court. . . . And the bright example of
that glorious Prince, (who by most is reckon'd a Free Mason) did influence the Nobility, the Gentry, the Wealthy and
the Learned of Great Britain, to affect much the Augustan
Stile. . . . And now under George I, the Modern Lodges of
Masonry in London flourish. . . .[28]

In addition to justifying the cultural status of Speculative Masonry, the *Constitutions* defines powers and operations of the London
Grand Lodge. Grand Masters were delegated executive, legislative,
and judicial functions and seemed to govern Masonry in light of Whiggish doctrines. As the prime minister of Masonry, the Grand Master
was to implement the provisions of the grand lodge constitution, was
to preside over assemblies, was to appoint committees to formulate
policies of the Craft, and was to preside over judicial proceedings.[29]
The office of Grand Master of Modern Masonry was related to the
Enlightenment in other ways. As a result of the approval of the recommendation of Desaguliers in 1721, the Grand Master was allowed
to appoint members to deliver lectures and speeches during grand
lodge meetings. As a result of the influence of Desaguliers, aristocratic enlighteners, who also held membership in the Royal Society,
served between 1720 and 1740 as Grand Masters of Modern Masonry;
these Grand Masters included the 2nd Duke of Buccleuch, the 2nd
Duke of Richmond, and the 4th Earl of Loudon. With assistance
from Desaguliers, these Masons appeared to be quite successful in
recruiting numerous members from the Royal Society to positions of
leadership in Modern Masonry. This special connection between the
Royal Society and Speculative Freemasonry was important to the development of the London Grand Lodge and suggested that Venetian
oligarchies consisting of London aristocrats and scholars would direct
the affairs of Modern Masonry.[30]

Other officers served in the hierarchy of the Modern Grand Lodge.
The Deputy Grand Master was second in command and was entrusted
with "the Chair" during the absence of the Grand Master.[31] What
can be said is that Desaguliers was the most influential Deputy Grand
Master, that from 1720 to 1740, many enlighteners, especially from
the Royal Society and including Martin Clare and Martin Folkes, held
this office, and that this position, in many cases, served as a stepping-
stone to the grand mastership. Many aristocratic patrons of the arts
and sciences from the Royal Society and other London learned so-

cieties served as Grand Warden and usually held this office for one year. Grand Wardens were appointed to advise the Grand Master about "the affairs of the Lodge" and in many cases were assigned specific responsibilities by the Grand Master.[32] The Grand Secretary was empowered to record minutes and to engage in correspondence with local and foreign lodges, and the Grand Treasurer was delegated authority to collect dues and to pay debts.[33] Grand lodge officers as well were required to comply with the custom of displaying their colors and jewels during assemblies. It appeared that Desaguliers introduced this custom and that colors associated with grand lodge offices reflected Enlightenment concepts. Blue represented liberty and white symbolized justice.

> None but the Grand Master, his Deputy and Wardens shall wear the Jewels in Gold or Gilt pedant to blue aprons about their Necks and white Leather Aprons with blue Silk.

> That all those who have served any of the three Grand Offices shall wear the like aprons lined with blue Silk in all Lodges or Assemblies of Masons. . . .

> That all Masters and Wardens of Lodges may wear their Aprons lined with white Silk and their respective Jewels with plain White Ribbons. . . . [34]

The London Grand Lodge between 1723 and 1740 operated as a viable and centralized body. Administrators of Modern Masonry succeeded in fulfilling several major objectives; they met with success in creating local lodges within the vicinity of London, assisted in recruiting enlighteners to these lodges, and capably supervised the operations of these bodies. Administrators of the Modern Grand Lodge as well recognized grand lodges in Europe and in America and received reports from grand and local lodges within its jurisdiction. Officials of the London Grand Lodge further succeeded in developing cordial relations with political leaders and discreetly suppressed the few anti-Masonic attacks directed against them.[35]

The Modern Grand Lodge became involved with philanthropy, a question of major concern to some London organizations and enlighteners. Charity certainly was embodied in Christian teachings and especially stimulated some Protestant churchmen, the Society for Promoting Christian Knowledge, and similar organizations in early Hanoverian London to act to assist the poor.[36] To Desaguliers and other administrators of the Modern Grand Lodge, philanthropy was a meaningful secular and ethical concept of the Enlightenment, revolving around the belief that Masons should engage in efforts to improve society and should act to raise the standards of public morality. To grand lodge officials, philanthropy also became associated with providing financial aid to needy Masons and with extending support to oppressed groups in English society. Desaguliers especially believed that the Modern Grand Lodge should become involved in philanthropic projects and in 1725 was named to head a grand lodge committee "to consider the best methods to regulate the Generall Charity."[37] Four years later, on July 11, 1729, Desaguliers proposed that the grand lodge take measures to establish a General Charity Committee.[38] His proposals concerning the operation of this committee were presented to the grand lodge on January 29, 1730 and were ratified by that body, after several debates, on April 21st of that year:

> There should be a Standing Committee for regulating and disposing of the Said Charity in such manner and such proportions as they shall Judge proper. . . . This committee shall consist of all those, who have been or shall be Grand Masters, Deputy Grand Masters, or Grand Wardens. The Grand Master shall always be deemed as the head of the said Committee. . . .[39]

The Charity Committee during the 1730s performed varying functions. This committee distributed funds to distressed Masons, to their families, and to orphans; it also allocated monies to several hospitals and schools in London. The Charity Committee as well became involved with a worthy project in America. Upon the recommendation of Desaguliers in 1733, grand lodge leaders authorized the Charity Committee to provide financial assistance to those London Masons who were going to America to start a new life in the Georgia Colony.[40] The activities of the Charity Committee were supported by local lodges in London and reflected pertinent teachings explained in Masonic ritualism.

3. The Rites of Modern English Speculative Freemasonry

The rites of Modern Masonry appeared to be quite distinctive and to serve many purposes. Although there is a lack of evidence about the evolution of the modern Masonic degrees, it is evident that Desaguliers and other early grand lodge leaders found the rites of Operative Masonry to be suitable teaching instruments. Accordingly, they significantly revised these old rites to meet their needs and consequently developed the new ritualistic system of Modern Masonry in order to explain salient Enlightenment ideas.[41] Modern Masonry ritualized Enlightenment culture and thus acutely differed from other secret societies in operation in early Hanoverian London. The language appearing in Modern Masonic ritualism was distinctive and unusual, but well served the purpose of explaining Enlightenment ideas in light of ancient legends and myths relating to architecture.[42] Symbols also abounded in the Modern Masonic degrees, became a hallmark of Speculative Freemasonry, and were effectively used to describe eighteenth century scientific, political, philosophical, and moral beliefs. The rites of Modern Masonry possessed other appealing features; the secrecy and the elaborate dramatization of the degrees enabled the candidate to associate himself with the exclusive world of Modern Masonry. In receiving the Modern degrees, the initiate was required to engage in ceremonies and thus was given the opportunity of interacting with lodge members. He further learned about the grips and signs of the order, was informed of their ethical and philosophical meaning, and thus became cohesively bound to the Masonic community.[43]

The Entered Apprentice Degree, or the first degree of Modern Masonry, revolved around the story regarding the building of the Temple of King Solomon and introduced the candidate to important Masonic and Enlightenment doctrines. In receiving this degree, the candidate was blindfolded and was ushered into the lodge by his guide. Having circumambulated the lodge with his guide, the candidate was informed that his travels resemble the perfect movements of the planets and moons around the Sun and attest to his willingness to purify his soul and to acquire an understanding of the principles of Masonry.[44] After ending his travels, the candidate was given an oath, had his blindfold removed, and was provided with light and with the teachings of the first degree. The candidate was informed that the lodge represents Nature and society and that his efforts should be devoted to understanding their laws and operations.[45]

He further was told what the tools of Masonry represent. Symbolic of proper moral conduct, the square and plumb are applied for the building of the three great pillars of the temple, which represent wisdom, strength, and beauty.[46] Prior to the closing of the Entered Apprentice Degree, the candidate was told about the importance of the twenty-four inch gauge and the level. He was told to use the gauge to design his spiritual temple and to apply the level in his quest to discover the wisdom and laws of Nature.[47]

The Fellow Craft Degree especially embodied Enlightenment concepts and revealed the commitment of Modern Masonry to education. The Master of the lodge told the candidate that he was a fellow of the Masonic society, was expected to be benevolent and virtuous, and was to follow the light of knowledge.[48] The candidate then ascended the winding stairs of the temple and was told that he had taken fifteen steps during his ascent. These steps represent the fact that Masonry is reliant upon mathematics and that mathematics enables Masons to discover the principles governing Deity and Nature.[49] Geometry, the candidate is told, is the queen of mathematics; geometry helps Masons to understand the laws of gravity and motion, the moral principles associated with the circle, square, and triangle, and the Divine Attributes of the Supreme Architect.[50] Before the termination of the Fellow Craft Degree, the candidate was shown a globe and was informed that this object symbolizes terrestrial knowledge acquired by Masons from their studies of the arts and sciences.[51]

Symbols and teachings of the Master Mason Degree contained pertinent moral and philosophical ideas; this degree also revolved around the completion of Solomon's Temple and was staged in its inner chamber. Being exposed to the square, compasses, and plumb, the candidate was told that reason and the five senses are essential for understanding the laws of Nature and the moral principles of society. The candidate learned that Masons lived according to the tenets of charity and fellowship and that temperance, prudence, and justice served as cardinal virtues of the order.[52]

This degree also stressed the belief concerning the immortality of the soul and the deistic qualities of God. The ceremony concerning the death of Hiram Abif, the chief architect of Solomon, was performed. The candidate then learned about the importance of the Hiramic legend; he was informed that the soul is immortal and is symbolized by the Sprig of Acacia, which was placed on the coffin of Hiram.[53] Before the conclusion of the Master Mason Degree, the candidate was told to seek the lost word during his travels. Known only by Hiram, this word was associated with the Attributes of Deity. Symbolized by the All-Seeing Eye, the Supreme Architect was described to the candidate as being Omnipotent and Omniscient.[54]

London Masons most likely viewed some major teachings of Modern Masonry as serving as the basis of a civil religion. These Masons discovered that the deistic interpretations in the three degrees in many cases were compatible with their views and that the Supreme Architect was the Source of the universal moral system of Modern Masonry. London Masons further found that ritualistic explanations of moral behavior were related to mechanistic principles and were embodied in the law of the square. This Masonic principle states that as the laws of motion and gravity describe the orderly operations of objects in Nature and in the universe, the law of the square explains how Speculative Masons in light of their conduct work to ameliorate and to bring harmony to society.[55] Embodied in the Modern Degrees and in the Charges of the *Constitutions*, significant Masonic teachings, which in some cases were a reflection of Whiggish ideas, affected the attitudes of London Masons. Masons were expected to respect the civil magistrate and his institutions and to comply with the laws of the state; Masons further were to subscribe to natural liberties, were to adhere to the doctrine of religious toleration, and were to be just and honest in their pursuits.[56] What consequently can be said about the degrees of Modern Masonry is that Desaguliers and other grand lodge administrators succeeded in their efforts to develop the tenets of a civic morality in light of architectural symbols and scientific concepts.

4. The Functions of Modern London Lodges during the Augustan Era

Blue lodges in London were multifaceted institutions, serving as ritualistic, cultural, and social centers.[57] These lodges functioned as voluntary associations, requiring candidates first to petition for membership and then to receive the unanimous approval of lodge members to be admitted to its ranks. Modern lodges operated as private and secret bodies, conferring the Blue Degrees upon qualified candidates and holding stated meetings to discuss lodge affairs.[58]

> A lodge is a place where Masons assemble and work. That Assembly, or duly organiz'd society of Masons, is called a lodge, and every Brother must belong to one, and must be subject to its By-Laws and General Regulations. . . .
>
> A Mason is oblig'd by his Tenure to obey the Moral Law. . . . Masons are to be good, honest, and honorable Men. . . . They [Masons] are to help their families and the neglected. . . . Masons are to cultivate Brotherly-Love, the Foundation and Cement of this Fraternity. . . .[59]

As indicated in the *Constitutions*, Blue lodges were to function as philanthropic institutions; these bodies contributed to the Grand Lodge Charity Fund, provided financial assistance to distressed Masons and their families, and gave donations to several charity schools and orphanages in London.[60] Local lodges in London also became social and cultural bodies. Lodge officers helped to promote the concept of fellowship among their members, encouraged them to visit other lodges in London, and were authorized to sponsor banquets and lectures.[61]

A Master and two Wardens served as the major officers governing the Modern Lodge in London. The Master was elected annually by a secret ballot, was installed during a special ceremony, and was referred to as "Right Worshipful."[62] He was authorized to stage degrees, to preside over stated and special meetings, and to appoint standing committees.[63] Wardens were elected to assist the Master in performing lodge duties; they were empowered to conduct the affairs of the lodge in the absence of the Master. The two Wardens also played central roles in ceremonies concerning the opening and the closing of the lodge.[64]

The local lodge in early Hanoverian London consisted of other officers. Two Deacons were elected; they were empowered to assist the Master and Wardens with conducting the activities of the lodge and to issue the messages of the Master to lodge members.[65] A Tyler was elected to help in preparing the lodge for meetings and was assigned the responsibility of protecting the lodge against intruders.[66] A Secretary was elected to keep the records of the lodge and to issue payments for its expenses.[67]

Symbols were used to describe the activities and roles of local lodge officers. The Master was viewed as being one of the "Lights of Masonry," and imparted to members of the Craft his knowledge of the liberal arts and sciences.[68] The Master wore a hat and during certain ceremonies tipped it, an act symbolizing his respect for Deity; the Master also wore a square jewel, a symbol of moral and natural laws and that of the Divine Attributes of the Supreme Architect. The Master was entrusted with a gavel and pounded it to demonstrate that Masons are honest and just in their dealings.[69] Wardens wore a plumb-rule, which represents the proper moral conduct of Masons; these officers also were seated near pillars, objects symbolizing the strength and harmony of the order.[70] The Tyler carried a sword, and this weapon represents the protective function of his office.[71]

Officers were attired in aprons of different colors. White symbolizes innocence and truth, blue fidelity and immortality, and red divine love and bravery. Purple is associated with temperance and justice, two tenets emphasized in rituals conferred in modern lodges.[72]

Modern lodges performed political functions and operated according to constitutional provisions. Local lodges maintained federalist relations with the Modern London Grand Lodge. These bodies, on the one hand, were established by the grand lodge and were required to obey its edicts, laws, and regulations; local lodges, on the other hand, were allowed to enact their own constitutions and laws and, for the most part, to function as independent institutions. By sending representatives to the annual Grand Lodge Assembly, local lodges revealed their willingness to participate in the Masonic community, demonstrated the importance of the federalist principle, and became involved in the legislative process. Other legislative functions, which reflected Whiggish ideas, were entrusted to local lodges. In operating as assemblies, these Masonic bodies elected their members and officers, permitted members to engage in debate about lodge matters, adhered to the principle of majority rule in the formulation of laws and policies, and appointed committees to study specific problems about lodge operations.[73] The Master, who might be envisioned as the Walpole of Masonry, and his "cabinet of officers" were delegated executive functions; they were authorized to implement the laws, regulations, and policies of their lodge and those of the Modern Grand Lodge. The Master also was entrusted with judicial functions. This officer was empowered to interpret the laws and edicts of his lodge and to protect the liberties and privileges of each of its members.[74]

Coffeehouses and taverns in early Hanoverian London also contributed to the operations of modern lodges. London lodges, in practically all cases, functioned either in coffeehouses or in taverns and depended upon many activities sponsored by these institutions to enhance the appeal of Masonry. As a result of their intimate attachment to the coffeehouse and tavern world of London, Masonic lodges served beverages and meals, had game and reading rooms, and sponsored concerts, artistic displays, and lectures about various topics.[75] Modern lodges also relied upon taverns and coffeehouses to recruit members to their ranks. Many clubmen, who for the most part were aristocratic and bourgeois enlighteners, patronized coffeehouses and taverns and as well were admitted to London lodges. It further seemed that certain groups of clubmen and enlighteners gravitated

to specific lodges in the districts of Covent Garden and Westminster.
Lodges located in the Blew Boar and Clare Market Taverns consisted
of painters who were affiliated with the St. Martin's Lane Academy.
Lodges meeting in the Chapter Coffeehouse and in the Bedford Head
Tavern consisted of some writers and actors. The Mitre Tavern Lodge
was comprised of numerous antiquarians, most of whom belonged to
the Society of Antiquaries. There were numerous circles of Masonic
physicians and scientists. Physicians seemed to gravitate to the Ship
without Temple Bar and Rummer Tavern Lodges. The Royal Society Club, whose poster included numerous Masons, met in the Mitre
Tavern. Scientists also played an active part in the Bedford Head,
Crown and Anchor, and Horn Lodges.[76]

B. The Cultural Functions of Modern London Masonic Enlighteners

1. Desaguliers and Other Masonic Mechanists

In addition to his central place in Modern Masonry, Desaguliers
served as a gospeler of mechanism. By serving as curator of the Royal
Society and by frequently lecturing in London coffeehouses and taverns, Desaguliers became the most important Newtonian demonstrator of his day and made many friendships. Some friends of Desaguliers
belonged to the Royal Society but were not involved in Masonry. Desaguliers seemed to be friendly with Henry Pemberton, giving this
mechanist assistance in preparing the third edition of the *Principia*.[77]
Desaguliers also cultivated a close friendship with Stephen Hales and
reviewed his *Vegetable Statiks*, a work that in the estimation of Desaguliers contained "a vast fund of the philosophy" of Newton.[78] Many
Masonic friends of Desaguliers, who were members of the Royal Society and who, for example, included Lord Coleraine, the Earl of Craw-
ford, and George Heathcote, were not, for the most part, professional
scientists. These friends were, however, aristocratic and bourgeois
patrons of science and, by attending London coffeehouses and taverns, were given the opportunity to interact with Desaguliers and to
learn about his mechanistic views. Desaguliers differed from other
prominent Newtonians, because he especially developed for the London coffeehouse and tavern crowd interesting and simplified scientific
lectures. He certainly was familiar with most of these convivial institutions located near the Covent Garden, but especially liked to

present his lectures in the Bedford Coffeehouse and in the Crown and Anchor Tavern.[80]

At the beginning of his lectures, Desaguliers told the audience that "only common sense and undivided attention" were needed for an understanding of his experiments and then proceeded to define the major aims and methods of Newtonian science.[81] To Desaguliers, experimental scientists "are to contemplate the Works of God, to discover Causes from their Effects, and to make Art and Nature subservient to the necessities of life, by a skill in joining proper Causes to produce the most useful Effects."[82] He maintains that scientists should rely upon empirical and observational methods for the exploration of Nature. "All the Knowledge we have of Nature depends upon facts. Without Observations and Experiments, our Natural Philosophy would only be unintelligible jargon."[83] Desaguliers believes that to determine the orderly operations of Nature in light of her causes and effects, experimental scientists should use precise mathematical instruments.[84] He further defends the inductive procedures of the Newtonians, maintaining that the Cartesians without mathematical evidence took "a few principles for granted, without examining their reality," and made "wild guesses about the motion of the planets and comets."[85]

Desaguliers in light of ancient scientific ideas identified varying attributes of matter. Like the Aristotelians, he thinks that simple bodies can be divided into four categories: the earth is cold and dry; water is cold and moist; air is hot and moist; and fire is hot and dry.[86] To Desaguliers, simple bodies possess motion as well.

1. The matter of natural bodies is the same; namely, a substance extended and impenetrable.

2. All natural bodies must have motion, in some or in all of their parts.

3. That local motion is the chief principle among second causes, and the chief agent of all that happens in Nature.[87]

Desaguliers explains that bodies are endowed with atoms and with attractive powers and are able to move as a result of the force of gravity. Like the ancient philosopher Democritus, Desaguliers claims that matter can be split into tiny particles, the smallest being known as "atomes."[88] These atoms form "the constituent or component Part of Natural Bodies, being created by the Wise and Almighty Author of Nature as the original Particles of Matter."[89] Desaguliers argues that atoms are solid and impenetrable, are incessantly in motion, and possess attractive powers.[90] He maintains that when atoms in bodies are drawn near to each other, the force of attraction will be strong; when these particles are moving away from each other, the force of attraction will decrease.[91] That force enabling particles to attract and to repel each other and causing Nature to be in a state of perpetual motion is gravity. Desaguliers attempts to demonstrate the relation between this mechanistic principle and the deistic and Masonic concept of God, claiming that the Purposeful Architect and gravity are responsible for the orderly and harmonious operations of all bodies in the universe.[92]

He lectured about concepts pertaining to motion and to gravity. Desaguliers defines mass as the quantity of matter in each body and velocity as "the swiftness with which a moving Body changes its Place."[93] He explains that when the mass and velocity of a body are increased, "the motion of the whole will be equal to the sum of the motion of all the parts."[94] He shows that the concepts of power and weight are related to those of mass and velocity. According to Desaguliers, any body sustained, raised, or depressed is defined as a weight; any object applied to raise a weight is considered a power. While a power moves according to its velocity in any direction, a weight can only move in one direction. Desaguliers applied these concepts to the study of the movements of terrestrial objects:

> The Line of Direction of a Weight is a Line drawn from its Center of Gravity to the Center of the Earth. As the Middle of the Weight of a Body, the Center of Gravity is a Point about which all parts of a Body are in *Aequilibrio*. . . .[95]

To demonstrate what the concept of the center of gravity means, he discusses the relationship of the planets to the Sun. Desaguliers claims that the Sun serves as the nucleus of the solar system and that the center of gravity of the planets and their moons are found within this immovable body.[96]

An important lecture of Desaguliers is devoted to an explication of Newton's first law of motion:

> Every Body perseveres in a state of rest, or of uniform motion in a right line, unless it be compelled to change that state by forces impressed thereon.[97]

He offers interpretations and examples to show the validity of this law. Desaguliers maintains that an object remains at rest or in a state of

Vis Inertiae until impressed by a force; upon its impression, an object is given motion and in many cases changes shape.[98] He advances a corollary to support the first law: when bodies with similar masses and velocities move from the same point or height, these objects will reach a common point.[99] To confirm this corollary, Desaguliers gives the example of similar balls fired from cannons located in the same place and reaching a common point at the same time.[100]

In another important corollary to the first law of motion, Desaguliers defined the essential features of centrifugal and centripetal forces and then took issue with important concepts of Cartesian physics. He explains that a centrifugal force makes a body move away from the center of motion and that a centripetal force makes a body move towards the center of motion. He further referred to these forces to repudiate the Cartesian theory of motion. Descartes advanced the vortex theory, believing that a "Whirlpool of celestial matter known as a vortex produces the motion of the planets around the Sun."[101] These whirlpools in turn force the Sun to rotate about its axis and give motion to celestial bodies. Descartes believes that the vortices are denser and heavier than the planets and that the orbits of the planets seem to move away from the Sun. Desaguliers argues that if the vortices are heavier than the planets, the centripetal forces of the planets "would make them go continually towards the Sun in a spiral line, until they fell into it."[102] He concludes that the vortex theory is invalid and that "gravity was that magnificent force keeping the planets and moons in their orbits about the Sun."[103]

Desaguliers extensively dealt with Newton's second law of motion: "The change of motion is always proportionable to the moving force impressed and is made in the right line in which that force is impressed."[104] Desaguliers interprets this law to mean that "if any force generates a motion, a double force will generate double the motion, and a triple force triple the motion."[105] Forces acting either at right or at acute angles upon a body will produce an increase in the velocity of the impressed object. Desaguliers further claims that the second law of motion is valuable to scientists, enabling them to determine the speeds of such descending projectiles as arrows and cannon balls.[106]

He cited numerous examples to illustrate the second law of Newton. With an organ circulating around the center of an axis, the fly is a machine which accumulates power impressed upon it and operates according to the second law of motion. Desaguliers explains that when the organ of the fly is attached to a large board, this machine can be used to impress coins and stamps.[107] He maintains that like the fly, the circular pendulum is capable of accumulating motion and of exerting its impressed force to move objects of great weight.[108] Desaguliers claims that the operations of the sling exhibit the validity of the second law. When not subjected to friction, this instrument accumulates power and has been used by ancient and modern engineers for the operation of the rammer and similar machines.[109]

Desaguliers also argues that the motions of the planets and comets help to confirm Newton's second law. According to Desaguliers, those planets nearest to the Sun perform their revolutions in shorter times than those at far distances from it. He claims that gravity enables the planets to maintain a balance between their centrifugal and centripetal forces and to revolve around the Sun in their elliptical paths. Desaguliers also demonstrates that the movements of a comet are related to the second law. He explains that as a result of its centripetal being greater than its centrifugal forces, a comet in moving towards the Sun is destined to fall into it.[110]

Desaguliers examined Newton's third law of motion; he informed his audience that "to every action, there is always an equal reaction; or the mutual actions of two bodies upon each other, are always equal, and directed to contrary parts."[111] In interpreting this law, Desaguliers explains that when a body strikes another one and alters by its force the motion of the struck body, the former body will also experience an equal change in its motion. The changes resulting from this interaction are equal, not in the velocities, but in the motions or momenta of the bodies.[112] Desaguliers gave numerous examples to demonstrate Newton's third law concerning action and reaction. He maintains that when a cannon is fired, the explosion of powder will push the ball forward and the cannon a little backwards; this law is applicable to the movements of swimmers. By pushing water backwards, swimmers are able to move forward.[113] As Desaguliers shows, the third law also explains the movement of the tides. As a result of the gravitational force of the moon, "the oceans ebb and flow, twice each day, the tides being greatest about the equinoxes, when the luminaries are nearest the earth."[114]

To demonstrate how the Newtonian system of the world functions, Desaguliers explained the operations of elastic and non-elastic bodies. He performed experiments with clay balls to show that non-elastic bodies operate according to the laws of motion and gravity;

when two clay balls strike each other, the magnitude of their blow will be proportionable to the velocity of the striking or the percutient body. When two non-elastic objects with opposite motions strike against each other, the magnitude of their blow will be the same as if one of the objects had remained at rest.[115] Desaguliers maintains that the principles governing the operations of elastic bodies are somewhat different than those of non-elastic objects. When two elastic bodies collide with each other, their velocities will remain the same before and after striking each other. Perfectly elastic bodies will also recede from each other with the same velocity which forced them to hit each other. After colliding with each other, two elastic bodies can restore themselves to their former shapes, with a force equivalent to that by which these bodies were compressed.[116] Desaguliers further speculates that the principles of attraction and repulsion are related to elasticity and could explain its cause. In subjecting elastic objects to fire and to various fluids, Desaguliers derived different results; fire and fluids cause some elastic bodies to cohere to each other and other elastic objects to repel each other. He consequently failed to discover the cause of elasticity.[117]

Desaguliers conducted experiments with vacuums to determine the properties of various objects where air is not prevalent and to exemplify Newton's principle regarding the resistance of matter. During one experiment, he dropped a guinea, a piece of fine paper, and a feather simultaneously into a glass-receiver exhausted of air; Desaguliers found that all three objects descend at the same time to the bottom of the receiver and that the interspersed vacuum provides no medium of resistance for the falling objects.[118] During another demonstration, he poured three pounds of mercury into a vacuum and three pounds of water into another one; he added hot and then cold water to the liquids in each vacuum. After the temperature of each liquid was taken, Desaguliers determined the quantity of each liquid remaining in the vacuums. He discovered that the mercury absorbs more heat than the water and that the amount of mercury remaining from the original three pounds is greater than that of water from the three pound quantity. Desaguliers concluded that bodies of similar bulk, subjected to an interspersed vacuum, do not always contain equal quantities of matter.[119]

Unlike other prominent Newtonians, Desaguliers delivered many lectures in London coffeehouses and taverns about topics concerning the application of mechanistic principles to technology.[120] There seemed to be several reasons to explain the interest of this Newtonian in technology; Desaguliers knew that the principles of motion helped to explain the operations of steam engines and that these engines were being used in Hanoverian England to improve transportation and to mechanize production. He also realized that many Londoners attending his lectures had invested capital in industrial enterprises and thus were interested in technology.

In one of his lectures, Desaguliers surveyed the development of the engine; he claims that "the fewest mechanical blunders came from civil and military architecture, since architects and engineers were skilled in the use of mechanical organs." [121] Desaguliers maintains that eighteenth century English engineers were familiar with ancient machinery, with the modern principles of hydrostatics and pneumatics, and with the operative skills of the mason, carpenter, and bricklayer. "Probing these crafts for the mystery of their art," modern engineers have combined the practical knowledge of these operative sciences with the Newtonian laws of motion to develop the steam engine. [122]

Desaguliers alluded to the views of Martin Clare about hydrostatics. A member of the Cross Keys Lodge in Henrietta Street and a Deputy Master of the Modern London Grand Lodge, Clare was elected to the Royal Society and acquired recognition for *The Motion of Fluids, Natural and Artificial*. In this work, he claims that the concepts of hydrostatics conform to Newtonian mechanical laws and can be used to improve industry, business, trade, and navigation. [123] Clare also vividly demonstrates that the forcing pump, fire-engines, and the machine for raising water by a multiplying-wheel function in light of hydrostatical principles.

> The Multiplying-Wheel Engine works in part by a Worm turning a Jack-fly and has raised enough water to fill the ponds of a Gentleman in Buckinghamshire. . . . The buckets of this engine can easily empty water anywhere. . . . Forcing pumps consist of a barrel and a forcer piston and are used to lift water from natural springs. . . . Engines for extinguishing Fire can be used to raise water and to lift bodies from the Earth. . . . [124]

Desaguliers examined the operations of the engine for driving piles, of the water engine of Joshua Haskins, and of the machine known as the jack-in-the box. Invented by Mr. Vauloué, the pile driving engine, Desaguliers explains, was in operation at the new

Westminster Bridge and is propelled by a great wheel; this wheel with cogs turns a trundle-head with a fly, forcing the great rope to pass over the pulley. According to Desaguliers, the pile driving engine served a useful purpose, in that it functioned to move objects from one place to another.[125] Desaguliers comments on the engine of Haskins, claiming that this machine effectively operated to pump water through pipes and into barrels.[126] He discusses the jack-in-the box, showing that this engine was designed to eliminate impurities in water pipes and pumped water from a reservoir near Cavendish Square to mansions in the vicinity.[127]

Desaguliers lectured about the steam engine. He explains that Captain Savery designed an engine to drain mines and that his engine converts water into steam and then forces the steam to lift water from mines. After observing the demonstrations of Savery's engine at York, Desaguliers advanced his views about problems entailed with the operations of this machine; he believes that the Savery engine functions awkwardly and that unregulated steam can damage parts of this engine. Desaguliers maintains that the atmospheric steam engine of Thomas Newcomen was superior to the Savery engine and was being used extensively in England. According to Desaguliers, the Newcomen engine, which operates by a piston moving in a great cylinder, pumped water from mines, helped in the lifting of coal from mines near Tyne and Wear, and assisted in supplying water to the Sion House of Lord Chandos and to the mansions of other English aristocrats.[128]

Desaguliers commented on the operations of the crane and believed that it could be applied for industrial purposes. He maintains that a "fixed crane with its moveable gibbet could raise stones from a great depth."[129] According to Desaguliers, the iron wheel of the crane rests on the gibbet and is propelled by the engine. He explains that capable of turning a complete circle, a "rat's tail crane" operates in accordance with the principles of the lever and the pulley, applying appropriate force to raise weights from the ground and to lower them into carriages for shipment.[130]

Desaguliers spoke of his mechanical inventions as well. He invented a pumping machine, which was equipped with a crank and with three regulators, to suck impure air from mines and to push fresh air into them.[131] Desaguliers informed his audience that the concept of circulating air also explains how his ventilating systems operated and that these systems were installed in London hospitals and in 1720 in the House of Commons.[132] Before ending his discussion about technology, Desaguliers referred to his invention used by British breweries. He explains that this machine blows warm air upon malt and thus facilitates the beer-making process.[133]

Desaguliers was one of the few British Newtonians interested in electrical studies. His work with electricity might be attributed to several reasons. He perhaps thought that the corpuscular theory of Newton was related to electrical studies and that the principles of motion, attraction, and repulsion governed electricity. Desaguliers might have believed that the study of electricity would lead to the discovery of the cause of gravity. Like Boerhaave, 'sGravesande, and other Dutch Newtonians involved with electrical studies during the 1730s, he probably believed that concepts governing electricity could be fruitfully applied to medicine, to industry, and to technology.[134]

The intention of the first experiments of Desaguliers was to determine "the property of electrical bodies and to discover what useful influence electricity has in Nature."[135] He experimented with numerous objects and even with a human. In his first experiment, Desaguliers produced friction from an iron bar and discovered that upon contact with the bar, many objects received electrical charges and included gold and silver medals, brass balls, sealing wax, ivory, human bones, and flesh.[136] In another experiment, he tied a heavy thread to a man suspended in air and transmitted electrical charges through the thread and the man to various objects; he discovered that woolen cloth, worsted tape, mercury, and wax became exceedingly electricized. This demonstrator discovered that ropes, sponges, and wire tubes transmitted with ease electrical virtues to other objects and that electrical virtues failed to excite and to pass through dampened wax, dried ox-guts, or a moistened silk string.[137]

In light of these and other experiments, Desaguliers defined the qualities and properties of electricity. He explains that electrical bodies are those capable of exciting electricity either by rubbing, patting, hammering, melting, or warming. According to Desaguliers, a non-electrical body cannot be transformed into an electrical object but in many instances can receive electrical charges from an electric *per se*.[138] He maintains that electrics *per se* are endowed with the powers of attraction and repulsion and that a body excited by an electrical charge, whether an electric or a non-electric, attracts and repels electrical objects. Desaguliers claims that when reduced to a non-electric state, an electric *per se* is not able to receive electricity from another electric *per se*. He further observes that an electric *per se* can be excessively electric in one part and can remain a non-electric in another part. According to Desaguliers, an electric *per se* gradually relinquishes its electrical charge, whereas a non-electric, upon receiving the electrical virtue, immediately loses its charge.[139]

Desaguliers in 1742, two years prior to his death, published "A Dissertation Concerning Electricity." This essay was considered an important contribution to experimental science, providing a concise account of major electrical concepts advanced by Desaguliers and receiving in 1742 the annual prize awarded by the Academy of Bordeaux. In this article, Desaguliers further speculates that electrical effluvia seem to be the basis of electrical motion and to be related to the principle of gravity.[140] This speculation and other electrical ideas of Desaguliers attracted the attention of mechanists not affiliated with the Craft and undoubtedly were of special importance to the young Benjamin Franklin and to other Masonic scientists.

Other London Masons, especially astronomers, were affiliated with the Royal Society and were proponents of mechanism. Several reasons might be suggested to explain why some astronomers wished to belong to Modern Masonry. They certainly knew Desaguliers from their involvement in science and in London club and tavern life; they also realized that the rites of the Craft contained astronomical and mechanistic concepts and recognized that their lectures well could be delivered in Masonic lodges. Lord George Parker attended Oxford with Desaguliers and during the early 1720s entered Masonry, being associated with the Swan Tavern Lodge in Chicchester; Lord Parker became a noted astronomer, charting the movements of the moon and stars from his well equipped observatory in Shirburn Castle. As a result of his observations, Parker was admitted in 1722 to the Royal Society and from 1752 until 1764 served as its president.[141]

John Machin and Brook Taylor belonged to the Bedford Head Lodge and as members of the Royal Society performed valuable functions. Dr. Machin served as Professor of Astronomy at Gresham College, was elected in 1710 as a member of the Royal Society, and was named as its secretary in 1718, holding this position until 1747. He served in 1712 on a committee assigned to investigate the dispute between Newton and Leibnitz and more importantly published "Law of the Moon's Motion according to Gravity," a chapter appended in 1729 to Motte's translation of the *Principia*.[142] Brook Taylor in 1712 sent a letter to Machin; this letter contained a solution to the problem raised by Kepler in the formulation of the second law of planetary motion and enabled him in 1712 to be elected to the Royal Society. Taylor published in 1719 an astronomical work entitled *New Principles of Linear Perspective* but primarily was known as a mathematician. Taylor's Theorem attempts to explain the expansions of functions of a single variable in an infinite series. Taylor further used the calculus to develop a differential equation concerning the relationship of light rays to a heterogeneous medium. Taylor also appeared to be active in Masonry, serving as Senior Warden of the Bedford Head Lodge.[143]

James Bradley was the most significant astronomer identified with Modern Masonry during the Augustan Era. He seemed to belong to the scientific circle of Desaguliers and was affiliated with the Three Kings Lodge in Spittlefields. Like Desaguliers, Bradley attended Oxford and studied under John Keill; Bradley earned his Bachelor and Masters Degrees from Oxford and in 1721 was appointed to the Savilian Chair of Astronomy in this university. Bradley was known for discovering the nutation of the Earth's axis; he was admitted to the Royal Society in 1718 and wrote papers concerning stars for the society to confirm Newton's principles of gravity and motion.[144] He demonstrates that "fixed stars" possess motion, "moving 20 degrees more southerly than when first observed."[145] From his observatory at Greenwich, Bradley, who was named as Royal Astronomer in 1742, calculated the distance between the Sun and the Moon and determined the elliptical movements of observed comets.[146]

A member of the Bedford Head Lodge and the President of the Royal Society between 1741 and 1752, Martin Folkes delivered papers to the Society concerning astronomy. Folkes, who was also an antiquarian, wrote about the characteristics and movements of Mock Suns,

> I was on a London street between 8 and 9 o'clock on March 30th and saw a light over the houses to the north. . . . I made haste into the fields, where I was for some time agreeably entertained with the sight of an *aurora borealis*. . . . The whole northern part of the horizon was in the same manner covered with something resembling a black cloud, from behind which there issued a considerable light, whose lower part was pretty well defined by the common edge of the cloud, but the upper died away more gradually. . . .
>
> On September 17, 1736, I was reading a little after 7 in the

morning and accidentally noticed an odd stream of colored
light, shooting upwards from the Sun. . . . I observed
that the stream of light was part of an arch concentric to
the Sun, tinged with red on the inside, and a bluish white
on the other. . . . These streams of light appeared as
Mock Suns and were always moving quickly as they gave off
luminous colors. . .[147]

Folkes offered no theories about Mock Suns; he perhaps thought their
movements resembled those of comets and conformed to laws advanced by Newton. Like other astronomers, Folkes probably believed
that Mock Suns, similar to comets, were mysterious celestial bodies
and that the principles governing these suns and comets were important for an understanding of the mechanistic operations of the solar
system.

Physicians constituted the other major group of mechanists. Many
London Masonic doctors belonged to the Royal College of Physicians
and to the Royal Society and believed that the mechanistic concepts
advanced in both societies were important to the study of anatomy,
physiology, pathology, and surgery; most Masonic physicians did not
play an active role in the affairs of the Royal Society, but many of
these medical men gave lectures to the College of Physicians.[148] The
attraction of English physicians to Modern Masonry seemed to be
attributed to several reasons. The Blue Degrees embodied the sensis-
tic and mechanistic views of John Locke and taught that as the Sun
is the center of the solar system, the heart functions as the nucleus
of the human body; these degrees also emphasized benevolence, an
important doctrine to physicians. It further seemed that Desaguliers
played a central role in recruiting William Rutty, Alexander Stuart,
William Graeme, and other physicians to Modern Masonry.

Thomas Pellett and Sir Richard Manningham, two Masonic doctors who belonged to the Royal Society and to the College of Physicians, were known for their work in pathology. Pellett received his
medical degree from the University of Padua, returned to London in
1718 to practice medicine, and in 1725 was admitted to the Bedford
Head Lodge. Pellett was quite active in the College of Physicians; he
delivered to the college the Harverian Oration in 1719 and lectured
about the symptoms of varying diseases prevalent in London at this
time. This pathologist between 1735 and 1739 also served as President of the College of Physicians.[149] Dr. Manningham, who was a
member of the Horn Lodge, published in 1750 a *Treatise on the Symp-*

toms, *Nature, Causes, and Cure of the Febricula or Little Fever.* In addition to commenting on this disease, he discussed the symptoms of varying fevers and the common cold, described the mechanistic operations of the body, and advocated the monistic or single cause theory of disease.[150]

Pathological investigations occupied the attention of other Masonic physicians. A fellow of the College of Physicians and a member of the Rummer Lodge at Charing Cross, Dr. Alexander Stuart obtained his medical degree from the University of Leyden and published several works about the diseases and functions of muscles.[151] Like Stuart, Nathaniel Cotton studied under the Newtonian physician Hermann Boerhaave at Leyden and returned in 1725 to London to begin his medical practice. Dr. Cotton, who was a member of the Castle Lodge, treated many cases of scarlet fever and in light of his extensive work with this disease published in 1749 a pamphlet entitled *A Kind of Scarlet Fever that lately appeared at St. Albans.*[152] Dr. Thomas Short, a member of the Queen's Head Lodge, was an obscure medical writer. He wrote in 1750 *New Observations on the Bills of Mortality*, commenting on major diseases causing deaths in early Hanoverian London and on the symptoms of these diseases.[153]

Some Masonic physicians engaged in anatomical investigations. Dr. James Douglas of the Freemason's Coffeehouse published a bibliography of anatomy entitled *Bibliographiae Anatomicae* in 1716 and delivered papers to the College of Physicians concerning the functions of the heart and the spleen; his lecture on the heart alluded to patients with heart murmurs, while that on the spleen dealt with amyloid degeneration, a question first examined by Virchow.[154] After receiving his medical degree from Oxford in 1729, Frank Nicholls went to London to practice medicine and in 1732 was elected to the College of Physicians. He delivered to this society lectures regarding blood vessels, arteries, aneurysms, and high blood pressure. Nicholls furthermore gave the Gulstonian Lectures in 1734. These lectures contained an explanation of the circulation of blood and the structure of the heart and were published in his 1738 work *Compendium Anatomico - oeconomicum.*[155]

Some Masonic anatomists and surgeons lectured about cancer. A member of the Swan Lodge in Ludgate Street and the chief surgeon of St. Thomas's Hospital, Dr. William Becket in 1712 gave a lecture to the College of Physicians entitled "New Discoveries Relating to the Cures of Cancers."[156] A colleague of Becket, the anatomist and surgeon Dr. William Rutty, who belonged to the College of Physicians and to the Royal Society, made observations of patients afflicted with this disease; he presented his findings to the Royal Society. Dr. Rutty described how tumors found in an infant had destroyed "nerves in the spine and the *medulla spinalis*."[157] In another lecture, he commented on the corrosive effects of throat and lung cancer, claiming that a tumor six inches long had been removed from the thorax of a patient and that cancer had completely blackened his lungs.[158]

Other surgeons were identified with Modern Masonry. Dr. John Radcliffe and the Jewish physician Meyer Schomberg practiced surgery in St. Bartholomew's Hospital. Both surgeons belonged to the College of Physicians but were not involved in medical research.[159] Dr. Samuel Sharp was the most noted Masonic surgeon, studying under William Hunter and then practicing as the chief surgeon of Guy's Hospital. Sharp furthermore lectured to naval surgeons in Covent Garden and published in 1739 *A Treatise on the Operations of Surgery*. This text contains significant chapters regarding amputations, concussions of the brain, and the removal of tonsils and gall-bladders.[160]

2. Literature and Modern English Masons

Although less numerous in the ranks of the Craft than physicians and scientists, some writers were involved with Modern Masonry in Augustan London. Minor writers from various fields of literature were admitted to London lodges and evidently perceived these institutions as being extensions of club and tavern life. These writers published works about ancient and modern ideas associated with Masonic rituals and with the Enlightenment; they, however, made little effort to relate the concepts of Masonry to those of the Enlightenment and thus failed to develop a London school of Masonic literature. Although most prominent London writers were not members of the Craft and seemed to be disinterested in its ritualistic operations, a few major writers affiliated with Modern Masonry but utilized literary societies rather than Masonic lodges to promote their ideas.

Alexander Pope was the most important Augustan writer to affiliate with Modern Masonry. The involvement of Pope in London literary clubs and coffeehouses helped to explain why he was inducted during the early 1720s into the Goat at the Foot Lodge in the Haymarket.[161] Although professing Catholicism and although never holding an office in this lodge, Pope subscribed to major Enlightenment ideologies and made some allusions to Masonic tenets and symbols in his writings. He probably perceived pertinent concepts of Masonry as being related to those of the Enlightenment.

Like many Masonic enlighteners, Pope wrote about science. In *An Essay on Man*, published in 1733, he portrayed in classical verse the accomplishments of Newton. To Pope, the discovery of gravity and the laws of motion epitomized the success of reason. Pope further maintains that the laws of Newton reveal the Grand Design of the Creator and explain the mechanical and orderly operations of bodies in Nature and in the vast universe.

> Heave'ns whole foundations to their centre nod, And Nature tremble to the throne of God. . . . Go, wond'rous creature! mount where science guides. Go, measure earth, weigh air, and state the tides; Instruct the planets in what orbs to run, Correct old Time, and regulate the Sun. . . .[162]

To Pope, Newton's laws of motion as well explain the operations of "gawdy Colours emitted from the Prismatic Glass" and thus are as applicable to the study of the microcosm as to that of the macrocosm.[163] Pope seemed to emerge as an advocate of the Great Chain of Being, suggesting in *An Essay on Man* that Newton's laws could be applied to understand the relationship between man and God and between man and Nature.[164]

In several works, Pope wrote as an enlightened Mason. In *The Temple of Fame*, published in 1715, he refers to Egyptian temples, suggesting that their columns, walls, and altars exemplified architectural perfection. Pope further speaks of "Aegypt's Priests" and believes that "they measur'd the Starry Spheres" and were familiar with the ancient mysteries.[165] In the "Universal Prayer," completed in 1738, Pope suggests ethical views resembling those of Freemasonry. He maintains that humans utilize reason to develop their spiritual temples and are benevolent, just, and tolerant in their relations with others. He further thinks that "men should sing one chorus to Thee, whose Temple is all Space and whose Altar is the Earth."[166]

In addition to Pope, other poets, who were quite obscure, were affiliated with Modern Masonry. Like many Masons, these poets exhibited interest in the classics and rendered English translations of Greek and Roman poetry. Although Dr. Johnson was not a Mason, the Masonic poets Moses Mendes and John Ellis belonged to the circle of this British writer. Mendes was known for his translations of the poetry of Vergil, and Ellis, who belonged to the Rose Tavern

Lodge, read to members of this lodge some of his translations of the epistles of Ovid.[167] The minor poet George Jeffreys belonged to the Crown and Anchor Lodge and was a member of the literary group meeting in the St. James's mansion of the Duke of Chandos. Jeffreys issued in 1721 a collection of poems entitled "Cato" and also wrote approximately five plays that centered on topics relating to ancient history.[168]

Many actors and playwrights were involved with Modern Masonry. Most Masonic dramatists were middle class, appeared to be interested in the ancient tenets embodied in the Blue Degrees, and patronized London coffeehouses and taverns. Plays performed in Augustan London provided Masonic playwrights and actors with the opportunity to explain to their audiences ancient themes, modern cultural achievements, and contemporary socio-political problems. Charles Beckingham served as a producer for the Lincoln's Inn Fields Theater and wrote several plays. He was especially interested in Roman history, writing *Scipio Africanus* in 1719 and staging a performance of this play the following year.[169] Another minor Masonic playwright was John Kelley. A member of the Cross Keys Lodge, Kelley wrote five plays and in 1747 published his most noted one, *The Universal Spectator*, a comedy in three acts.[170] Joe Miller, James Quinn, and John Palmer were Masonic actors associated with the Drury Lane Theater; Miller appeared in 1726 in *The Siege of Damascus* by Hughes, and Palmer in 1729 played the role of Captain Plume in *High Life Below the Stairs*. Quinn was recognized as one of the finest actors in Augustan London and between 1717 and 1732 played leading roles in ancient tragedies staged in the Drury Lane Theater.[171]

The literature of deism, which revolved around ancient and modern concepts, was important to some Masonic writers. In the preface of his translation of the *Mathematical Elements of Natural Philosophy* by the Dutch Newtonian s'Gravesande, Desaguliers speaks as an enlightener and attempts to explain deistic ideas in light of mechanistic concepts. Desaguliers in this work describes the attributes of the Supreme Creator and the moral qualities of humans in light of geometrical figures.

> The Supreme Architect is Infinite, Eternal, Omnipotent, and
> Omniscient. His duration reaches from eternity to eternity,
> and His presence from infinity to infinity. . . . The Architect
> is everywhere. . . . He is all eye, all ear, all brain, and all
> power to perceive, to understand, and to act. . . . Circles,

Squares, and Triangles represent the Divine Attributes of Him, the laws of Nature, and the moral qualities of man. . . [172]

In the *Constitutions*, Desaguliers and Anderson speak as enlightened Masons and perceive the ancient God of Modern Masonry in mechanistic terms. To Anderson and Desaguliers, God is "the Center of Union" and is the Source of morality.[173] By permitting Nature to function in light of the laws of motion and gravity, the Supreme Architect likewise expects Masons to apply such moral concepts as benevolence, justice, toleration, and virtue to improve society.

Other Protestant ministers in London, who were connected with the circles of Desaguliers and Anderson, subscribed to the ancient or "pagan" ideas of Masonic deism and renounced Christian deists associated with John Toland.[174] The Presbyterian ministers John Ball and John Newman in 1724 lectured to members of the Sun Tavern and Swan Lodges; they told members of these lodges that if admitted to Masonry, Toland and his followers would secure control of the Craft and would vitiate its ancient deistic teachings.[175] In a lecture to members of the Freemason's Coffeehouse Lodge in 1725, the Congregational minister John Evans maintained that the deistic views of Toland were in opposition to the nonsectarian principles of Speculative Freemasonry and that London Masonic lodges had succeeded in thwarting the efforts of Christian deists to enter the ranks of the Craft.[176]

Numerous Masons in London, who were involved with the study of the ancients, helped to promote the literature of antiquarianism and were affiliated with the Society of Antiquaries. Several reasons might be suggested to explain the close connection between Modern Masonry and the Society of Antiquaries. By meeting between 1718 and 1726 in the Mitre Tavern, which also housed a Masonic lodge, and by fostering the study of history and of "valuable Relicks of former Ages, especially those of the Romans," the Society of Antiquaries enlisted the support of many Masons.[177] Masons also played active roles in the Society of Antiquaries and in some cases held leadership positions in this organization. Henry Hare, the third Earl of Coleraine, belonged to the Craft and was a charter member of the Society of Antiquaries. Known for his prints of Roman temples designed in the Augustan Style, the Earl of Coleraine actively recruited Masons to this society.[178]

Dr. William Stukeley, another important charter member of the

Society of Antiquaries, was affiliated with several major cultural institutions in London. He was elected during the early 1720s to the Royal Society and to the College of Physicians.[179] At this time, Stukeley devoted considerable attention to antiquarian studies; he belonged to the Gentleman's Society of Spalding and frequently lectured to members of this historical and literary society about topics regarding ancient history. Stukeley in 1721 was also "made a Freemason at the Salutation Tavern in Tavistock Street."[180] It appeared that the interests of Stukeley in deism, in the ancient mysteries, and in Greek and Roman architecture and history motivated him to seek admittance to Masonry. After his election as Master of the Fountain Tavern Lodge in 1723, Stukeley delivered to the members of this lodge a lecture about ancient remains discovered in the Dorchester amphitheatre.[181]

During the 1720s and 1730s Stukeley served as secretary of the Society of Antiquaries and acquired prominence for his historical research. He showed to members of this society in 1722 his drawings of the ancient ruins at Alchester, Blenheim, and Chipping Norton.[182] Stukeley the next year "read a discourse upon the use of brass instruments call'd Celts, showing that they were British and appertaining to the Druids."[183] He also during the late 1720s gave lectures to the Society of Antiquaries about the circles and remains of the Druids discovered at Avebury and Stonehenge. Stukeley proposed a theory to explain the religious rites of the Druids; he maintained that the monuments within the small circles at Avebury and Stonehenge contained evidence of their worship of the moon and that those remains within the large circles suggested their worship of the Sun.[184] Samuel Gale, the first treasurer of the Society of Antiquaries and an active member of the Gentleman's Society of Spalding, worked with Stukeley at Stonehenge and in 1730 published his views about the findings at this site in the pamphlet *A Dissertation on Celts*.[185]

Other Masons affiliated with the Society of Antiquaries investigated topics relating to English History. Peter Le Neve, a Unitarian minister, delivered papers to the society regarding the history of Norfolk County; he also compiled exhaustive notes on genealogy and heraldry and assisted Tanner in writing the *Bibliotheca*. After the death of Le Neve in 1729, materials from his valuable collection were sold in the Bedford Coffeehouse; many sources from this collection were purchased and were used by John Bridges for his work entitled *The History and Antiquities of Northamptonshire*.[186] The Anglican bishop Richard Rawlinson was quite active in the Society of Antiquaries; he donated to the society his valuable collection of coins, engravings, and pictures. Rawlinson further wrote for the society *Antiquities of Salisbury and Bath* and *The History and Antiquities of the Cathedral Church of Hereford.*[187] Philip Webb gave lectures to and wrote several books for the society about Medieval English History. Webb published *A Short Account of Danegeld* and *A Short Account of the Domesday Book.*[188]

As a result of the influence of Webb and other Masonic antiquarians, Martin Folkes, whose involvement in the Egyptian Club attested to his interest in the ancients, was elected in March 1750 as President of the Society of Antiquaries. During his presidency, Folkes and members of the society especially devoted their attention to topics pertaining to ancient history. Folkes received approval and funds from members of the Antiquarian Society to publish his "very learned dissertation concerning the value of ancient moneys."[189] He also presented to the society several papers regarding the discovery of Roman coins in England. While Folkes served as president, Thomas Hunt delivered several important lectures. Hunt spoke to the society about the evolution of Hebrew, about Egyptian architecture, and about the career of Hippolytus.[190]

Ephraim Chambers, who was not a member of the Society of Antiquaries but who knew many intellectuals in London, engaged in a literary enterprise to promote major ideas of the British Enlightenment; he published in 1728 the *Cyclopedia* or *The Universal Dictionary of Arts and Sciences.* It seemed that Masonic support of the *Cyclopedia* was quite probable, for Chambers was a member of the Royal Society and the Richmond Lodge; he also was involved in Masonic groups headed by Desaguliers, by Folkes, and by the Duke of Montagu. The efforts of Chambers to disseminate ancient and modern knowledge of the arts and sciences certainly were compatible with the teachings of Masonry. The work of this Mason was invaluable and contained articles about astronomy, physics, ancient history, music, art, and architecture.[191]

3. The Fine Arts and English Masons

The development of the Augustan Style and the evolution of Modern Masonry in England appeared to be related to each other. Developed by the ancient Roman architect Vitruvius and revived during the Renaissance by Palladio, concepts of this style were described in the rites of Modern Masonry and were to be amenable to many "learned gentlemen and nobles of Great Britain" who were associated with the Craft.[192] Masons learned in the Blue Degrees that the Augustan Style reflected the laws of Nature and revolved around the concepts of order, harmony, and symmetry.[193] In light of their exposure to these degrees, Masons also learned about the walls, porches, arches, and Doric and Ionic columns of buildings erected in the Augustan Style.[194]

London Masons revealed interest in classical architecture. The Dukes of Chandos and Richmond, the Earl of Paisley, Martin Folkes, and some architects associated with the Craft went to Italy to study classical architecture. Some Masonic aristocrats also hired architects to build their London and residential mansions in light of major concepts of ancient architecture. Employed by Chandos, the Masonic architects George Dance and John Price designed Cannons, Edgware, and Marylebone. Indicative of the Augustan Style, these three mansions of Chandos were designed to resemble ancient Roman temples; they had domes, Doric columns, large porches, gardens, vaulted walks, baths, obelisks, and villas.[195] Nicholas Hawkesmore also built mansions in the Augustan Style in Hanover Square for the Duke of Richmond and the Earl of Coleraine.[196]

Like architects, artists also were attracted to Modern Masonry. Masonic artists in London discovered that the Blue Degrees emphasized important teachings of the ancients, placed stress on the orderliness of Nature, and associated colors with themes from Nature and with concepts of morality. Most Masonic artists also patronized taverns and coffeehouses located near the Covent Garden and were affiliated with lodges in this district.

Sir James Thornhill occupied a major place in Augustan art and in Masonry. Thornhill studied art in Italy and upon his return to England in 1712 was commissioned by Queen Anne to paint works for Hampton Court and for Greenwich Palace. He further painted frescoes on the dome of St. Paul's Cathedral. Thornhill in approximately 1721 opened an art academy and offered courses in engraving and in portrait painting; he recruited some Masons to his academy. Thornhill taught the engraver Richard Cooper, gave instruction to the painter Thomas Hudson who did portraits of the Duke of Montagu and Meyer Schomberg, and supervised the young artist William Hogarth who was to marry his daughter Jane.[197] Thornhill seemed to perceive Masonry as an important institution. He served as Master of the Swan Lodge, was appointed in 1729 as Senior Grand Warden of

Modern Masonry, and prior to his death in 1734 convinced Hogarth to affiliate with the Craft.[198]

As head of the St. Martin's Lane Academy, Hogarth significantly contributed to Augustan art. By depicting social problems in the British capital and by satirizing in his "pictur'd morals" the lives of the wealthy and the poor, this painter provided art in London with a new direction. Hogarth well portrayed in 1724 in *An Emblematical Print on the South Sea Scheme* speculators broken by the wheel of fortune.[199] In *Rake's Progress*, Hogarth in 1735 portrayed the adventurer Rake in the taverns of Covent Garden; there Rake met aristocrats, merchants, and beggars and was exposed to individuals promoting culture and corruption in Augustan London.[200] Hogarth in 1751 displayed *Gin Lane*, superbly depicting a drunken woman with children at her knees, and thus vividry revealed the "poisonous" problems entailed with this beverage.[201] In addition to his satirical works, Hogarth did portraits of Dr. Desaguliers, Martin Folkes, Lord Parker, Dr. Thomas Pellett and numerous other Masons, thus suggesting his interest in and connection with members of the order. Hogarth also trained Thomas Worlidge, a painter doing etchings of the level, square, and other Masonic symbols.[202]

Some Masons, who evidently wished to write musical compositions about Masonic teachings and symbols, affiliated with the ephemeral *Philo-Musicae et Architecturae Societas*. This society was organized in March 1725, consisted of merchants and musicians primarily from the Queen's Head Lodge, and admitted to its ranks approximately twenty members. The administrators of this society were minor merchants and included Thomas Bradbury, Charles Cotton, and Edmund Squire. The *Philo-Musicae et Architecturae Societas* admitted Francisco Geminiani, William Gulston, Obadiah Shuttleworth, and several other obscure Masonic musicians.[203] This society appeared to hold few meetings, did little to promote the study of music in London, and in 1727 disappeared as a result of lacking support from its membership.

John Heidegger, who was not affiliated with the *Philo-Musicae et Architecturae Societas*, emerged as one of the few important Masons in London during the 1720s and 1730s involved with music. Heidegger came to London in 1707, was known as the "Swiss Count," and invested money in ventures relating to music; he bought the Haymarket Theater, became a director of the Royal Academy of Music, and along with Handel owned the Italian Opera Company of London. As a result of poor attendance and management, this opera company went bankrupt, and its closing led to the financial demise of Heidegger.[204]

Musical performances at Cannons, an estate owned by the Duke of Chandos, were important to John Immyns and to other Masons. Immyns seemed to go frequently to Cannons, which was approximately five miles from London to direct the private orchestra of Chandos.[205] Under the direction of Immyns, the orchestra of the duke played many works of Handel, the eminent composer living at Cannons during the 1720s and 1730s.[206] This orchestra played his funeral anthems, his oratorios *Solomon* and *Belshazzar*, and his pastorals *Acis* and *Alexander's Feast*. These works emphasized ancient and secular ideas and evidently were meaningful to enlighteners and Masons attending musical performances at Cannons.[207] Desaguliers, the Dukes of Montagu and Richmond, and other Masons and Whigs frequently came to Cannons to listen to concerts, were the guests of Chandos for dinner, and afterwards stayed for a short time to discuss political matters.

4. Whigs, Tories, and Masons

There were various reasons for some Whigs to affiliate with Modern Masonry. The Blue Degrees emphasized some Whiggish principles. Justice, religious toleration, and other natural liberties were explained in these degrees. Many Whiggish ideas also were reflected in the operations of the lodges of Modern Masonry. Like Parliament, these lodges were required to comply with constitutional provisions, entrusted their chief officer with executive powers, appointed committees to study major proposals and problems, and enacted legislation in light of the principle of majority rule. Despite the Masonic regulation prohibiting the discussion of political matters during lodge meetings, some minor Whiggish leaders felt that affiliating with Masonic lodges would be advantageous to them.[208] What seemed to be important to these Whigs were the activities conducted outside of Masonic lodges and in various coffeehouses and taverns in London. Although Robert Walpole was not a member of the Craft, his arisocratic and bourgeois Masonic supporters held party dinners, circulated pamphlets, and campaigned especially in the Bedford and the Chapter Coffeehouses and in the Vine and Queen's Head Taverns to popularize the ideas of Robinocracy.[209]

Several Masons connected with the Whigs vindicated the doctrine of religious toleration. Raphel Courteville, the editor of the

Gazeteer, and Dr. Thomas Pyle advanced similar views about this doctrine. These two writers believed that members of Protestant sects should be entitled to vote, to hold political positions, and to worship without fear of persecution from the state.[210] John Asgill, a parliamentary minister from Enniscorthy, favored the abolition of restrictions imposed upon various religious groups in England. In an address to the House of Commons in 1719, Asgill spoke against the repeal of the Occasional Conformity Act and favored legislation granting civil and religious liberties to Protestant dissenting groups in England.[211] In another speech, he called for the repeal of the Test and Corporation Acts and for the removal of civil and religious disabilities imposed upon Catholics. Asgill also emerged in 1724 as one of the early proponents of Jewish emancipation but was not alive when the Whig Ministry under Pelham in 1753 introduced the Jew Bill.[212]

Numerous Masonic Whigs derived benefits from the patronage system of Walpole and were appointed to plum positions in the ranks of the Robinocracy.[213] The Duke of Chandos served as Paymaster General under Walpole and succeeded in increasing his fortune; the duke pocketed monies appropriated for the army and navy, stole funds from Chelsea Hospital, and purchased for a pittance Richmond Park and other lands previously used for deer hunting.[214] As Treasury Secretary, the Honorable Charles Stanhope engaged in practices similar to those of Chandos, using tax revenues for his personal investments. Appointed as a justice of the peace, Nathaniel Blackerby was delegated considerable power in the Robinocracy. Like other justices of the peace, Blackerby in many instances functioned quite independently of parliamentary authority; he was empowered to appoint some local administrative officials and to issue levies for parish needs. Blackerby also heard minor cases and received for his services sizable commissions.[215]

Many Whigs connected with Masonry were fortune hunters, were engaged in commerce and trade, and were well rewarded by Walpole; they envisioned themselves as being virtuous patrons of the state, but in fact only served themselves. Masonic Whigs involved with the East India Company gave extensive support to Walpole. As a result of the precipitous decline of the stock of the South Sea Company in 1720, Walpole convinced Parliament to approve legislation enabling the Bank of England and the East India Company to assume a major share of the stocks and debts of this failing company. This maneuver of Walpole resulted in the sudden rise of the stock of the East

India Company and in profits for the Masonic merchant John Clark and for other investors in the company.[216] As a consequence of the influence of Walpole, Sir William Billers was appointed as a director of the East India Company in 1723 and for approximately twenty years bribed parliamentary members to vote for bills concerning the exclusive trading privileges of the company.[217]

Walpole provided assistance to other Masons involved in commercial enterprises; he made Martin Bladen the Comptroller of the Mint and then appointed him as a commissioner of the Trade and Plantations.[218] The prime minister in 1724 helped John Gurney to obtain votes for a parliamentary bill concerning the Norwich wool trade; the bill was enacted, and Gurney was entrusted with powers to supervise the wool trade in this county.[219] By patronizing Walpole, the merchant Richard Cantillon in 1726 was granted special privileges for importing French cloth into England.[220] John, Lord Hervey of Ickworth defended these and other actions of Walpole. In *Sedition and Defamation Displayed*, published in 1731, he maintains that Walpole significantly increased the commerce and trade of England and that if brought to power, the Tories would destroy the economic foundations of the state.[221]

A few Tories were associated with Modern Masonry. Tories belonging to the Masonic order dined and caucused in the Bell and the Swan Taverns and also gave speeches during meetings of the Brothers Club and the Beef-Steak Society.[222] Masonic Tories tended to engage in pamphleteering and published articles to support the views of their leader Bolingbroke.[223] What Masonic Tories shared in common was the view that the gentry and independent representatives of Parliament should coalesce their efforts to oppose the oppressive policies of Whig ministries.[224] After losing his position in the army, Richard Temple, the Viscount of Cobham came to London and affiliated with the Tories and with Masonry; he further issued scathing attacks against Walpole, arguing that this Whig prime minister was one of the most corrupt leaders in English History.[225] The views of the Tory pamphleteer John Byram resembled those of Cobham; Byram denounced the commercial soldiers of fortune, called for the abolition of the Venetian oligarchy, and looked to the gentry for the moral and political regeneration of England.[226] In his poems during the 1720s, Edwin Ward satirized Walpole and his opportunistic colleagues. Ward perceived Whiggish merchants, financiers, cabinet officers, and parliamentary ministers as mere cheats.[227]

In looking to the monarchy for support during the late 1730s, leaders of the Modern London Grand Lodge probably wished to demonstrate to Whigs and Tories and to critics of the Craft that Masonry was above party politics. As a result of the influence of Desaguliers and of John Lumley, who was a groom to the bedchamber of the Crown, Frederick, the Prince of Wales, made the decision to enter Masonry. During a special meeting on November 5, 1737, Desaguliers inducted the Prince into the Kew Lodge.[228]

> We hear that on Saturday last was held at Kew a Lodge
> of Freemasons, where Dr. Desaguliers presided, when there
> was admitted several persons of high distinction as brethren
> of that Order. . . .[229]

Desaguliers evidently believed that Frederick would provide Masonry with leadership and would defend the order at the royal court. Frederick became, however, a great disappointment to the Craft. He surrounded himself with dispossessed political leaders, incessantly annoyed George II, and exhibited minimal interest in the affairs of Modern Masonry.[230]

C. The Demise of Modern Masonry in Eighteenth Century London

By the 1750s Modern Masonry in London began to decline. Until the death of Desaguliers in 1744, Modern Masonry in the British capital had succeeded in recruiting enlighteners from various fields of the liberal arts and sciences. After his death, Modern Masonry appeared to lack an effective recruiter and failed to attract many members of London cultural elites to its ranks. Most members of the Royal Society, during the middle and late years of the eighteenth century, were involved with the study of chemistry and biology, but did not affiliate with Modern Masonry. These materialists evidently viewed the Craft as being unimportant to their scientific investigations.[231] Moreover, a few artists, antiquarians, and writers during the last half of the eighteenth century gravitated to Modern Masonry; they found the ancient and deistic concepts embodied in the rites of Modern Masonry as being of minimal value to them. It was also apparent that the cultural and social operations of Modern Masonry after 1750 were not very meaningful to London patrons of culture and that most Whig and Tory leaders, who were concerned with the problems of the British Empire, felt little need to become involved in the affairs of the Masonic order.[232] To revitalize itself during the last half of the eighteenth century, Modern Masonry consequently needed leadership and members.

What Modern Masonry experienced at this time was strident competition from another Masonic institution known as the Antients. This schismatic body in Masonry was established in London in 1751 and in many respects resembled its modern counterpart.[233] The officers, organization, and operations of the Antient Grand Lodge and its local lodges closely resembled those of the Modern Grand Lodge and its local bodies. Local lodges under the jurisdiction of the Antients even conferred the first two degrees of Modern Masonry. The major point of departure between the Antients and the Moderns stemmed from the fact that the Royal Arch Mason Degree was conferred as the third degree in Antient Masonry. To the Antients, this degree served as the "root, heart, and marrow of Freemasonry."[234] The Royal Arch Degree, whose origins are nebulous, revolves around the story regarding the rebuilding of the Temple of Solomon. This degree lucidly explains the efforts of Prince Zerubbabel and of Haggai the Prophet to accomplish this task and contains symbols relating to ethical conduct. The hexalpha, or the Solomon Seal, symbolizes architectural and moral perfection, and the arch, which was needed to hold the reconstructed temple together, represents the keystone or moral cement of Freemasonry.[235]

By conferring the Royal Arch Degree, the Antients in London recruited members from various groups and consequently successfully rivaled the Moderns for approximately sixty-two years. Under the Grandmasterships of the Earl of Blessington and the third Duke of Atholl, Antient lodges in London during the last half of the eighteenth century recruited to their ranks many artisans, shopkeepers, soldiers, and a few Irish and Scottish nobles who resided in the British capital.[236] Antient lodges in London, which consisted of few intellectuals, functioned as the Country Party in British Masonry and until 1813 opposed the policies and operations of the Moderns. By agreeing that the three Blue Degrees would be exclusively conferred in local lodges and that separate bodies known as chapters would only stage the Royal Arch Degree, administrators of Modern Masonry that year reconciled their differences with officials of Antient Masonry. Leaders of Antient and Modern Masonry furthermore consented to unite in order to form a new body known as the Grand Lodge of England.[237]

Even before its competition and its compromise with the Antients,

Modern Masonry in several ways made an imprint upon the cultural life of Augustan London and became established in other European cities. The ritualistic system of Modern Masonry seemed to be a new and a rather important cultural invention in early Hanoverian London. Characterized by a special language and by distinctive symbols, the Blue Degrees provided London Masons with ritualistic explanations of salient Enlightenment ideologies. The relation of Masonry to the Enlightenment in the British capital can be illustrated from another standpoint. By enlisting the support of many London enlighteners, Modern Masonry functioned as the cultural wing of the fraternity. Specific behavioral patterns of Masons in Modern London lodges also appeared. These Masons participated in the ritualistic operations of London lodges, viewed these bodies as a source of Enlightenment and as fraternal associations, and consequently acted as Masonic enlighteners. Modern Masons held membership in numerous cultural organizations in Augustan London, engaged in social and cultural activities sponsored by clubs and taverns in the British capital, and, unlike their counterparts in Paris, felt little need to transform a London lodge into an Enlightenment learned society. Some modern London Masons during the 1720s also played an active role in establishing lodges in Paris. Modern Masonry then served as a vehicle for the dissemination of Enlightenment concepts in Paris and induced many French Masons to engage in cultural activities. In the next chapter, attention will be directed to topics concerning the origins and organization of Parisian Masonry and the cultural functions of members of the Lodge of the Nine Sisters.

III. PARISIAN MASONRY, THE LODGE OF THE NINE SISTERS, AND THE FRENCH ENLIGHTENMENT

A. The Evolution of Masonic Systems in Paris

1. The Origins and Operations of the Grand Lodge of France

Modern London Masonry during the 1720s and the 1730s affected the development of the Craft in Paris. With approval from the Grand Lodge of London, the Grand Lodge of France was established in 1725 in Paris.[1] With the consent of the Modern London Grand Lodge, Lord Derwentwater, an Englishman residing in Paris, was appointed as Grand Master of the French Grand Lodge. He, in turn, named the Duke d'Antin and several English and French nobles living in Paris as officers of this new grand lodge. Derwentwater, until approximately 1736, dominated the affairs of this Parisian grand lodge.[2] More importantly, the Grand Lodge of France, whose administrative operations between 1725 and 1736 were quite routine, emerged as a source of Anglophilism. This body received at this time administrative direction from the Grand Lodge of London and established lodges in Paris to promote significant ideas associated with English culture.[3]

The Lodges *Louis d'Argent, Coustos-Villeroy*, and *Bussi-Aumont* operated in Paris between 1727 and 1740 and were important to Masons in the French capital for several reasons. The organizational functions of these lodges resembled those of London lodges and, for the most part, permitted Parisian Masons, who were accustomed to monarchical institutions, to engage in new activities. Parisian lodges permitted Masons to elect their members and officers, to learn about natural liberties, to enact laws according to the majority rule principle, and to serve on committees. Those Masons serving as lodge officers, in many instances, were entrusted with new responsibilities and roles of leadership. Parisian lodges especially functioned as social centers. These bodies functioned as clubs, sponsoring many banquets and some lectures and thus allowing English and French Masons to interact with each other. Parisian lodges recruited many aristocrats, numerous middle class individuals, and some intellectuals. There was, however, another important facet of Parisian lodge life. Parisian Masons looked to these lodges for explanations of doctrines and symbols of the Blue Degrees.

Some concepts and symbols of the Modern degrees proved to be of special importance to Parisian Masons. These Masons seemed to perceive the Blue Degrees as a special source of the ideas of antiquity.[4] Parisian Masons learned from these degrees about important ideas concerning ancient architecture, mathematics, and science; moreover, the Blue Degrees explained to them ancient concepts regarding justice, temperance, and virtue.[5] Deism was quite fashionable in Paris, and the tenets of this ancient moral philosophy were well presented in the Blue Degrees. As a result of their exposure to the All Seeing Eye, to the three lesser lights of Masonry, and to the square and compasses, Parisian Masons were given ritualistic explanations concerning Deity, the powers of Nature, and the proper moral conduct of man. Ancient deistic concepts of the Blue Degrees consequently served as an alternative to the teachings of modern religion. These concepts also helped to shape the views of Parisian Masons towards the state and influenced their ethical conduct.[6]

Modern Enlightenment ideas appearing in the Blue Degrees stimulated the interest of Parisian Masons and, in many instances, were identified with a civil religion in France. These degrees revealed to Masons in the French capital significant Enlightenment concepts pertaining to education. In light of their exposure to the middle chamber of the Temple of Solomon and to the globe, Parisian Masons learned that knowledge is derived from reason and the senses and that Masons should strive to promote the study of the liberal arts and should probe Nature to ascertain her laws.[7] To aristocratic and bourgeois Masons in Paris, the Blue Degrees contained important social and political ideas. Parisian Masons were taught to be benevolent, just, and prudent and to work for the implementation of liberty, religious toleration, and other natural rights. These Masons evolved secular interpretations in explaining the moral legends, tenets, and symbols of the Blue Degrees and, in many cases, became ardent proponents of natural liberties. Numerous Masonic symbols helped to exemplify concepts of a French civil religion based on political reforms. The square, the plumb, the gavel, and the columns of Solomon's Temple were associated with this religion and appeared frequently during the *ancien régime* and the French Revolution.[8]

Some members of Parisian lodges during the 1720s and 1730s

performed cultural functions to promote Enlightenment concepts. Established in 1727, the Parisian Lodge *Louis d'Argent* consisted of numerous nobles of the robe and of some middle class intellectuals. French judges belonging to this lodge meeting in the *Hôtel de Bussy* furthermore served as patrons of the arts and sciences. Judge Davy de la Fautrière belonged to the *Club de l'Entresol*, was a proponent of economic and legal reforms, and published a history of French commerce and finance. He also revealed interest in Newtonian concepts, publishing an article in 1739 in the *Journal de Trévoux* concerning the importance of mechanical laws to metaphysics.[9] Count Chauvelin, also a judge in the Parisian Parlement, behaved as a Masonic enlightener; he was an associate member of the Academy of Sciences and also possessed interests in history and in literature. Chauvelin allocated funds for the publication of *Charles XII* by Voltaire. He furthermore developed a large library containing works about the Enlightenment and prior to his death donated them to the lodge.[10]

Two other minor intellectuals were involved with the *Louis d'Argent* Lodge. Jacques Pernetti was a Benedictine priest, who left Rome to reside first in Lyon and then in Paris. He was admitted to the lodge in 1730 and was known as a minor writer; Pernetti in 1732 published *Repos de Cyrus*, lauding the accomplishments of the ancient king. Pernetti also wrote a short work about Masonry, claiming in *Les Conseils de l'Amitié* that the Craft functioned to promote benevolent and cultural activities.[11] The former Jesuit and poet Jean Gresset evidently envisioned Masonry as a cultural vehicle of the Enlightenment. He maintained that Masonry taught its members ancient philosophical views espoused by Aristotle, Plato, and Socrates. According to Gresset, Masonry revolved around important concepts of the Enlightenment.

> Reason reigns supreme and is needed for the study of Nature.
> . . . Reason reveals to men their natural rights and liberties.
> . . . Masons, use reason to erect your spiritual temples and
> to improve society. . . .[12]

Montesquieu, who was inducted into the Horn Lodge in 1730, visited the *Louis d'Argent* Lodge in 1734. Several reasons might be suggested to explain his interest in Masonry and his visit to this Parisian lodge. Montesquieu during the late 1720s visited England, became friendly with the Duke of Richmond and Desaguliers, and evidentiy was convinced by these two Masonic enlighteners to affiliate with the Craft.[13] From an ideological viewpoint, Montesquieu evidently sympathized with Masonic teachings pertaining to the Enlightenment. Like many Masons, he was interested in experimental science and believed that the laws of Newton could be applied to the study of other disciplines. Like many Masons, Montesquieu exhibited interest in the political thought of the ancients and in 1748 argued in *L'Esprit des lois* that the Greeks and Romans should be commended for issuing constitutions, for developing viable legal systems, and for implementing the principle of the separation of powers.[14] He became an Anglophile; he believed that the government of early eighteenth century England resembled successful ancient ones and succeeded in operating in light of the doctrine of the separation of powers and in protecting the natural liberties of its citizens.[15] As an enlightener and as a Mason, Montesquieu subscribed to the doctrine of religious toleration; he denounced in *L'Esprit des lois* the persecution of the Jews in Europe. Montesquieu also explained in *Lettres persanes* that the teachings of Judaism, Islam, and Christianity were similar to each other and that European monarchs during the eighteenth century should enact laws to recognize the civic rights of religious groups in their states.[16] In knowing that several French enlighteners and some of his judicial colleagues from the Parlement belonged to the *Louis d'Argent*, Montesquieu visited this lodge. He knew, moreover, that the *Louis d'Argent* and other lodges in Paris sponsored some Enlightenment activities. After his visit to the *Louis d'Argest*, Montesquieu appeared, however, to lose interest in the affairs of the Craft and evidently was disappointed to see that no Parisian lodge functioned as a Masonic learned society.[17]

Established in 1736, the Lodge *Bussi-Aumont* consisted, for the most part, of French aristocrats affiliated with the army and of a few enlighteners. A prominent French general, Bertin du Rocheret, played a central role in the lodge and recruited to its ranks French nobles of the sword.[18] A member of the Rocheret circle, Charles Francois de Calvière, served as a general in the French army and displayed interest in Enlightenment activities. Admitted to the *Bussi-Aumont* in 1737, Calvière also belonged to the French Academy of Painting and was known for his collection of paintings and busts. An obscure English painter, Mr. Collins, belonged to this lodge and presumably during the 1730s was in Paris to study art.[19] The *Bussi-Aumont* Lodge, by and large, failed to recruit many enlighteners and consequently did not stage many cultural events. This lodge also had a small membership and engaged in minimal relations with the Lodges *Louis d'Argent* and *Coustos-Villeroy.*

The *Coustos-Villeroy* Lodge was established in 1736, consisted of approximately twenty French Masons, and seemed to develop into a center for numerous European Masonic aristocrats residing in Paris. Some enlighteners as well were affiliated with this lodge; a group of French opera singers was associated with the *Coustos-Villeroy* and consisted of Jean Guignon, Jacques Naudot, and Pierre Jeliote,[20] Joseph Baur was a Huguenot banker, providing the lodge with financial assistance and writing several articles about deism.[21] A friend of Baur, the lawyer Pierre Meyzieu was a minor proponent of legal reforms and a financial contributor to the *Encyclopédie.*[22] Residing in Paris during the late 1730s, Central and East European nobles in some cases were patrons of the arts and sciences and exhibited interest in affiliating with the *Coustos-Villeroy.* It seemed that the Duke of Villeroi encouraged many of his aristocratic friends to become involved with the lodge. As a result of his efforts, the *Coustos-Villeroy* in 1737 inducted into its ranks the Venetian ambassador Count Farsetti, Prince Caraffa of Lombardy, the Swedish diplomat Baron Scheffer, the Danish ambassador Count Platte, Prince Wemille of Nassau, Prince Lubomirski of Poland, and Prince Nariskin of Russia. The lodge consequently reflected a diverse ethnic composition, and many of these aristocratic Masons also belonged to Parisian learned societies.[23]

There were, however, challenges posed to the operations of the Lodges *Coustos-Villeroy* and *Louis d'Argent* during the 1730s. Authorities of the Catholic Church and administrators of the Bourbon Monarchy suspiciously viewed the activities of these bodies. Yet the alleged connection between the Jacobites and Parisian Masonry posed a serious threat to the functioning of these lodges.

Although concrete evidence has not been produced to demonstrate the precise relationship between Parisian Masonry and the Jacobite movement, there probably were some members of the *Coustos-Villeroy* and *Louis d'Argent* Lodges who supported efforts to restore the Stuarts to the English throne.[24] What might be suggested is that a Jacobite faction arose in Parisian Masonry in 1736, was headed by Lord Derwentwater, and attracted support from members of the *Coustos-Villeroy* and *Louis d'Argent* Lodges. That year, another Masonic group consisting of members from both of these lodges ascended to oppose and to discredit the Jacobite faction. As a result of the successful efforts of the anti-Jacobite group, Derwentwater probably was forced to resign as Grand Master. Moreover, his successor, the Duke d'Antin, evidently initiated measures to suppress French Masons involved with the Jacobites and to exonerate Parisian Masonry from the attacks of political and religious authorities.[25]

Louis XV in 1737 was concerned about the operations of Masonic lodges in Paris. The king, who in many instances had provided assistance to sympathizers of the Stuart cause, was probably not disturbed about the alleged connection between the Jacobites and Masons, but for other motives favored the probing of Masonic activities in the French capital. Louis presumably was apprehensive about the teachings of Masonry, believing that its rites contained antimonarchistic doctrines. Moreover, he probably was concerned about the composition of Masonic lodges, thinking that many members of the Craft were *frondeurs* and might use these lodges to conspire for the overthrow of his throne. The 1737 Decree issued against Masonry reflected the concerns of the king. This decree stipulated that royal advisers and administrators were forbidden from belonging to Masonic lodges and that the police would be empowered to search these bodies for traitors.[26]

Rene Hérault, the head of the police in the French capital, conducted investigations of Parisian Masonry between 1737 and 1743 and showed that Masons were not involved with seditious activities. During these investigations, Hérault made no arrests, submitted frequent reports to *L'Arsenal*, and revealed important perceptions about Parisian Masonry.

> The Masonic order was established in England and first appeared in Paris in 1725. . . . Three lodges have operated in the city, have conferred degrees based on the teachings of King Solomon, and have prided themselves for their charitable activities. . . . Members of the order in Paris have thought of themselves as brothers and are comprised of nobles, of merchants, and of individuals in the arts and sciences. . . . Important and less known individuals have been received into the order, and some of my friends have been admitted to it. . . . Count Maurepas, the Duke of Villeroi, and Bertin du Rocheret have been active in the order and have told me that political matters are not discussed in Masonic assemblies. . . .[27]

The reactions of Louis to the reports of Hérault were mixed; the king, on the one hand, was probably surprised to know that some prominent nobles of the robe and his friend the Duke of Villeroi actively participated in Parisian Masonry. Louis, on the other hand, evidently was relieved to be informed that the operations of the order were not subversive. For six years, he received reports from the Paris police commissioner, but as a result of the influence of Villeroi, d'Antin, and other French Masonic nobles decided in approximately 1739 not to take action to suppress the Craft. During the remainder of his reign Louis maintained cordial relations with members of the Craft and more importantly permitted the operations of Masonic lodges in Paris and in other French cities.[28]

Like the edict issued by the French king in 1737, the bull announced by the pope in 1738 posed a threat to the functioning of Parisian lodges. This bull of Clement XII stipulated that Catholics were forbidden to affiliate with Masonic lodges and that Catholic monarchs and clergymen should cooperate to suppress the order.[29] The bull did not, however, thwart the growth of Parisian Masonry; Louis XV and ranking church officials seemed to ignore its provisions. Moreover, the gradual increase of the rosters of Parisian lodges in 1740 suggested that Catholic Masons in the French capital disregarded the provisions of the bull and that the operations and rites of the Craft satisfied their cultural and emotional needs.

The enigmatic career of Andrew Michael Ramsay illustrated quite a bit about Catholicism, Masonry, and the Enlightenment. On the one hand, Ramsay was a Catholic enlightener and, on the other, contributed to raising the status of Parisian Masonry during the late 1730s and early 1740s. The son of a Calvinist baker and an Anglican mother, Ramsay was reared in Ayr, Scotland, attended for a short time the Universities of Edinburgh and Leyden, and in light of his exposure to the views of Boerhaave became a proponent of deistic and mechanistic ideas. The incessant travels of Ramsay helped to shape his thinking; this adventurer and enlightener studied under Fenelon in Cambrai, became a Catholic, went to Rome in about 1724 to serve as a tutor for the sons of the old Pretender Charles Edward, and during his stay in Italy seemed to support the Jacobite cause. Ramsay during the late 1720s resided in England and seemed to be well received in the world of the British Enlightenment. He was awarded a doctorate in civil law from Oxford, was admitted to the Royal Society and to the Gentlemen's Society of Spalding, and was inducted into

the Horn Lodge.[30] Ramsay left London in 1730 and from that year
until his death in 1743 lived in Paris. As a result of his friendships
with Masons who opposed the designs of Derwentwater, Ramsay in
1736 denounced the activities of the Jacobites and the next year was
appointed as Orator of the French Grand Lodge. He used this position to support Parisian Masons against their political and religious
foes, proclaiming that the teachings of Masonry were not subversive.
Ramsay also believed as a Catholic enlightener that the principles of
the Craft reflected salient doctrines of Catholicism and those of other
major religions of the world.[31]

Like Desaguliers and other Modern English Masonic enlighteners,
Ramsay perceived the ancients as significant contributors to Masonic
thought. In *Les Voyages de Cyrus*, published in 1731, Ramsay claims
that Egyptian priests, Solomon, Cyrus, and other ancient monarchs
and sages were familiar with the teachings of the ancient mysteries. He further maintains that many ancient kings and philosophers
worshiped the Supreme Creator, subscribed to the moral doctrines
of deism, promoted the study of Nature, and thus helped to lay the
foundations of Modern Speculative Freemasonry.

> The teachings of the ancient mysteries were the remnants
> of an ancient religion practiced by Noah and the patriarchs,
> These teachings were transmitted from one society to an-
> other in the ancient world. . . . Egyptian priests held
> great feasts to induct candidates into their mystery cults. .
> . . Inspired by the teachings of Moses and David, Solomon
> ordered the erection of a magnificent temple which was ded-
> icated to the Supreme Creator and whose parts symbolized
> the operations of Nature and the moral conduct of men. Af-
> ter the temple was completed, Solomon instructed his priests
> to admit learned Jews and gentiles into its chambers and to
> convey to these select individuals the teachings of the mys-
> teries. . . . After the destruction of the first temple, Cyrus,
> who was initiated into the ancient mysteries by Zorobabel,
> ordered the rebuilding of the temple and served as a great
> philosopher king who attempted to improve the status of
> Masonry and learning in the ancient world. . . .[32]

The Masonic thought of Ramsay also emphasized the importance
of the Craft during the Middle Ages. In *Le Discours*, published in
1738 or the same year that the papal bill was promulgated, Ramsay

claims that the Templars functioned as a significant brotherhood and that members of this order were loyal to the Catholic Church, lived according to the principles of Masonry, and in many cases were French nobles. To Ramsay, the Templars promoted the ancient concepts of benevolence, justice, and virtue and also believed that the teachings of Masonry were compatible with the doctrines of monarchy and with those of Catholicism.[33] In *Le Discours*, Ramsay presented some new interpretations of Masonic philosophy and attempted to justify salient doctrines of the Craft to the hierarchy of the Catholic Church, to Louis XV, and to French aristocratic and bourgeois Catholics. Moreover, he helped to provide Masonry with new direction and to lay the foundations of Scottish Rite Masonry.

2. The Scottish Rite and Masonic Rivalry in Paris

Scottish Rite Masonry, which in fact had little to do with Scotland, originated during the early 1740s in Paris.[34] This new system, which by the late eighteenth century would consist of thirty-two degrees, served as an alternative to Modern Masonry in Paris. Scottish Rite Masonry developed, however, upon the foundations of Modern Masonry and used legends, ideas, and symbols from ancient and medieval history to explain in other ways major concepts appearing in the Blue Degrees. Moreover, the Scottish Rite was intended to provide Parisian Masons with a distinctive Masonic heritage and identity, but on many occasions provoked considerable dissension within the Parisian Masonic community.[35]

The evolution of Scottish Rite Masonry led to the formation of a new grand lodge in Paris. The English Grand Lodge of France was established in 1743 to replace the French Grand Lodge and strangely enough succeeded in securing recognition from officers of the Grand Lodge of London and in acquiring support from Parisian leaders of Scottish Rite Masonry. The Duke of Clermont that year was appointed as the Grand Master of the new grand lodge and was expected to effect a compromise between the Blue Lodge and Scottish Rite factions. A patron of the arts and sciences and a cousin of Louis XV, the Duke of Clermont seemed to be an excellent choice for this position and introduced measures to strengthen the English Grand Lodge of France.[36]

Clermont for several reasons issued the 1743 and 1755 statutes; he wished to centralize the new grand lodge, to entrust local lodges with the power of conferring the English and Scottish Degrees, and to secure aristocratic and bourgeois support for Parisian Masonry. The 1743 Statutes gave immense powers to the Grand Master, enabling him to hold his position for life and to appoint grand lodge officers and special committees. The statutes further confirmed the regulations specified in the 1723 *Constitutions* and permitted the staging of the Blue Degrees and of three Scottish Degrees.[37] The 1755 Statutes reconfirmed the powers of Clermont and his grand lodge officers and defined the duties of officers of local lodges. These statutes also acknowledged the conferring of the Blue Degrees and of five Scottish Degrees and required Parisian Masons to comply with the provisions of a new ethical code issued by the grand lodge.[38] The enaction of the 1743 and 1755 Statutes suggested that the English Grand Lodge of France provided Parisian Masonry until approximately 1757 with valuable administrative direction and succeeded in housing under the same roof leaders of the English and Scottish Rite factions.

However, factional disputes within the English Grand Lodge of France occurred in late 1758 and brought an end to the era of compromise in Paris. Some factions remained loyal to Clermont and continued to confer the Modern Blue Degrees and the first five Scottish Degrees. But others severed ties with the English Grand Lodge of France and established bodies known as councils and chapters to stage the higher degrees of Scottish Rite Masonry. As a consequence of these factional feuds, rivalry among lodges, chapters, and councils persisted within the Parisian Masonic community until the early 1770s.

Various features characterized the organizational operations and membership of Parisian lodges, councils, and chapters during the 1760s. The titles and powers of local lodge officers in Paris were similar to those of local lodge officials in London. Councils of the Emperor of the East and West and Chapters of the Rose Croix, on the other hand, gave their officers medieval titles; officers of these two bodies were known as princes, commanders, and knights and were granted powers resembling those of officials in Parisian lodges.[39] Parisian lodges, chapters, and councils adhered to strict recruiting procedures, and competition for members among these bodies was excessive. Further, the composition of these three bodies somewhat differed. Parisian lodges, for the most part, consisted of middle class officers and members, while councils and chapters in the French capital conversely were comprised of aristocratic officers and members.[40] Parisian chapters and councils sponsored some banquets and lectures, but the noble army leaders, judges, and royal advisers who belonged to these institutions primarily viewed them as centers for the staging of colorful ceremonies associated with the high degrees of Masonry.[41]

The Scottish Degrees presented new interpretations of Masonic doctrines and contained ethical concepts associated with a French civil religion. The Scottish Degrees of the Secret Master, the Perfect Master, and the Perfect Elect were conferred in Parisian lodges. These three degrees revolved around teachings concerning the Temple of Solomon and provided further insight into concepts developed in the Blue Degrees. In the Secret Master Degree, Masons learned that the secrets of the Craft and the Temple of Solomon should never be divulged to individuals not affiliated with the order. This degree further emphasized that Masons should provide for and protect their families and should obey the laws of the state.[42] By stressing the civic virtues of ambition, honesty, and hard work, the Perfect Master Degree offered pertinent explanations of ethical behavior to Catholic and Protestant bourgeois Masons and illustrated to them the importance of their economic positions in French society.[43] Like the Modern rites, the Perfect Elect Degree explained concepts regarding the conduct of Masons in the state. This Scottish Degree emphasized the doctrines of benevolence, justice, and liberty and encouraged members of the Craft to work for the creation of a republic of humanity.[44]

By emphasizing Christian doctrines in many of their degrees, councils and chapters operating in the French capital succeeded in giving to Parisian Masonry a distinctive ideological character. The Degree of the Knights of the East and West and that of the Prince of Jerusalem were staged in Parisian councils. The Knights of the East and West Degree centered on ethical teachings common to the major religions of the world. Knights of the East and West met in the Holy Land during the Crusades and were taught that Moses, Jesus, and Mohammed were great prophets and preached similar moral and religious doctrines. The knights recognized that these religious leaders were inspired by the Deity governing all nations and imbued their followers with the teachings of brotherhood, charity, justice, and virtue.[45] The Prince of Jerusalem Degree was based on a meeting of Christian monarchs during the Crusades. These kings agreed that bravery, honor, and love of their religion motivated Christian knights in their efforts to secure control of Jerusalem.[46] The Knight of the Rose Croix Degree was the most significant one performed in Parisian chapters and was based on the activities of the Templar Order and on those of its leader Jacques De Molai. This degree emphasized that the ancient Roman eagle symbolized honor and military strength and that the rose represented heroic conduct and the sacrificing of life in battle. The Rose Croix Degree further revealed that despite the burning of De Molai at the stake and their subsequent suppression during the early fourteenth century, French Templars during the Crusades had exhibited loyalty to the Catholic Church and to their kings.[47] As a consequence of the moral and religious teachings of this degree, Parisian chapters especially enlisted the support of French Masons belonging to the armed services.

The evolution of the Scottish Degrees produced major effects upon Parisian Masonry. These degrees, on the one hand, contained Christian principles, but, on the other hand, offered vivid explanations of moral and secular concepts. The ancient and medieval tenets of these degrees concerning deism, honor, virtuous conduct, civil obedience, and religious toleration seemed to reflect a character of cultural universality and were associated with ideas of the Enlightenment. The concepts of the Scottish Degrees also were intimately involved with ethical behavior and enabled Parisian Masons to be identified with a distinctive French Masonic culture and community.[48] While its degrees were associated with significant cultural functions, Scottish Rite Masonry caused jurisdictional feuds among bodies of the Craft in the French capital. These feuds, in turn, led during the early 1770s to the fragmentation of Parisian Masonry and threatened to destroy it.

3. The Grand Orient and the Parisian Masonic Compromise

The Duke of Chartres helped to resolve the factional disputes within Parisian Masonry. The Duke of Clermont, who refused to negotiate with leaders of Parisian councils and chapters, died in 1771 and that year was succeeded as Grand Master of the English Grand Lodge of France by the Duke of Chartres. Unlike his predecessor, Chartres was willing to meet with Parisian Scottish Rite leaders and in 1772 entered into parleys with them. The results of these negotiations led to the Parisian Masonic compromise of 1773. The Duke of Chartres and Scottish Rite officials agreed that the Grand Orient would be established as the new governing body of Parisian Masonry. They also wished to transform the Grand Orient into a French national grand lodge. Chartres and Parisian Scottish Rite officials consequently agreed that the Duke of Montmorency-Luxembourg, who was appointed as general-administrator of the Grand Orient, should be authorized to consult with Masonic leaders outside of Paris, so that lodges, councils, and chapters in various provinces of France could be given the opportunity to affiliate with the new grand lodge.[49]

Montmorency-Luxembourg, who proved to be a very capable grand lodge administrator, drafted in 1773 the constitution of the Grand Orient. According to the provisions of this document, administrators of the Grand Orient were empowered to recognize other grand lodges, were to authorize the conferring of the Blue and Scottish Degrees in local Masonic bodies, and were to work in conjunction with an annually elected grand lodge assembly to formulate policy. The constitution further stipulated that grand lodge officers were to review and to give their approval to the constitutions and rosters of local lodges and that grand lodge inspectors were to be sent to local lodges to investigate their affairs and to file reports about their operations.[50]

Major effects resulted during the 1770s from the effective governance and operations of the Grand Orient. By holding annual assemblies, administrators of the Grand Orient permitted representatives of local Masonic bodies to participate in the decision-making process and helped to bring stability to Parisian and French provincial Masonry. By recognizing local bodies which conferred the Blue and Scottish Degrees, leaders of the Grand Orient succeeded in reducing rivalry and internal dissension within Masonry and in transforming this body into an operable and a centralized institution. As a consequence of the efforts of the Dukes of Chartres and Montmorency-Luxembourg, the Grand Orient received the tacit support of the crown, successfully resisted the few attacks of anti-Masonic groups, and continued to induce aristocratic and bourgeois Frenchmen to affiliate with provincial and Parisian lodges.

Masonry and the Enlightenment during the middle years of the 1770s proved to be of importance to Paris. The viability of the Grand Orient and the operations of learned societies and salons in the French capital enabled Paris to evolve into a Masonic and an Enlightenment hub. Jerome Lalande, who was an Orator of the Grand Orient, realized that Parisian Masonry had enlisted the support of numerous enlighteners. In recognizing the need for a Masonic learned society in Paris, Lalande in 1776 proposed the establishment of the Lodge of the Nine Sisters and thus began his efforts to fulfill the idea of his deceased friend Helvétius.[51]

B. The Origins, Organization, and Operations of the Parisian Lodge of the Nine Sisters

1. The Establishment of the Lodge of the Nine Sisters

For varying reasons, the astronomer and Grand Orient administrator Lalande favored the creation of a Parisian Masonic learned society. He believed that the promotion of the liberal arts and sciences was a fundamental objective of Masonry. Lalande further thought that the operations of a Masonic learned society would enable this laudable aim to be accomplished and would reveal to Masons and to intellectuals not belonging to the Craft the intimate connection between Masonry and the French Enlightenment. What Lalande evidently envisioned was a Masonic lodge explicitly designed to service the cause of the Enlightenment; his intention also was to have this lodge serve as the cultural locus of Masonry in Paris. Lalande, moreover, thought that a Parisian Masonic learned society would provide prominent and obscure Masonic intellectuals with the opportunity to interact with each other, to deliver lectures about various topics, to display paintings and sculpture, to perform scientific experiments, and to sponsor special projects pertinent to Masonry and to the Enlightenment. He evidently did not anticipate problems concerning the recruitment of members for his proposed society. This enlightener expected to recruit Masons affiliated with the Paris Academy of Sciences and with other learned societies in the French capital. Lalande also thought that Masonic intellectuals belonging to French provincial academies and to European and American learned societies would like to serve as members of a Parisian Masonic academy. In light of his involvement in the Salon of Madame Helvétius, or the "Estates General of the *philosophes*," Lalande knew that support of many of its Masonic enlighteners could be enlisted for his proposed society.[52]

> At Auteuil, an intimate academic atmosphere was created to enable the blossoming of the arts and sciences. Cabanis and Lalande were moving spirits of the salon. Volney gave historical lectures there; and Garat, Franklin, and Tracy engaged in stimulating philosophical debates. These and other guests of the salon discussed, listened, and truly philosophized. . .
> [53]

Lalande on March 11, 1776 submitted to officers of the Grand Orient his proposal concerning the establishment of a Parisian Ma-

sonic learned society and met with opposition from some of its conservative administrators. Lalande responded to his opponents in terms
of the language of Masonry, but failed to explain why these administrators objected to his proposal.

> My proposal concerning the creation of the Nine Sisters met
> with opposition. I favored erecting a temple but found it
> necessary to imitate the example of Zorobabel. I held the
> trowel in one hand, and the sword in the other. . . .[54]

Motives concerning the opposition to the proposal of Lalande might
be suggested. Conservative officers of the Grand Orient knew that
the functions of this proposed society would vastly differ from those
of regular Masonic lodges. They might have believed that if established, this Parisian learned society would be difficult to administer
and might not adhere to grand lodge regulations. Opponents of this
proposal realized that French Masonry just recently had been reunited
and had been fortunate to operate in an atmosphere relatively free of
anti-Masonic attacks; they further might have thought that members
of this society would embrace political causes offensive to the French
Crown and would precipitate major problems for the Grand Orient.
Conservative administrators finally might have viewed the proposed
name of the learned society as being strange and might have disliked
Lalande.[55]

Officers of the Grand Orient between March and July engaged
in debate about the recommendation of Lalande. There were at least
three heated sessions about the establishment of the Nine Sisters, and
Lalande with great adamancy defended his proposal. With obvious
reluctance, officers of the Grand Orient by a five to four vote approved
on July 5, 1776 the creation of the Lodge of the Nine Sisters and that
same day issued its constitution.[56]

2. The Structure and Leadership of the Nine Sisters

The constitution of the lodge explained the aims of the Nine
Sisters. According to this document, Masons admitted to the society
were to devote their attention to studying natural and moral laws,
to investigating the arts and sciences, and to engaging in cooperative
enterprises for the promotion of the Craft and the Enlightenment.
These objectives were defined in the constitution in light of Masonic
and ancient philosophical concepts.

> The Lodge of the Nine Sisters in making virtue its base has
> dedicated itself to fostering the arts and sciences. The aim
> of the lodge is to restore them to their place of dignity. Did
> not the arts and sciences serve as the foundations of great
> civilizations and nations?

> Work then with zeal to preserve and to advance civiliza-
> tion and our fraternity. Remember then that the base sup-
> ports the edifice. Decorate both remembering that orna-
> ments should not mask the dignity of Freemasonry. . . .[57]

Appearing on the first page of the constitution, the emblem of the
Nine Sisters contained Masonic symbols relating to the objectives
of the society. A pyramid appeared on the lodge emblem and represented moral perfection and the orderly operations of Nature. In-
scribed within the pyramid were the square, compasses, and the motto
"Truth, Union, and Force."[58] By employing these tools in their work,
members of the Nine Sisters were to demonstrate the validity of the
ancient, Masonic, and Enlightenment belief that virtuous men could
cooperate to advance the arts and sciences.[59]

The constitution revealed how this Parisian society would operate as a Masonic lodge. This document stipulated that the lodge
would comply with the regulations of the Grand Orient, that stated
meetings of the Nine Sisters would be devoted to operational matters,
and that special meetings and assemblies would be held to stage degrees and cultural events. During stated meetings, the lodge was to
adhere to Masonic procedures, allowing its members to hear committee reports, permitting them to engage in debate about recommendations, and enforcing the principle of majority rule for the adoption of
policies and resolutions. The Lodge of the Nine Sisters was to operate according to the principle of benevolence and during stated meetings was empowered to initiate measures to require its lawyers and
physicians to render their services without charge to its members.[60]
The constitution also provided that during stated meetings, the lodge
would adhere to the principle of unanimity for the election of new
members and that during special meetings and assemblies, candidates, who were elected as active members of the Nine Sisters but
who were never affiliated with the Craft, could be inducted by the
lodge into Masonry.

The constitution indicated how the Lodge of the Nine Sisters
would function as a learned society. According to the lodge charter,

the lodge was not to restrict membership to French Masons, but was to recruit members of the order from other European states and from America. Although the constitution mentioned nothing about membership quotas, the lodge during most of its history had an annual average roster of 100 members and recruited to its ranks French, European, and American Masons residing in Paris. The lodge charter stipulated that there would be active and associate members in the Nine Sisters and that newly elected active members were expected to give before the lodge presentations concerning their contributions either to the arts or to the sciences. This document also provided that assemblies and special meetings of the lodge for the most part should be devoted to cultural operations and that the lodge should award monies from a special fund to members who made outstanding contributions to science, to the humanities, and to the fine arts. According to the constitution, the lodge upon the recommendation of its officers was empowered to fund and to sponsor ancillary cultural institutions.[61]

Leadership played a significant role in fostering the development of the Nine Sisters. A Master, a Secretary, and the Orators served as the major officers of the Nine Sisters and generally speaking were annually elected. Masters of the Nine Sisters were entrusted with the power of conferring rites to candidates and occasionally performed this function. Lodge Masters were responsible for the coordination of the cultural operations of the Nine Sisters and were expected to assist in the recruiting of members. Jerome Lalande and Benjamin Franklin, the first two Masters of the Nine Sisters, staged numerous assemblies and meetings and were quite successful in recruiting Masons from the Paris Academy of Sciences, the Parisian Academy of Painting and Sculpture, the *Académie Française*, and the Salon of Madame Helvétius. The minor enlighteners Beaumont, Dupaty, and Pastoret served as Masters of the Nine Sisters during the 1780s and provided the lodge with minimal administrative direction. These three Masters became personally involved in matters concerning state reforms, but revealed little interest in recruiting new members to the lodge and in holding assemblies and special meetings to promote the cultural activities of the Nine Sisters. Orators of the lodge as well were involved with cultural functions. They were entrusted with the responsibilities of arranging lectures, scientific demonstrations, and artistic displays and of delivering eulogies of eminent enlighteners and Masons. It seemed that friends of Masters of the Nine Sisters were elected as Orators and that Orators for the most part were minor Parisian intellectuals. The Secretary of the lodge was allowed to engage in correspondence with other lodges and was expected to call the roll; he, however, was not obligated to record the minutes of lodge meetings and assemblies. In deciding against taking notes, Gébelin and other Secretaries of the Nine Sisters evidently wished to preserve the secret character of the lodge and unfortunately have provided historians with no information about the inner organizational workings and the cultural operations of this Masonic learned society.[62]

3. Cultural Operations and Special Projects of the Nine Sisters

During his first term as Master between 1776 and 1777, Lalande cautiously governed the lodge and seemed to do little to stimulate its cultural activities. The resignation of Lalande in 1776 as Orator of the Grand Orient and the lack of cultural operations of the Nine Sisters suggested that he evidently was attempting to conciliate his grand lodge opponents. Lalande further directed his attention to the recruitment of members to the Nine Sisters and attracted to its ranks minor Masonic enlighteners connected with important cultural institutions in Paris.

Two founding fathers of the Nine Sisters were scientists. Pierre Le Changeux and Jean Chauvet evidently wished to become involved with the lodge to further their scientific careers. Minimal evidence about the career of Chauvet has been discovered. Chauvet belonged to the Bordeaux Academy of Sciences and was a corresponding member of the Paris Academy of Sciences. He came to Paris in the early 1770s and, upon the suggestion of his friend Lalande, decided to affiliate with the newly established Parisian Masonic learned society. Chauvet contributed nothing of significance either to French science or to the Nine Sisters.[63] Pierre Le Changeux differed from Chauvet, publishing several minor scientific works and assuming a leadership position in the lodge. Le Changeux belonged to the Paris Academy of Sciences and to the Salon of Madame Helvétius, knew Lalande, and in 1776 was elected as an Orator of the Nine Sisters. He was a mechanist and eventually acquired some prominence in the Parisian scientific world. Le Changeux conducted experiments with the barometer, wrote an article about this instrument for the *Journal de Physique*, and in 1781 published *Le Barométrographie et autres machines météorlogiques.*[64]

Most of the founding fathers were writers; many were connected with Parisian literary circles and probably envisioned affiliation with the Nine Sisters as being important for the publicizing of their works. Cailhava, who wrote *L'Egoisme*, and Saint-Firmin, who published *La Jeune Esclave ou les Français à Tunis*, were playwrights and members of the *Académie française*. Both Masonic dramatists realized that scenes from their plays could be staged during lodge assemblies.[65] Fallet and Garnier were two minor poets and evidently thought that their connection with the Nine Sisters would provide them with new literary opportunities. Fallet in 1775 composed "Mes premices" and the next year the heroic poem "Phaeton," while Garnier during the 1770s wrote poems for the *Mercure de France*.[66] It seemed, however, that these two poets never acquired prominence in the Parisian literary world and that their participation in the cultural operations of the Nine Sisters was minimal. Abbé Robin conversely became a significant member of the Nine Sisters. This minor writer published works to defend the principles of the American Revolution, played an active part in lodge projects designed to support leaders of this revolution, and at a later time delivered a lecture to the lodge about Masonic rites.[67]

The induction of Voltaire into the lodge in 1778 was the first major cultural operation of the Nine Sisters and was recognized as being important for several reasons. In light of his affiliation with the Paris Academy of Sciences, Lalande knew Voltaire and evidently in early 1778 was the Mason to convince this eminent enlightener to apply to the Nine Sisters. Lalande realized that the initiation of Voltaire into the Nine Sisters would impress authorities of the Grand Orient and would help to enhance the stature of the Lodge.[68] Lalande also realized that numerous Masons would favorably view the lodge as a result of this initiation. Minor Parisian Masonic writers would want to join the Nine Sisters, realizing that they would be given the opportunity of meeting and of even working with the philosopher of Ferney. Lalande probably thought that, motivated by the ideas of Voltaire and by the teachings of the Craft, Parisian Masonic intellectuals from the humanities and sciences would flock to the lodge, would perform significant cultural functions, and thus would help to transform the Nine Sisters into a viable Enlightenment institution. He further believed that the affiliation of Voltaire with the Nine Sisters would prompt Masonic enlighteners from other nations in Europe to become members of the lodge and thus would enable it to evolve into an international Masonic learned society. It also appeared that some enlighteners not affiliated with the Craft would notice the connection of Voltaire with the Nine Sisters and would recognize the cultural importance of this lodge.[69]

Some unusual developments were associated with the induction of Voltaire into the Nine Sisters. Although not a member of the Craft, Voltaire in flagrant violation of Masonic regulations was allowed on March 21, 1778 to attend as a visitor the meeting of the Nine Sisters. After this meeting, the philosopher of Ferney, who evidently enjoyed this session of the lodge, informed Lalande that he would consent to be initiated into the Nine Sisters during its next meeting.[70] The induction ceremonies of Voltaire were held on Tuesday, April 7, 1778 and were not conducted according to stated Masonic procedures. Because of the age and the poor health of the philosopher of Ferney, the Master Lalande was constrained to abbreviate the initiation ceremonies. Leaning on the arm of his guide Benjamin Franklin, the blindfolded Voltaire was escorted into the lodge chamber and was asked several questions about his moral conduct. Without being required to receive the three mandatory degrees of Blue Lodge Masonry, he was informed of the signs, secrets, and symbols of the Craft and then was proclaimed a member of the order and the Nine Sisters.[71]

During this meeting, more time was devoted to paying tribute to Voltaire than to inducting him into the Nine Sisters. Benjamin Franklin, Count Stroganoff, Dr. Guillotin, and other lodge members extended their congratulations to Voltaire, and then the minor painter Monnet presented this eminent enlightener with a portrait. After the lodge orchestra played several pieces, Court de Gébelin delivered a short lecture about ancient and modern Masonic ceremonies; Gébelin maintained that like Voltaire, the ancient and modern ceremonies of the Craft emphasized the importance of the Supreme Creator, natural laws, religious toleration, and natural liberties.[72] Lalande then gave a major speech, explaining the importance of the occasion and assessing from a Masonic perspective the achievements of Voltaire.

> My dear brother, we have marked a great moment in our lodge and have admitted to our ranks an Apollonian and a friend of humanity. We are delighted with your zeal about being admitted to the Nine Sisters and know that you will continue to promote the arts and sciences. . . . In entering

Masonry, know that your efforts should be directed to ending fanaticism and superstition. You have raised a temple to the Eternal and were a Mason in spirit prior to receiving your degrees. You have used the square in your actions and worn the apron during your fruitful career.[73]

To Lalande, the lodge was fortunate to receive into its ranks the indisputable leader of the French Enlightenment and the Party of Humanity. Lalande perceived the accomplishments of Voltaire, the concepts of the Enlightenment, and the teachings of Masonry as being intimately related to each other. To Lalande, members of the Nine Sisters were perceived as disciples of Voltaire and as Masonic enlighteners. Members of the lodge relied upon reason to discover the natural laws of experimental science, revived salient philosophical teachings of the ancients, and utilized literature as a vehicle to encourage the implementation of legal and religious reforms in France.

Approximately seven weeks after his induction into the Nine Sisters, Voltaire on May 30, 1778 died. Similar to other Parisian learned societies, the lodge on November 28, 1778 held a special meeting to pay tribute to this deceased brother. Ninety-five members of the Nine Sisters and 150 Masonic visitors were present during the lodge of mourning directed by Lalande. During this meeting, La Dixmerie delivered the major eulogy, the lodge orchestra played the march from the opera *Alceste*, and the bust of Voltaire done by Houdon was placed on display.[74]

The lodge in 1778 sponsored other cultural activities. A lodge banquet was held in July at Passy to honor Benjamin Franklin. During this session, a plaque containing the silhouettes of Helvétius and Voltaire was presented to this American enlightener, and then theatrical performances were staged.[75] The lodge on September 30, 1778 held a special banquet to celebrate St. Jerome's Day and to honor its Master Jerome Lalande. Many speeches were given about his contributions to science. These speeches praised Lalande for publishing *Traité sur la Navigation* and for writing articles in the *Encyclopédie* about Egyptian astronomy and about the manufacturing of paper. In their addresses, members of the lodge also referred to his observations of Venus and to his views about the parallax of the moon.[76] La Dixmerie sang a song in honor of Lalande and well portrayed this Masonic mechanist:

Do you know in this canton a certain savant and a fine gentle-

man, who, from his study of Copernicus and Newton, wrote
a tome? We know him as Monsieur Jerome.

The body that he observed so closely was the planet Venus.
All these things are known about this genius. . . . When he
speaks and writes, we applaud him in great chorus. . . .[77]

La Dixmerie as well spoke of the Masonic achievements of this astronomer; he claimed that Lalande helped to develop French Masonry into a significant cultural institution and that his *Mémoire historique sur la Maçonnerie* and his article regarding the order in the
1777 supplement of the *Encyclopédie* well explained the importance
of Masonry during the *ancien régime*. Before this session closed, La
Dixmerie sadly announced that Lalande was serving his final term as
Master of the Nine Sisters.[78]

Prior to the conclusion of his third term, Lalande in April 1779
presided over a session to honor the lodge members Vernet and Lemierre.
Vernet was a painter, and Lemierre was a writer who was admitted
to the *Académie française* two years hence. During this celebration,
Cubières presented a brief oration and identified these two Masonic
enlighteners with their ancient counterparts.

Muses, open your temple, to these two distinguished artists.
One imitated Linnus, the other Zeuxis: One teaches by pre-
cepts and writings, the other by his brilliant paintings.[79]

With the departure of Lalande as Master, the lodge needed a
prominent Masonic enlightener to direct its cultural operations and
thus on May 21, 1779 elected Benjamin Franklin as his successor.
Members of the Nine Sisters were certainly familiar with the reputation of Franklin as an enlightener; they knew about his electrical
experiments, his invention of the lightning rod, his founding of the
Pennsylvania Academy, and his creation of the American Philosophical Society.[80] As members of the Nine Sisters realized, Franklin was
an active Mason. As a young man, he was inducted in 1731 into
the St. John's Lodge of Philadelphia, published on his printing press
copies of the *Constitutions*, and served in 1749 as Deputy Grand Master of Pennsylvania.[81] While in Paris during the late 1770s to secure
financial and military assistance for the Second Continental Congress,
Franklin displayed interest in Enlightenment and Masonic activities.
He frequently participated in the Salon of Madame Helvétius, met at
Auteuil many prominent members of the Nine Sisters, and willingly
consented to become involved in the cultural operations of the lodge

and to serve as its Master.[82]

During the mastership of Franklin between 1779 and 1780, two major assemblies devoted to cultural activities were held. The activities of August 16, 1779 revolved around literature and the fine arts. Greuze and Houdon arranged an impressive display for this session. Greuze showed his recent paintings of French villages and his portraits of eminent Frenchmen, and Houdon exhibited his busts of Franklin, La Dixmerie, and other lodge members.[83] La Dixmerie, who was re-elected as a lodge Orator, gave his *Eloge de Montaigne*, and Roucher read stanzas from his poem "Novembre." In this poem, he explained to members of the lodge the importance of state reforms and encouraged them to work for their implementation.[84] After the reading of this poem, Abbé Robin delivered a lecture concerning the relationship between ancient literature and Masonic rites. In presenting to the lodge important ideas from his *Recherches sur les initiations anciennes et modernes*, published in 1779, Robin claimed that important myths and legends of Egyptian, Greek, and Roman literature constituted the foundations of Modern Speculative Freemasonry.[85]

The cultural operations of this assembly and those of the May 1, 1780 session revealed that the Nine Sisters would function as a center for Masonic supporters of the American Revolution. These activities flagrantly violated Masonic regulations, but for unknown reasons were never questioned by Grand Orient authorities. The cultural operations encouraged by Franklin conversely permitted the lodge and French Masonry to become identified with this American political and cultural movement. During the August assembly, Hilliard d'Auberteuil read the preface of his *Essais historiques et politiques sur les Anglo-Americains*, one of the first works about America to appear in France.[86] In the preface of this detailed work composed from newspaper accounts, d'Auberteuil perceives Americans as advocates of natural liberties and virtue; he further is impressed with the operations of American state assemblies and with American efforts to detach themselves from the British monarchy.[87]

> State assemblies are elected and are designed to operate for the welfare of their citizens. . . . Most state legislatures are empowered to collect taxes and to levy monies for state projects. . . .
>
> Americans are fighting against the tyranny of the English king and nation. This nation has enslaved her American

colonies economically and politically. If these virtuous colonies
are to end this enslavement by George III and his minister
Pitt, French assistance is needed. . . . Since 1763, the
English have dominated the economic and political institutions of the American colonies and Canada and have posed a
threat to the French colonies of Guadeloupe and Martinique.
. . .[88]

D'Auberteuil admired the constitutions of New York, Pennsylvania,
and Virginia. The constitutions of these three states embodied the republican principles of the separation of powers, of legislative represen-
tation, and of freedom of speech, press, and religion.[89] D'Auberteuil
as well was present during the lodge feast of May 1780. He gave a
lecture about the contributions of Franklin and Washington to the
American Revolution and maintained that these two Masons had ac-
tivated the principles of the Enlightenment and those of the Craft.
After this speech, John Paul Jones was honored by members of the
Nine Sisters and received tribute from La Dixmerie for "his meritori-
ous service and heroic deeds."[90]

After the mastership of Franklin, members of the Nine Sisters
still continued to display interest in America and during two sessions
in 1785 engaged in significant cultural activities. During the mastership of the obscure lawyer Elie de Beaumont, a Lodge of Mourning
was convened on March 7, 1785 to honor the memory of the Americanophile and lodge Secretary Court de Gébelin. As a tribute to
him, Roucher, the new Secretary of the lodge, read his ode entitled
"L'Immortalité de l'homme." This ode confirmed the Masonic belief
concerning the afterlife and referred to the sprig of acacia.

> Man knows that at the end of life on Earth, the spirit sep-
> arates from the body and seeks its destiny in heaven. . . .
> There a Voice informs the immortal soul of its triumphant
> earthly glories. . . .[91]

A lodge assembly was convened in June to honor Franklin prior to his
return to the United States. Louis Alexandre, the Duke of Rochefoucauld d'Anville presented to the lodge his translations of American
republican writings; the duke distributed to lodge members copies of
the Declaration of Independence, the Articles of Confederation, and
six state constitutions. Rochefoucauld maintained that these documents well explained concepts concerning natural liberties, bicamer-
alism, unicameralism, and the separation of powers and in his view

were considered as major contributions to the political thought of the Enlightenment.[92] Before this assembly terminated, Houdon displayed his marble statue of Washington, and Beaumont announced that the lodge would offer a prize of 600 *livres* for the best paper on the topic of "Benjamin Franklin *vivant.*"[93]

It appeared to be unusual that with the exception of these two meetings, the lodge between 1781 and 1789 held no other assemblies for the staging of cultural events. Administrators of the Grand Orient perhaps discouraged officers of the Nine Sisters from holding assemblies and were worried that the activities of the Nine Sisters might revolve around French political problems and consequently would pose a threat to the monarchy. The election of minor enlighteners as Masters of the Nine Sisters during this decade also appeared to be related to the lack of cultural operations of the lodge. The Masters Milly, Dupaty, Beaumont, and Pastoret were not of the stature of Lalande and Franklin and were not that well known in Parisian cultural circles. Dupaty, Beaumont, and Pastoret were proponents of state reforms, but did not hold lodge assemblies to propagandize the cause of reform.[94] These three Masters continued, however, to promote the special projects of the lodge.

Members of the lodge financed and edited *Affaires de l'Angleterre et de l'Amérique.* Edited by Jean Robinet, Rochefoucauld, and Gébelin, this journal was published between 1776 and 1780 and was intended to furnish news about the War of Independence and to support the cause of the American revolutionaries. The journal contained descriptive accounts about military and political developments in America and summaries of political events in England and in France. The volumes of *Affaires* also contained an occasional editorial and many translations of important American political documents. By publishing the Declaration of Independence and the constitutions of several American states, the Masonic editors of this journal succeeded in revealing to their French subscribers American perceptions of natural liberties and of republican institutions. After securing diplomatic recognition and financial assistance from Louis XVI, Franklin during his second term as Master of the Nine Sisters convinced the editors of this journal to terminate its publication.[95]

Support of the Nine Sisters was extended to the Gallo-American Society. A member of the lodge, Brissot de Warville established this society in 1787 with the intention of fostering mutual understanding and commercial relations between America and France. The society succeeded in encouraging a few Parisian Masons to purchase land in America and in stimulating several lodge members to write articles about American society. This society however was ephemeral and with the outbreak of the French Revolution no longer functioned.[96]

The operations of educational institutions sponsored by the Nine Sisters were more successful than those of the Gallo-American Society. Masonic and Enlightenment ideas explained why the lodge decided to operate schools. Members of the Nine Sisters believed that orders of the Catholic Church dominated French education and that the state should fund and control the educational system. They further believed that state schools should be open to the public, should be inexpensive, and should place emphasis upon the humanities and sciences. In recognizing that the French Crown had done little to promote public education and that a valuable need would be filled, Franklin recommended that the lodge should allocate funds for the creation and the maintenance of a school. After the members of the lodge approved this proposal, Franklin on November 17, 1780 announced the opening of the Apollonian Society. This school was open to the public and offered inexpensive courses. Many members of the Nine Sisters were involved with the Apollonian Society; Gébelin frequently lectured about linguistics and ancient philosophy. The teaching of ancient music by Rozier and that of European literature by La Dixmerie suggested that the Apollonian Society emphasized the importance of courses in the liberal arts. Prior to closing its doors in 1781, the society also published a journal which probably contained significant lectures given by members of the Nine Sisters who taught in the school.[97]

The lodge during the 1780s sponsored two *musées*. A *musée* under the direction of Gébelin was opened in late 1781 and, similar to the Apollonian Society, offered an envisaging program in the humanities; students attending the *musée* took ancient philosophy from Gébelin, European literature from Saint-Firmin, and French drama from Cailhava. This *musée* held several special events. It sponsored lectures, displayed many busts sculptured by Houdon, and honored Benjamin Franklin for negotiating the 1783 Treaty of Paris.[98] The lodge in 1782 opened a second *musée* and after the death of Gébelin decided in 1784, probably for financial reasons, to merge the operations of both schools. Officers of the lodge appointed Pilâtre de Rozier to supervise the operations of the newly created *Musée de Paris*. This school was designed to promote the arts, sciences, and commerce and offered a wide selection of courses. Students took physics from Sue and chemistry from Fourcroy.[99] Students enrolled in scientific courses were granted permission to utilize the facilities of the Paris Academy of Sciences. The *Musée de Paris* also offered courses in mathematics, in anatomy and physiology, in geography, in ancient and modern literature, and in textile manufacturing. After the death of Rozier in 1785, this school was closed.[100]

In 1785 the lodge established the *Lycée de Paris* to replace the *musée* of Rozier. The *lycée* was known for offering extensive programs in the arts and sciences to male and female students. This school also was known for its well qualified faculty; Condorcet, Fourcroy, La Harpe, and Marmontel held chairs in the *lycée*. This institution operated until the outbreak of the French Revolution and proved to be a successful project sponsored by the lodge.[101]

C. The Cultural Functions of Enlighteners of the Nine Sisters

1. Mechanists of the Nine Sisters

There were not many mechanists associated with the Nine Sisters. Several physicians belonged to the lodge. While the cultural activities and projects of the Nine Sisters were not directly related to medicine, physicians retained their affiliation with the lodge and evidently were interested in the various facets of its Enlightenment operations. The lack of astronomers and physicists in the Nine Sisters certainly was related to the shift of interest from mechanistic to materialistic concepts and paradigms.[102] While not presenting many papers or experiments during lodge assemblies, some mechanists, however, supported projects of the lodge and taught in its schools.

Chabanneau was one of the few physicists to belong to the lodge. He was a minor physicist, not holding membership in any important scientific society and evidently perceiving affiliation with the Nine Sisters as being important to his career. Chabanneau during the early 1780s taught in Paris, was admitted to the Nine Sisters, and became friendly with the Masonic and Spanish enlightener Count Pena Florida. As a result of the efforts of Pena Florida, Chabanneau in 1785 was granted a chair in physics in the University of Madrid and five years later published in Spanish a comprehensive work concerning significant eighteenth century discoveries in physics.[103]

The astronomer Jean Bailly affiliated with the Nine Sisters for several reasons. He belonged to the Paris Academy of Sciences and knew Lalande. The occasional visits of Bailly to the Salon of Madame Helvétius also suggested his connection to an important circle of the Nine Sisters and helped to explain why he became friendly with Roucher and Gébelin. Like these two officers of the Nine Sisters and other members of the lodge, Bailly subscribed to deistic ideas. He believed that the study of ancient astronomy and mythology would reveal pertinent insights about the attributes of the Supreme Creator and about His relationship to Nature and to man.[104]

Bailly became an important contributor to the astronomy of the French Enlightenment. In 1759 he determined the orbit of Halley's Comet and in the following year determined from his observatory in Paris the positions of Mars, Jupiter, and Saturn. In cooperation with his friend and teacher Lacaille, he also observed in 1760 the transit of Venus—a development enabling a more accurate measurement of the parallax of the Sun.[105] Five years later, Bailly delivered lectures to members of the Paris Academy of Sciences about the moons of Jupiter and in detail described their inclinations and nodes.[106]

Cardinal ideas of Bailly appeared in *Histoire de l'astronomie ancienne.* In this work published in 1775, he maintains that the ancient Egyptians, Chinese, and Greeks shared similar astronomical views; astronomers of these ancient civilizations devised lunar and solar calendars, made records of lunar eclipses, identified seven planets of the solar system, and offered speculations about the distances between the Earth and the fixed stars.[107] In this history, Bailly claims that ancient astronomers and philosophers became advocates of the great order and advanced myths to explain how the universe, Nature, and man functioned. He describes some important myths. Prosperine is known for living both above and below the Earth and symbolizes the appearance of the Sun in the morning and its disappearance in the evening. The struggle between Hercules and the Amazons represents the conflict between the forces of light and those of darkness. The tales of Adonis and Osiris reveal the themes of life, death, and resurrection.[108] As attested to by these and other myths, the ancients, according to Bailly, believed that moral and natural laws were closely interrelated to each other and were to be traced to a Single Cause.

The several physicians of the Nine Sisters believed that clinical and pathological studies would help in determining mechanistic principles relating to the operations of the body. These doctors further worked to improve facilities of Parisian hospitals and to promote the public health movement in the French capital.[109] Victor de Seze was a minor Parisian physician connected with the circle of Guillotin and espoused mechanistic ideas. In *Recherches philosophiques sur la sensibilité ou la vie animale,* published in 1786, De Seze maintains that physicians should investigate and classify body organs and sensations in light of their functions.[110] While known for his device for decapitation, Dr. Joseph Guillotin made other significant contributions to Parisian medicine and Masonry. He served as one of the founders of the French Academy of Medicine, was appointed as a regent of the University of Paris Medical School, and played an active role during the 1780s in attempting to improve the conditions of hospitals in the French capital. Guillotin as well denounced Mesmer and his followers as quacks and believed that they would thwart the advancement of Parisian clinical medicine. He identified Masonry as a reform institution, served as master of the Parisian Lodge *Concorde Fraternelle,* but was not actively involved in the cultural operations and projects of the Nine Sisters.[111]

Like many members of the lodge, Dr. Pierre Jean George Cabanis was an intellectually versatile individual. Cabanis was interested in ancient literature and in 1777 was honored by the *Académie française* for his French translation of *The Iliad.* He further during the late 1770s earned his medical degree, became the "adopted son" of Madame Helvétius, and gave frequent lectures in her salon about the sensationalistic philosophy of John Locke.[112] As a result of his friendships with Lalande, with Franklin, and with other Masons of this salon, Cabanis in 1779 decided to affiliate with the Nine Sisters. He envisioned the lodge as being a significant institution for the promotion of his medical ideas.

The philosophy of Cabanis was significant to Parisian medical thought; he believed that inductive techniques and sense observations were essential for the proper practice of medicine.

> Until the appearance of Sydenham, inductive techniques in medicine were unknown. This seventeenth century English physician gave to medicine the true spirit of observation. Locke adhered to the observational techniques of Sydenham. . . . Locke showed that babies at birth have a clear mind and in light of their sense observations acquire knowledge. . . .[113]

To Cabanis, medicine as well was indebted to the natural philosophy of Newton, utilizing its "precise language and reasoning procedures for the examination of the parts of the body and for the treatment of diseases."[114] According to this medical philosopher, clinical investigations enabled numerous French physicians to discover new remedies for diseases.[115] Cabanis maintains that clinical studies enabled physiologists to classify organs and parts of the body and to explain digestion, muscular movements, and the functioning of nerves and veins. According to Cabanis, French physicians probed the mind and explained its operations in light of sense impressions.[116]

2. The Materialists of the Lodge

Numerous proponents of materialism affiliated with the Nine Sisters. Most materialists of the lodge held membership in the Paris Academy of Sciences and belonged to the circles of Fourcroy and Rozier. Some materialists offered courses in schools sponsored by the Nine Sisters. Materialists for the most part wished to utilize the lodge as a vehicle for the promotion of their chemical writings.

Antoine Fourcroy made significant contributions to late eighteenth century French chemistry. His *Elémens* served as one of the major texts of inorganic chemistry during the late eighteenth century and contained many and varying experiments regarding metals, acids, alkalis, and salts.[117] A member of the Paris Academy of Sciences, Fourcroy in 1777 delivered to this society a lecture concerning the reaction of iron salts to alkalis and acids. He maintained that iron salts reacted more to acids than to alkalis and that upon exposure to acids, these salts emitted an inflammable gas.[118] As Fourcroy explained to members of the academy, these experiments suggested that iron ores could be decomposed. In other experiments, he ascertained the properties of gold, silver, platinum, and mercury and showed that when mixed with strong acids, these chemicals were difficult to decompose.[119] Fourcroy also studied human blood. He succeeded in determining the properties of blood and advanced the view that additional chemical investigations of this substance might lead to an understanding of the causes of various diseases.[120]

The Englishman John Forster, who spent considerable time in Paris during the 1780s, and Claude Berthollet were connected with the circle of Fourcroy. The influence of Fourcroy evidently explained why both of these chemists chose to affiliate with the Nine Sisters and why Cadet de Vaux, a lodge member and an editor of *Journal de Paris*, decided to publish some of their experiments.[121] Berthollet performed valuable experiments concerning bleaching and dyeing. He demonstrated that if placed in a tub of muriatic acid, cloth containing vegetable colors would be bleached.

> When vegetable colors are immersed in oxygenated muriatic acid, they are completely destroyed. A mixture of different colors, in a similar exposure, suffers from the same change. . . . We may conclude that the coloring vegetable matters, which have been acted upon and deprived of their properties of producing color, have taken away the oxygen from the acid by a strong chemical attraction, and have, by means of this combination, acquired new properties, whilst they have lost that of producing color. . . .[122]

Berthollet and Forster believed that experiments would lead to an understanding of some chemical compounds and would demonstrate their usefulness. Forster developed methods for assaying metals. He performed experiments with iron ores and showed that when exposed to fire, iron could be separated from compounds and could be used for industrial purposes. The experiments of Forster further demonstrated that substances could be classified into four groups: earths, salts, metals, and gases.[123]

Joseph and Jacques Montgolfier belonged to the Nine Sisters and the Paris Academy of Sciences, were members of the scientific circle of Rozier, and demonstrated that heated gases could propel their aerostatic balloon. The Montgolfiers in 1782 conducted experiments concerning the density of heated air and concluded that an object filled with hot air could rise from the surface of the Earth. On June 5, 1783, they gave a public demonstration of their machine. When inflated with hot air and released, their aerostatic machine, made of paper and approximately thirty-five feet in diameter, ascended to a height of about 6,000 feet and descended gradually as the air in it cooled. As a result of the excitement aroused by this flight, Louis XVI insisted that the Montgolfiers present a demonstration of their invention to the royal family. With animals as its passengers, the aerostatic balloon on September 19, 1783 was released at Versailles, ascended to a height of 1,500 feet, and then fell to the ground without injuring its passengers.[124]

Rozier wished to experiment with the machine of his two friends. He was a minor scientist in Paris during the 1780s and was known for teaching chemistry to ladies, for inventing the phosphoric candle, and for experimenting with hydrogen. Rozier in October 1783 offered his services to the Montgolfiers and evidently recognized that he could acquire fame for being the first person in history to make a successful flight in an aerostatic balloon. Rozier that year made two successful ascents, rising on October 15th to a height of eighty-three feet. During his second ascent on November 21st, Rozier was accompanied by the Marquis d'Arlandes, remained in the air for twenty-five minutes, crossed the Seine at 3,000 feet, and descended safely having completed a trip of six miles. After several ascents in 1784, Rozier was convinced that he could direct a flight across the English Channel. In an effort to accomplish this objective, he was launched in an aerostatic balloon on June 16, 1785 and reached a height of 1,700 feet. Rozier then encountered problems with fire, crashed the balloon several miles from Boulogne, and was instantly killed.[125]

3. Neoclassicism and the Nine Sisters

Members of the Nine Sisters associated with the humanities and the fine arts shared in common several important beliefs; they believed that the revival of ancient ideologies and paradigms would enable them to become modern enlighteners. These enlighteners concentrated their efforts on portraying the features of Nature and the qualities of man and probably realized the importance of Masonic teachings regarding the ancients and Nature. Many of these enlighteners actively participated in the assemblies of the Nine Sisters and were provided with splendid opportunities to read their poems, to stage scenes from their plays, and to exhibit their paintings and statuary. Most of these savants of the lodge held membership in Parisian learned societies and belonged to varying cultural circles in the French capital.

Artists of the Nine Sisters identified major concepts of the ancients with themes of naturalism. Many of these artists became known for their vivid portrayals of ancient and modern leaders and society. Many painters of the lodge as well belonged to the French Royal Academy of Painting. Claude Notté belonged to this society and acquired prominence as a portrait painter. Notté did portraits of Franklin, Milly, Dupaty, and other modern enlighteners of the lodge. Claude Vernet painted a few portraits, but was elected to the Royal Academy of Painting as a result of other works. Vernet conveyed themes of naturalism in his paintings of French port cities, rivers, farms, and forests.[126]

Jean Greuze was recognized as the most noted artist in the Nine Sisters. After studying in a studio in Lyon, Greuze in 1747 at age twenty-two moved to Paris, became known for *Un Écolier endormi sur son livre* and for *Portrait de M. Sylvestre* and consequently in 1755 was elected to the Royal Academy of Painting.[127] He became involved in the salon life of Paris during the 1760s and painted several important portraits. In *Comte d'Angivillers*, Greuze superbly depicted the cold and stern qualities of this French noble. Praise was offered in 1765 for *La Mère Bien-aimée*; this work well conveyed the half-open mouth, the swimming eyes, and the relaxed position of the subject.[128] He also painted in 1765 *Sévère et Caracalla* which showed Severus reproaching his son for attempting to assassinate him. Greuze during the 1770s painted two portraits of members of the Nine Sisters; he did colorful portraits of Benjamin Franklin and Count Stroganoff.[129] Some of the paintings of Greuze during the late 1770s revealed astute perceptions of French society. In *L'Accordée de Village*, Greuze portrayed the life of French peasants and exhibited concern for their plight. In *The Death of the Paralytic*, Greuze recreated the scene of a dying middle class man and in cleverly using colors conveyed the ruefulness expressed by the immediate members of the family.[130]

Features of naturalism were embodied in the sculpture of Jean Antoine Houdon. In addition to doing busts of American Revolutionary heroes, he sculptured statues of French enlighteners involved with the Nine Sisters. Ancient and modern legal expressions and symbols appeared in his statutes of Dupaty and Pastoret and suggested his concern for the cause of natural liberties. Perceived as the modern Phidias, Houdon sculptured an enormous statue of Jerome Lalande, portraying this Masonic astronomer as he viewed the heavens with his telescope.[131]

The few musicians of the Nine Sisters belonged to the Royal Academy of Music and expressed interest in the ideas of the ancients. They were involved with the lodge orchestra, staged several operas based on ancient legends, and during lodge assemblies gave musical renditions of ancient lyrics. Nicolas Piccinni served as conductor of the lodge orchestra and became a spokesman for dramatic opera. He believed that the legends and heroes of ancient civilizations should be emphasized in a modern operatic setting. Piccinni was known for revising the operas *Atys* and *Didon* to conform to his standards and presented to the lodge select acts from these two works. The singing of Pierre Tirot and Jean Lays and the violin solos of Pierre Lahous-

saye were featured to dramatize the themes of these operas.[132] Like
Piccinni, John Palza and Charles Turschmidt served as conductors of
the lodge orchestra, composed several minor pieces, and in 1786 left
Paris to accept positions in the orchestra of Frederick William II. The
departure of these two conductors and the lack of musicians in the
Nine Sisters suggested that the lodge did not develop into a major
center of Parisian music.[133]

Minor Parisian poets belonged to the lodge and displayed great
interest in the ideas and models of their ancient counterparts. Most of
these poets participated in Parisian salons and evidently envisioned
the Lodge of the Nine Sisters as another cultural agency enabling
them to reveal their literary talents. Some of these poets were given
the opportunity to read eulogies and lyrics during lodge assemblies.
Others attended meetings of the lodge as interested observers, but
were known in Paris for stimulating interest in ancient ideas through
their translations. Jacques Delille was educated in the classics and
translated into French the "Georgics" of Vergil. Voltaire regarded
this translation as one of the finest works in French literature. Indicative of his interest in the ancients, Delille also rendered a translation of the "Aeneid" and wrote the poem "L'Homme des Champs
ou les Georgiques françaises."[134] Louis Fontanes believed that many
poems of Alexander Pope contained significant ideas of the ancients.
Fontanes in 1783 translated into French "An Essay on Man."[135] He
further composed in 1778 "Forêt de Navarre" and in this poem praised
the ancients for their views concerning Nature.[136]

Jean Roucher wrote "Les Mois" in 1779 and explains in this poem
that ancient and modern enlighteners were involved in the study of
Nature. He pays tribute to ancient Greek and Roman natural philosophers and to Newton. Roucher maintains that the laws of Newton
enabled modern enlighteners to explain the systematic operations of
Nature.

> Before Newton, Nature concealed her laws. . . . Newton
> made the heavens his domain and through his discoveries
> made the world humane. . . . All men can understand his
> system, for gravity, motion, and attraction serve as the basis
> of the solar system. . . . Attest then to the honor and the
> glory of his work. . . . Oh, man and Nature be indebted to
> this genius. . . .[137]

Like Roucher, the obscure Masonic poet Barthelemy Imbert perceived the importance of the contributions of Newton to the Enlightenment. Imbert offered praise to Newton and to French enlighteners in "L'Utilité des découverts dans les sciences et dans les arts sous le regne de Louis XV."[138]

Francois Turpin and Constantin Volney, who did not play an active role in the activities of the lodge, were known in Paris for their works concerning political and cultural developments in ancient history. Members of the Nine Sisters perceived Turpin as the Plutarch of eighteenth century France.[139] Turpin was in fact a minor enlightener, and little evidence has been discovered about his career. He published in 1769 *Histoire du gouvernement des anciennes républiques* and envisioned ancient monarchs as being capable administrators. To Turpin, these monarchs selected qualified advisers, did not usurp the powers of legislatures, and assisted the courts in promoting justice.[140] Turpin and Volney viewed ancient history somewhat differently. An active participant in the Salon of Madame Helvétius, Volney, like Gébelin and other members of this circle, emphasizes in *Les Ruines* the importance of ancient myths. Volney maintains that Egyptian priests and Greek and Roman philosophers developed myths to explicate the operations of Nature and the concepts of civic morality. He also believes that the decline of cultural and moral values led to the demise and to the eventual collapse of the political and economic institutions of ancient civilizations.[141]

The works of Gébelin concerning ancient language, myths, and mystery cults revealed the efforts of this minor enlightener to promote the study of linguistics and anthropology. In *Histoire Naturelle De La Parole*, published in 1776, Gébelin explains salient functions of language. He maintains that humans were endowed by the Creator with the ability to speak and thus differed from animals. To Gébelin, humans utilized language to reveal their thoughts and sentiments.

> God gave man those organs necessary to speak. Speech is the painting of our ideas and constitutes the essence and glory of man. Animals and men eat, drink, and sleep, but only men through speech can convey their pleasures, pains, and thoughts.[142]

He maintains that language allowed individuals to understand the operations of Nature and to engage in the study of the arts and sciences. Gébelin also believes that language was needed to permit humans to function in society and to achieve their material and moral objectives through secular and cultural institutions.[143]

> Language enables humans to express ideas derived from hear-
> ing, seeing, smelling, and touching. . . . Words convey ideas
> and thoughts about the beauties in Nature and in the heav-
> ens. . . . Speech allows individuals to express their thoughts
> about experiences in society. . . .[144]

Monde Primitif was the voluminous dictionary published by Gébelin in 1773 and contained detailed explanations about words from
varying ancient languages. In this work, Gébelin cogently demonstrates that the origins and meanings of words were related to specific
functions performed in ancient civilizations. He as well shows that
the meanings of words reflected significant cultural concepts, morals,
and social values of ancient civilizations.

> Language and words provide the anthropologist with an un-
> derstanding of the functions of a specific society. Social cus-
> toms, cultural heritage, and scientific discoveries of a civ-
> ilization are revealed through the study of language and
> words. . . .[145]

In this dictionary, Gébelin examines nouns, verbs, and adjectives
from Chinese, Hebrew, Greek, and Latin; he develops an etymologi-
cal scheme to classify ancient words and to compare their meanings.
Words are categorized according to their universal meanings, to their
nuances, and to their prefixes and suffixes.

> The Greeks developed the study of etymology. They studied
> the meanings and the structure of ancient words and showed
> that the meanings of words were associated with the knowl-
> edge of Nature. . . .The Greeks discovered that words from
> Egyptian, Hebraic, and Chinese civilizations conveyed sim-
> ilar meanings. . . . The knowledge of ancient words thus
> contributed to the development of the arts and sciences. . .
> .[146]

Monde Primitif contained a lengthy account about the Eleusinian
Mystery Cult. Gébelin recognizes that this ancient cult and Modern Masonry possessed similarities; both societies performed valuable
cultural functions, conveying in their rites important moral doctrines
and cultural values of ancient civilizations. Both societies as well
functioned as cohesive communities and admitted into their ranks
enlighteners.[147]

The sacred rites of the Eleusinian Mystery Cult were admin-
istered with great pomp and embodied cultural ideals cher-
ished in ancient empires. The Eleusinian Mysteries served as
a rallying point for the ancients and emphasized the beliefs
of virtue, justice, and human liberty. . . .[148]

Gébelin explains activities pertaining to the conferring of the
Eleusinian rites in Greece. Prior to his entry into this ancient cult,
the initiate pledged that he would aspire to purify his soul and to lead
a virtuous life. As an indication of his desire to cleanse his soul, the
candidate submerged himself in a river near the plains of Attica; he
then received a wreath of flowers, a symbol of the purity of Nature.
The candidate proceeded to the Temple of the Gods, went to its altar,
and drank a glass of wine. Hierophant, the head priest administering
the Eleusinian mysteries, told him that wine symbolized the fertility
of the Earth. Hierophant then offered prayers to the Supreme Being,
the Sun, and the Earth and explained to the candidate the secrets
of the cult. This priest escorted the new member of the order to the
banquet hall and ended the lengthy ceremonies with a feast.

The Eleusinian Mysteries revealed the fecundity of Nature
and agriculture and symbolized the prosperity of ancient
civilizations. . . . Candidates were required to acknowledge
the Attributes of the Supreme Creator and the powers of the
Earth and other heavenly bodies. Candidates recognized the
importance of the forces of Nature and of the harmony of
bodies moving in the heavens. . . .[149]

In light of his studies regarding ancient civilizations, Gébelin became a proponent of the great order. He believed that the ancients
established similar secular institutions, developed similar languages,
and endorsed similar cultural and moral teachings. Gébelin maintained that like modern enlighteners, those in the ancient world advanced theories to explain how the universe, Nature, and man were
interrelated to each other. To Gébelin, the ancients and the moderns were deists and realized that an Omnipotent Spirit governs the
operations of the great order.[150]

4. Perceptions of Lodge Members of America

Some writers of the Nine Sisters envisioned America as a utopia
of the Enlightenment and belonged to the Americanophile faction
of the lodge. Many writers of this group were recruited from the

Salon of Madame Helvétius and directly supported lodge operations to popularize the cause of the American Revolution. Several members of the American faction however only wrote about this nation.

Abbé Robin was known for participating in Americanophile activities of the lodge and for writing *Nouveau voyage dans l'Amérique Septentrionale*. In this work published in 1782, Robin perceives America as a major center of the Enlightenment. He maintains that the colleges of this nation and the American Philosophical Society significantly contributed to the arts and sciences and that reason motivated Americans to make new discoveries about the operations of Nature. Robin lauds American political institutions for functioning in light of precisely defined constitutional principles and for protecting natural liberties. He also equates the commercial activities conducted in American cities with material progress.[151]

> The commerce of Bostonians consisted of a variety of articles and was extensive prior to the outbreak of the American Revolution. Bostonians supplied England with timber, codfish, beef, and turpentine. The town has a superb wharf which extends two thousand feet into the sea and which permits the city to have a large amount of commerce. . . [152]

The views of Brissot de Warville about America resembled those of Robin. Brissot in *Nouveau Voyage* regards this nation as a paradise of the Enlightenment. To Brissot, America consisted of reasonable and virtuous citizens and served as a mecca of republicanism and science. He further perceives Philadelphia as the nucleus of the American Enlightenment.[153]

> Philadelphia may be considered as the major metropolis of the United States. It is certainly the finest town and the best built in America; it is the most wealthy, although not the most luxurious. You find here men of great political and scientific knowledge. . . .[154]

There were other American propagandists in the lodge. Jean Démeunier was known for his French translations of American writings and for his *Essai sur les États-Unis*. Démeunier in this work emphasizes the achievements of state legislatures in America, maintaining that these bodies consisted of elected representatives, enacted laws to guarantee the economic, political, and religious rights of their citizens, and asserted their position against the English crown.[155] The dramatist Sébastien Chamfort reveals in *La Jeune Indienne* his interest in America. In this play, Chamfort presents portrayals of Indians, merchants, and Quakers; he perceives these three groups as being advocates of the concepts of American liberalism.[156] After the *Académie française* staged a performance of this play, Chamfort told Franklin that "America was the place in the universe where the rights of man are best understood."[157]

5. Lodge Proponents of State Reforms

Several members of the Nine Sisters hoped that France would become a nation in which the inalienable rights of man could be respected. Spokesmen of state reforms from the Nine Sisters were familiar with American republican and natural rights ideologies and certainly believed that some American doctrines could be applied to improve conditions in France. These Masonic advocates of reform were not connected, however, with the Salon of Madame Helvétius. They envisioned their affiliation with the lodge as being essential for the dissemination of their views, but were not involved either with any important Parisian cultural groups or with any monarchical institutions. These Masonic enlighteners exhibited minimal interest in the physiocratic views of the royal minister Turgot, but championed major reform proposals of Voltaire and those of the Milanese *philosophe* Beccaria and thus helped to promote the concepts of a civic morality.

It was evident that in light of their views regarding religious toleration, Louis Sebastian Mercier and Elie de Beaumont drank from the same bottle as their Masonic brother Voltaire. Mercier was a minor Parisian satirist and became known for his *L'an deux mille quatre cent quarante*. In this work published in 1771, he maintains that Frenchmen should do penance for the St. Bartholomew's Day Massacre and for the revocation of the Edict of Nantes. Mercier further claims that Louis XV should recognize the religious and civil liberties of the Huguenots and that their emancipation was required for the improvement of French banking and commerce.[158] The persecution of the Huguenot Jean Calas disturbed Beaumont. A minor Parisian trial lawyer, Beaumont published in 1762 *Memoire pour les Calas* and argues that "an innocent man had been convicted and executed because of religious prejudice."[159] He as well implored Louis XV to end the religious and civil disabilities of French Protestants. The commitment of Beaumont to the cause of reform well explained why he became involved in the Nine Sisters. This disciple of Voltaire and Master of the lodge, however, never wrote another work about state reforms, appeared to be frightened of Grand Orient and royal authorities, and consequently decided against holding lodge assemblies to advance the reform movement.

A Master of the lodge, Dupaty wrote about legal reforms, and his problems with the crown justified the concerns of Beaumont. Dupaty served in the Bordeaux *Parlement* between approximately 1768 and 1774 and at this time distinguished himself as a writer. He wrote a eulogy dedicated to L'Hopital and was elected to the La Rochelle Academy. Dupaty in 1774 left Bordeaux to reside in Paris and three years later issued a French translation of *Dei delitti e delle pene* by Beccaria. Major views advanced in this work were important to Dupaty. He like Beccaria believed that criminals were entitled to fair trials, that punishments should be determined in light of the severity of crimes, and that prison conditions should be improved.[160] The year 1785 was a significant one for this Masonic spokesman of reform. Dupaty served as Master of the Nine Sisters, published *Réflexions sur le Droit criminel*, and, in light of pressure from royal officials who disapproved of the views advanced in this work, was constrained to leave France and to reside in Italy for approximately a year. He criticized the crown in *Réflexions*, arguing that trial procedures of French courts were unjust, that criminal laws and punishments were stern, and that Louis XVI displayed minimal concern about implementing legal reforms. After his return to France, the obstinate Dupaty refused to alter his position regarding legal reforms; the Rouen *Parlement* arrested, tried, and convicted him for treason. Before receiving his sentence, Dupaty in September 1788 died, believing that "the French *Parlements* lacked dignity, honesty, and tolerance."[161]

Claude Pastoret served as Master of the Nine Sisters between 1786 and 1789 and wrote to vindicate the cause of legal reforms. This Parisian lawyer during the early 1780s issued short works about Zoroaster, Confucius, Mohammed, and Voltaire. Pastoret perceived these philosophers as enlighteners and as advocates of justice.[162] While serving as Master of the Nine Sisters, Pastoret was writing *Des Loix Pénales* and in 1790 published it. He maintains in this work that the legal institutions of ancient Greece and Rome functioned according to principles of justice and that legal and penal systems of modern France were degenerate. Pastoret exhibited concern for Frenchmen accused and convicted of crimes.

The condemnation of the innocent is unfair. Until a judg-

ment of condemnation is rendered, a defendant is considered innocent. Proof against the accused must be accurate and decisive. If the accused is proven guilty, the punishment should be equivalent to and not greater than the crime. Punishments should be just, constructive, and useful. Punishments should be assigned for rehabilitative purposes. . .
.[163]

In *Des Loix Pénales*, he calls for the termination of cruel punishments in France. Pastoret condemns the cutting of feet, the mutilation of ears and noses, and the throwing of bodies into scalding water. He implores Louis XVI and French representatives in the National Assembly to end inhumane techniques of capital punishment: flogging until death, burning in the public square, and decapitation.[164] Pastoret further believes that capital punishment for minor crimes was wrong and was excessively used in France and that the French king and legislature, similar to those in ancient history, should be empowered to grant pardons.[165]

Most members of the Nine Sisters probably agreed with the reform proposals advanced in *Des Loix Pénales* and realized that Pastoret during his mastership discreetly managed the affairs of the lodge; they knew that the paucity of lodge meetings during the late 1780s was related to pertinent developments occurring in France. Members of the Nine Sisters realized that with the eruption of the French Revolution, the lodge eventually might be forced to cease its operations.

As spring gives way to the heat of summer and to the harvest of the fall, the muses of our lodge await the opportunity to relive their golden years. . . .[166]

D. The French Revolution and the Disappearance of the Nine Sisters

Such proved to be the case. During the heat of revolution, the lodge found it difficult to function. The lodge by early 1790 significantly decreased its activities; this body discontinued funding the *lycée* and staged few sessions. The attitudes of lodge members towards the Nine Sisters explained why lodge meetings were infrequently conducted. Most members were concerned about the affairs of the French Revolution and not about those of the Nine Sisters.[167] Other members did not want to become involved in the revolution and refused to attend meetings of the Nine Sisters. They believed that their participation in the lodge would result in attacks from political and anti-Masonic authorities.

Administrators of the Grand Orient first tried to justify the operations of the lodge and then decided to terminate them. Officers of the Grand Orient changed in late 1790 the name of the lodge to the *Société Nationale des Neuf Soeurs*. This action was taken to demonstrate to leaders of the National Assembly that the society was involved with cultural and social activities rather than with political matters.[168] The Grand Orient even permitted this new society to hold open meetings, but discovered that former members of the Nine Sisters were not interested in its activities. In recognizing that the few sessions of the *Société Nationale des Neuf Soeurs* were poorly attended and that the Jacobins, who viewed the Craft as a threat to their regime, would act to suspend Masonic activities, officers of the Grand Orient in November 1792 issued an edict to dissolve this society and thus to end "the golden age of the muses."[169]

Even before the French Revolution, both achievements and failures characterized the operations of the Lodge of the Nine Sisters. In light of major organizational functions of the lodge, its members made some contributions to the Enlightenment in Paris. During assemblies and banquets of the Nine Sisters, members behaved as Masonic enlighteners; they performed scientific experiments, suggested state reform proposals, read poems and eulogies, and saw new works of art and sculpture. Yet, the most significant organizational function of the Nine Sisters revolved around the lodge's sponsorship of surrogate institutions; the lodge succeeded in promoting educational institutions and in supporting groups which favored the cause of the American Revolution. Failures too marked the cultural operations of the Nine Sisters. Unlike its counterpart in Vienna, the Lodge of the Nine Sisters failed to publish journals containing articles about the Enlightenment and Masonry and consequently did little to encourage its members to write as enlightened Masons.

Born and other Viennese Masons knew about the operations of the Lodge of the Nine Sisters and in some respects designed the True Harmony Lodge to resemble its Parisian counterpart. Like the Lodge of the Nine Sisters, the True Harmony Lodge functioned to promote Enlightenment activities within the context of Masonry and recruited to its ranks many Masons from the Habsburg Empire. The organizational and cultural functions of the True Harmony Lodge differed, however, in many respects from those of the Nine Sisters.

In the next chapter, the origins, structure, and cultural functions of this lodge will be examined. Attention in that chapter will also be directed to the organization, rites, and operations of eighteenth century Austrian and Bohemian Masonry.

IV. PRAGUE AND VIENNESE FREEMASONRY, THE ENLIGHTENMENT, AND THE OPERATIONS OF THE TRUE HARMONY LODGE OF VIENNA

A. The Organization, Ritualism, and Cultural Operations of Prague Freemasonry

1. The Prague Lodge of the Three Stars: A Mecca of Blue Lodge Masonry in Bohemia

Like Paris and London, Prague during the eighteenth century evolved into a locus of Freemasonry. In comparison to these two West European capitals, Prague lacked cultural and social institutions, and consequently Masonry in Prague filled varying important needs. Masonry functioned in Prague as a social agency, enabling aristocratic and bourgeois Czechs and Germans to associate with each other and providing them with the opportunity to sponsor special festivities. Masonry in the Bohemian capital served, moreover, as a vehicle for the promotion of the Enlightenment. The degrees of the Craft offered to Prague Masons a ritualistic synthesis of pertinent ancient and modern ideologies concerning the liberal arts and sciences and provided them with interpretations of West European morals and values.[1] By functioning in some cases as learned societies, Masonic lodges in Prague, in another way, served as cultural centers.[2]

As the first Masonic body in the Habsburg Empire, the Prague Lodge of the Three Stars was established on June 26, 1726 and functioned as a local Modern lodge.[3] As stipulated by its constitution, which was granted by the Grand Lodge of London, the Three Stars Lodge was authorized to elect its officers and members, to confer the three degrees of Modern Masonry, and to engage in cultural and charitable activities.[4] This Prague lodge elected Count Franz Anton Sporck as its Master and as a result of his efforts recruited to its ranks such Bohemian aristocrats as Counts Kaiserstein, Kinsky, Paradis, Sternberg, and Wrabna.[5]

Some Enlightenment and ethical concepts of the Blue Degrees proved to be of importance to members of the Three Stars Lodge.

Members of this lodge seemed to associate the globe with the knowledge of the ancients and the moderns and with Newtonian laws explaining the operations of Nature.[6] Prague Masons also equated teachings and symbols of the Modern degrees with a civil religion. Masonic concepts regarding deism, which are explained in light of the All-Seeing Eye, and those regarding natural liberties, which are described in terms of the plumb and square, affected the moral conduct of Prague Masons and especially seemed to stimulate them to support the cause of religious toleration.[7] Members of the Three Stars Lodge became known, moreover, for their benevolence and thus recognized the importance of the Masonic handshake, a symbol of brotherly love and charity.[8]

As a result of the efforts of Sporck, the Three Stars Lodge during the late 1720s made significant philanthropic and cultural contributions to Prague. Under the Mastership of Sporck, this lodge donated money for the building of a hospital and an orphanage in Prague.[9] In an attempt to project a favorable civic image for Masonry, the Lodge of the Three Stars, too, allocated funds for the operations of a theater, an art gallery, and a library in the Bohemian capital.[10] There was also another cultural dimension to this lodge. Sporck, who had frequently toured Western Europe and had become a proponent of mechanistic, deistic and Jansenist ideas, on numerous occasions held meetings of the Three Stars Lodge in the Angelus Gardens of his Kukus palace.[11] During meetings at this estate located near Prague, members of the Three Stars performed some scientific experiments, exhibited paintings and sculpture, and gave lectures about the emancipation of Jews, Protestants, and peasants in Bohemia.[12] However, after 1729, meetings of this lodge were no longer held in the mansion of Sporck.

Sporck in 1729 encountered problems with the Jesuits and with imperial authorities. As a result of advocating Jansenist beliefs and of supporting the cause of Protestant emancipation in Bohemia, Sporck became involved in a feud with the Jesuit Konias; imperial authorities arrested Sporck in 1729 and charged him with committing treasonable acts against the crown and with being involved with efforts to undermine the Catholic Church. The trial of this Bohemian noble lasted seven agonizing years and culminated in his exoneration in 1736 and in his death in 1738.[13]

After the death of Sporck, the Three Stars Lodge continued to operate but suffered from factional disputes. Members of the lodge violated Blue Lodge regulations; they discussed political problems during lodge meetings and consequently divided into three factions. The Bavarian Party, or the first faction, was headed by Count Paradis and in 1740 favored recognizing Charles Albert, the Elector of Bohemia, rather than Maria Theresa as the Habsburg monarch. The Austrians, the second lodge faction, supported the succession of the young princess to the imperial throne, while the neutrals, or the third faction, wished to take no stand on the question of imperial succession, viewing the lodge as no place for the promotion of political activities.[14]

Involvement with the issue of imperial succession produced major effects upon the operations of the Three Stars Lodge. Paradis, Kaiserstein, and other leaders of the Bavarian faction were arrested, tried, and pardoned. Count Kinigl, the leader of the Neutrals, by 1743 succeeded in uniting the members of the lodge and guaranteed imperial authorities that the lodge would confine itself to ritualistic and philanthropic operations. Kinigl attempted to ameliorate relations with imperial authorities and in late 1743 secured their consent to create a new lodge known as the Prague Three Crowned Stars Lodge. This new Masonic body replaced the Three Stars Lodge, functioned under the Strict Observance jurisdiction, and enhanced the status of Prague as a hub of Masonry in the Habsburg Empire.[15]

2. The Supremacy of Strict Observance Masonry in Prague

Strict Observance Masonry, which was prevalent in Central and Eastern Europe during the 1760s and 1770s, was the invention of Baron von Hund and secured extensive support from members of the Prague Lodge of the Three Crowned Stars. An aristocrat from Lausitz with a great interest in the Templars, Hund in 1764 held a Masonic convention in Altenberg to acquire support for his Strict Observance System.[16] This new system proposed by Hund centered on the conferring of the English, Scottish, and Templar Degrees in Strict Observance lodges. Hund also suggested that the Strict Observance System should be organized into nine provinces which would extend from Bavaria to Russia and from Sweden to Greece.[17] Pracht, Schmidburg, and Skolen represented the Three Crowned Stars Lodge at Altenberg and favorably viewed the new Masonic system of Hund. After their return to Prague, these three representatives filed a report to members of the Three Crowned Stars and claimed that by recognizing the Strict Observance Rite, the Three Crowned Stars Lodge

would become one of its major grand lodge bodies. After hearing this
report, members of the Three Crowned Stars Lodge overwhelmingly
voted to affiliate with the Strict Observance Rite.[18]

What also seemed to be of great importance to Prague Masons
were major Enlightenment and moral concepts contained in the degrees of the Strict Observance Rite. Members of the Three Crowned
Stars Lodge received the three Blue Degrees and such Scottish Degrees as the Perfect Elect, the Knights of the East and West, and
the Knight of the Rose Croix. By taking the Perfect Elect and the
Knights of the East and West Degrees, members of this lodge learned
about Enlightenment concepts concerning justice and religious toleration and about ethical ideas regarding charity, honor, and virtue.[19]
In the Rose Croix or Templar Degree, Prague Masons were provided
with explanations concerning medieval chivalry and concerning loyalty and service to the state.[20] Degrees of the Strict Observance Rite
produced several effects upon Masonry in Prague. Although in many
cases containing religious teachings of the Middle Ages, these degrees
succeeded in imparting to Prague Masons secular and ethical ideas of
the Enlightenment. By conferring the Strict Observance Degrees, the
Lodge of the Three Crowned Stars attracted the support of numerous
groups in Prague. This lodge consisted of Catholics and Protestants,
of military men, of imperial bureaucrats, and of some intellectuals.

In addition to serving as a ritualistic center, the Three Crowned
Stars Lodge performed other functions and was comprised of several
Prague enlighteners. During the early 1770s and under the mastership of Count Kinigl, the lodge sponsored an important philanthropic
project; this body operated the Masonic Orphanage of Prague and adhered to the policy that orphans of all religions and nationalities could
receive support from this institution.[21] The Three Crowned Stars
Lodge also engaged in social and cultural activities, sponsoring banquets and some lectures.[22] Several imperial administrators belonged
to this lodge, succeeded in defending it from political and religious
critics, and perceived it as being an important agency of the Enlightenment in Prague. Counts Charles Francis Martinitz and Joseph
Thun were members of the *Hofkanzlei* and frequently attended meetings and banquets of the Three Crowned Stars.[23] Two other imperial
administrators behaved as enlighteners in this lodge. Karl Fursten-
berg, who was Governor of Bohemia, presented to the lodge several
papers about ancient history, and Count Philip Clary-Aldringen, who
was a graduate of the *Theresianum* and a member of the *Hofkanzlei*,

lectured to this body about the ideas of Plutarch.[24]

An important organizational function also characterized the operations of the Three Crowned Stars Lodge; this lodge functioned as a grand lodge of Strict Observance Masonry and consequently served as a center of Masonry in the Habsburg Empire. General Leopold von Pracht was named in 1765 as Commander of the Bohemian Provincial Grand Lodge of the Three Crowned Stars. He established lodges in Bohemia, Austria, Hungary, Transylvania, and Poland. Pracht, too, appointed such officers as Prefects, Priors, and Knights to govern the operations of lodges in these lands.[25] As a result of the 1772 Strict Observance Convention in Kohlo, Pracht was granted additional powers. He was allowed to create six new lodges and to establish administrative districts known as capitular governments to assist in directing the affairs of lodges under his vast jurisdiction.[26]

This special grand lodge status of the Three Crowned Stars Lodge seemed to be quite advantageous to Masonry in Prague. The Three Crowned Stars Lodge developed a centralized and effective administrative system and consequently expanded the base of operations of Strict Observance Masonry in the Habsburg Empire. By holding conventions in Prague to formulate policies for local Strict Observance lodges in the Habsburg Empire, the Three Crowned Stars Lodge helped to promote inter-Masonic relations within the empire. Until the gradual disappearance of Strict Observance Masonry, which resulted from the rise of the Zinnendorf Rite during the late 1770s, this lodge enabled Prague to achieve dominance over Vienna in the world of Habsburg Masonry.[27]

B. The Structure, Rites, and Cultural Operations of Viennese Freemasonry

1. Blue Lodge Masonry in Vienna

Modern English Masonry in Vienna, which arose during the early 1740s, served numerous functions and, in some respects, resembled that in Prague. Blue Lodge Masonry in Vienna, like that in Prague, sponsored special social events and thus helped to fill important needs. Modern Masonry in the imperial capital functioned as a club, but unlike the Craft in Prague, recruited to its ranks aristocratic and bourgeois members of different nationalities and religions. Modern Masonry in Vienna, like its counterpart in Prague, served as a source of West European Enlightenment ideas and sponsored special cul-

tural activities. Although their ritualistic and cultural operations
aroused the suspicion of imperial authorities, the Viennese Lodges of
the Three Cannons and the Three Hearts received support from the
Mason and Emperor Francis I and successfully met the challenge of
their opponents.[28]

The Blue Degrees contained concepts and symbols important
to members of these two Viennese lodges. These degrees offered to
Viennese Masons interpretations of Enlightenment ideas. Masons in
the imperial capital associated the globe and the three lights of the
Craft with the laws of motion, with the orderly operations of Nature,
and with the importance of education.[29] Viennese Masons exhibited,
moreover, interest in the tenets of deism and interpreted the symbol
of the All-Seeing Eye in terms of being the Omnipotent Legislator
of moral and secular laws.[30] Many Viennese Masons, who believed
that the policies of Maria Theresa would lead to the amelioration
of imperial institutions, viewed some ethical and secular concepts
contained in the Blue Degrees as constituting a civil religion based on
state reforms. As a result of receiving the degrees of Modern Masonry,
members of the two lodges in Vienna learned that religious toleration
was a fundamental principle of the order, that justice was one of the
cardinal Virtues of Masonry, and that the square was identified with
proper ethical conduct in society.[31]

The Three Cannons Lodge of Vienna was established on September 17, 1742 and was designed to operate as a local Modern lodge.
Granted by the Grand Lodge of London, the constitution of this Viennese lodge described its operational guidelines. This document stipulated that the Three Cannons Lodge would be empowered to recognize other local lodges and to engage in inter-Masonic relations. The
constitution also specified that lodge officers would confer the three
Blue Degrees either in English or in German, would direct special
cultural sessions of the Three Cannons, and would collect two thalers
yearly from each member for philanthropic projects.[32] During the first
meeting of the lodge, the election of officers was conducted. Count
Albrecht Joseph Hoditz was elected as Master, Gilgens as Steward,
Colmann as Treasurer, and Czernichew as Secretary. Before the closing of this meeting, the lodge inducted into its ranks the Britisher
Hamilton, the Italian Benedetto Testa, and the Austrian Engel. On
this and other occasions, the Three Cannons Lodge admitted individuals of varying nationalities.[33]

Under Count Hoditz, this lodge performed ritualistic and cultural functions. A court chamberlain, Hoditz held an important meeting at Rosswalde, his large estate with streams and fountains, with a theater, and with an enormous mansion resembling a Roman temple. During the October 1742 meeting, officers of the Three Cannons were attired in ancient costumes and inducted several aristocrats into the lodge. The Hungarian noble Gabriel Bethlen, who was to become the chancellor of Transylvania, Samuel von Bruckenthal, a statesman who also donated funds for medical and geological research, the French Count Charles de Ligny, and Count Seilern, who had served as imperial ambassador to England, received during colorful ceremonies the degrees of Modern Masonry. After these initiations, members of the lodge proceeded to play music, to stage scenes from several ancient plays, and to hold a lengthy banquet.[34] What these activities at Rosswalde demonstrated was that members of the Three Cannons Lodge behaved as Masonic enlighteners and attempted to revive cultural and social traditions of the ancients through the institution of Freemasonry.

Under de Grossa, who in November 1742 replaced Hoditz as Master, the Lodge of the Three Cannons continued to engage in ritualistic activities, but there was a threat posed to its operations. The lodge inducted into its ranks Count Casimir Draskovich, Lieutenant Anthony von Freyenthal of the Bavarian Grenadier-Regiment, and the Jew Joseph Riga, who translated from Hebrew into German select writings of King Solomon to reveal the relationship of ancient Jewish history to the development of Freemasonry.[35] Believing that the lodge should be protected from intruders, de Grossa decided to hold meetings of the lodge in the homes of different members. However, the protective strategy of de Grossa culminated in failure, for imperial soldiers on March 7, 1743 interrupted a session of the Three Cannons Lodge; they proceeded to arrest de Grossa, Lord Hamilton, Count Starhemberg, and other members in attendance and to charge them with conducting treasonable activities.[36] After these arrests, soldiers then searched the room in which the meeting had been conducted, confiscated the possessions of the lodge, and discovered its records and minutes. In their investigation of the minutes, imperial authorities discovered only the roster of the lodge and no incriminating evidence against the accused members.[37] What also happened was that Francis I came to the defense of the arrested members of the Three Cannons Lodge; he convinced Maria Theresa of their innocence and persuaded her to have imperial authorities release and pardon them.[38] After this episode with the Crown, the Lodge of the Three Cannons well might have continued to function between 1743 and 1765. However, evidence concerning its operations has not been discovered.[39]

The Viennese Lodge of the Three Hearts, unlike that of the Three Cannons, functioned as a deputy lodge. In light of its special status as a deputy lodge, the Three Hearts Lodge, which was created in 1754 and consisted of aristocratic and bourgeois members of varying nationalities, was accountable for its operations to the Hanover Lodge Friedrich. This Hanover Lodge was entitled to appoint the Master and other presiding officers of the Three Hearts, to establish a structure of dues for its members, and to regulate the activities of the Viennese lodge. The constitution granted by the Hanover lodge to the Three Hearts stipulated that the Blue Degrees would be conferred in this Viennese lodge, that a Master, two Wardens, and a Secretary would direct lodge affairs, and that monies derived from dues would be forwarded to Hanover.[40] This Viennese lodge, on the one hand, was responsible to a German Masonic body and, on the other hand, assisted in the diffusion of English Enlightenment and Masonic ideas in the Habsburg capital.

The Lodge of the Three Hearts first operated under the direction of John Frederick Raban de Sporcke. Named as Master of this lodge on May 22, 1754, Sporcke, who was a Danish gentleman of the bedchamber, was delegated considerable authority. He was entrusted by the Hanover lodge with control over the books, records, and furniture of the Three Hearts Lodge. During the mastership of Sporcke, the English lawyer Hobart, the French physician Jolive, the Hungarian Count John Joseph Kinsky, and the Austrian Baron Schenck were inducted in 1754 into this Viennese lodge. As the lodge that year continued to attract new members, Sporcke, for inexplicable reasons, resigned as Master and suddenly left Vienna. Yet before his departure, Sporcke had received consent from officials of the Hanover Lodge to entrust responsibility for the operations of the Three Hearts to Hinuber, an obscure aristocrat about whom little is known.[41]

Odd developments between October and December 1754 occurred under the mastership of Hinuber. In engaging in ritualistic activities, officers and members of this Viennese lodge were required to assume names associated with ancient culture; Schenck was known as Minerva, Hinuber as Cleander, Kinsky as Xerxes, Hobart as Liberty, and Jolive as Titus. By assuming these names, members of the Three

Hearts, perhaps, either were displaying respect for classical culture or were attempting to protect themselves in case of being infiltrated by imperial authorities. For no apparent reason, the Three Hearts Lodge in December 1754 terminated its operations. Prior to the closing of this lodge, imperial officials did not infiltrate its ranks, and Masonic administrators of the Hanover lodge did not rescind its constitution.[42] With the sudden disappearance of the Three Hearts Lodge, a void occurred in Viennese Masonry and was not filled until the rise of the Strict Observance Rite.

2. Strict Observance Masonry in Vienna

Strict Observance Masonry in Vienna, which first appeared in 1765, was characterized by various patterns. Vienna did not develop into a grand lodge center of Strict Observance Masonry, and its local lodges functioning under this system were accountable and subordinate to the policies of the Prague Three Crowned Stars Lodge. With no problems either from authorities of the crown or from those of the Catholic Church, Strict Observance local lodges in Vienna were able to engage in varying activities. These bodies, from an organizational viewpoint, performed valuable functions. Strict Observance lodges in Vienna elected their officers and members, delegated responsibilities to committees, held banquets, and thus provided their aristocratic and bourgeois members with the opportunity to serve in new positions of leadership and to sponsor social events. In also functioning as cultural centers, these lodges conferred rites, sponsored some lectures and concerts, and thus assisted in the diffusion of salient eighteenth century ideas in Vienna.[43]

Viennese Masons viewed the Strict Observance Degrees as being a source of Enlightenment and ethical ideas. Interpretations and symbols concerning civil obedience, religious toleration, justice, and philanthropy appeared in many degrees of Strict Observance Masonry and helped to explain why some Viennese writers and imperial administrators, who were proponents of state reforms, affiliated with the Craft during the 1760s and 1770s. In its high degrees, the Strict Observance Rite contained, furthermore, significant moral tenets. By vividly describing through medieval legends the concepts of honor, virtue, courage, and self-sacrifice, the Templar and the Knights of the East and West Degrees assisted in the development of a civil religion in Vienna and were especially enticing to Catholics and to military leaders belonging to lodges in the imperial capital.[44]

The Generosity Lodge, which was established in 1765 and was the first Masonic body in Vienna to operate under the banner of the Strict Observance Rite, primarily functioned as a ritualistic center, but did stage some special cultural sessions. A captain in the Habsburg army, Baron George von Kuffstein served as Master of the Generosity Lodge between 1765 and 1774 and inducted into this body military men, imperial administrators, writers, and merchants.[45] In addition to conferring degrees, the Generosity Lodge between 1772 and 1774 established cordial relations with the Prague Lodge of the Three Crowned Stars and received from its administrators numerous favors. George Weiler, who served in Prague during this two year period as the representative of the Generosity Lodge, convinced Commander Pracht of the Three Crowned Stars Lodge to allocate funds to this Viennese lodge for special cultural projects. Officials of the Generosity Lodge sponsored several lectures and musical performances and donated money to the University of Vienna Medical School.[46] However, officers and members of the Viennese lodge during the late 1770s regarded Commander Pracht as being too domineering and thus wished to obtain independence from Prague.[47]

The Vienna Lodge of the Three Eagles during the 1770s also functioned under the jurisdiction of the Strict Observance Rite. Leaving Prague in 1771 to reside in Vienna, Count Schmidburg, who had been a member of the Three Crowned Stars Lodge, established the following year the Lodge of the Three Eagles and for eight years served as its Master.[48] Besides its ritualistic operations under Schmidburg, the Lodge of the Three Eagles promoted some social and cultural activities and acquired support from individuals of various groups in Vienna. The army major Count Josef Franz Thun, the imperial administrators Count Auesberg and Konrad von Pufendorf, the banker Puthon, and the merchants George Malvieux and Johann Puchberg belonged to this Viennese lodge, attended its monthly dinners, and perceived this body as a convivial meeting place and as a point of reference.[49] Joseph Franz Hermann and the ex-Jesuit Franz Eder von Odenstein, who were professors in the University of Vienna, were associated with the Lodge of the Three Eagles and presented in this lodge several lectures concerning geology.[50] Despite its special cultural and social operations, the Lodge of the Three Eagles during the later 1770s suffered from a sharp decline in membership, terminated its relationship with the Prague Lodge of the Three Crowned Stars in 1780, and two years later secured consent from its members to affiliate with a new Masonic jurisdiction known as the Zinnendorf Rite.[51]

The Vienna Crowned Hope Lodge, which like the Three Eagles Lodge was established in 1772, first operated under the jurisdiction of Strict Observance Masonry and then under that of the Zinnendorf Rite. Under its Master John Paul Roder, the Crowned Hope Lodge developed into a ritualistic center and sponsored some banquets and special cultural sessions. As a result of its varying operations, this lodge admitted to its ranks the historian and the director of the *Hofbibliothek* Adam Kollar, the poet Franz Rosalino, the aristocratic patron of the arts Count Esterházy, and several other Viennese enlighteners.[52] Although the crowned Hope Lodge during the late 1770s continued to increase its membership, Roder and many members of the lodge objected to being dominated by Strict Observance leaders in Prague. Officials of the Crowned Hope Lodge in 1778 opened negotiations with administrators of the Zinnendorf Rite. As a consequence of these meetings, the Crowned Hope Lodge that year became affiliated with the Zinnendorf Rite and, like its two sister lodges in the imperial capital, acquired its independence from Prague.[53]

3. The Zinnendorf System and the Viennese Masonic Achievement

The Zinnendorf Rite seemed to play a central role in the development of Vienna as a center of Masonry and the Enlightenment. This rite, which with the exception of its Templar Degree closely resembled Strict Observance Masonry, originated in Sweden in the late 1760s, swept through the Germanies during the 1770s, and by 1777 was recognized in Vienna. The Austrian Provincial Grand Lodge between 1777 and 1783 and then the Grand Lodge of Austria between 1784 and 1787 served as the administrative institutions of Zinnendorf Masonry in the Habsburg Empire, were located in the imperial capital, and more importantly enabled Vienna to replace Prague as the locus of Masonic operations in the empire. Prince Dietrichstein between 1777 and 1787 headed both Zinnendorf grand lodge bodies, appointed numerous intellectuals from Vienna to administrative positions in these two bodies, and governed a large Masonic empire which consisted of local lodges in Austria, Croatia, Hungary, Transylvania, and Silesia.[54] What also happened was that an imperial decree concerning the status of the Craft in Habsburg lands especially benefited Zinnendorf lodges in Vienna. As a consequence of the 1781 Josephinian Patent legalizing the activities of Masonry in the empire, these lodges through their cultural operations helped to advance the cause of the Enlightenment in Vienna and evolved into havens for intellectuals in the imperial capital.[55] After the promulgation of this patent, imperial bureaucrats, writers, Catholic clergymen, and former Jesuits were admitted to Zinnendorf lodges in Vienna, served in some instances as lodge officers, and for the most part perceived these bodies as being valuable agencies for the diffusion of ideas concerning state reform. This edict evidently implied to Viennese enlighteners affiliated with Zinnendorf lodges that Joseph II viewed the Craft as a respectable institution and that in implementing its reform program, the crown looked to Masonry for support.

The Zinnendorf Rite, which was a synthesis of the Blue and the Strict Observance Degrees, served, moreover, as a source of Enlightenment and moral tenets and contained ideas relating to a civil religion based on state reform. The Zinnendorf Templar Degree, which favorably portrayed the role of the medieval Catholic Church, was of special importance to Catholic Masons in Vienna. The degree vividly described the ethical teachings of Jesus and his disciples and emphasized the concepts of faith, hope, charity, honor, virtue, and brotherhood.[56] Yet, equally instructive to Viennese Masons were concepts presented in the Blue Degrees. In addition to being provided with symbolic interpretations regarding the laws of motion, the operations of Nature, and the importance of education, Viennese Masons learned from the Blue Degrees about concepts concerning natural liberties. These Masons, who in many instances embraced the cause of state reform, became advocates of a civil religion which centered on feudal and Enlightenment ideas. In their writings, many Masons in the imperial capital endorsed, on the one hand, such ethical teachings of Templarism as benevolence and honor and subscribed, on the other hand, to such concepts of the Enlightenment as civil obedience, justice, and religious toleration.[57] Like Lessing these Viennese Masons consequently believed that Masonry should help to foster civic responsibility and should extend its support to those monarchs committed to the cause of state reform.[58]

> Masonry aspires to promote an international community based on benevolence and tolerance. . . . Masons are dedicated to the study of Nature and to the improvement of civil society. . . . Masons are instructed to comply with the laws of the state and to endorse the principle of religious toleration. . . .[59]

Although its organizational operations were quite routine and thus resembled those of other Zinnendorf lodges in the imperial capital, the Vienna Crowned Hope Lodge during the early 1780s engaged in some cultural operations. Under the direction of Count Johann Esterházy, who served as its Master between 1778 and 1785, the Crowned Hope Lodge held annual assemblies. Cultural events especially marked its 1783 assembly; Samuel Matolay, who was senior warden of the Crowned Hope Lodge, read several of his recently published poems, and the lodge orchestra gave a short performance. Under the direction of Paul Wranitzky, this orchestra played the specially composed Masonic cantata "Joseph der Menscheit" and several pieces from the opera *Oberon*.[60] The lodge, too, in 1783 funded a special project. This body sponsored a library and appointed the bookseller Adam Bartsch, who served as Secretary of the Crowned Hope, to head it.[61]

The Crowned Hope Lodge during the early 1780s consisted of several writers. They came from the circle of Count Esterházy and considered affiliation with this lodge as being important to their literary careers. Ladislaus Biró, a literary critic from Hermannstadt, and the Czech Alexander Pronay were obscure writers, were not active participants in the affairs of the Crowned Hope Lodge, and in 1783 left Vienna without making any significant contributions to the literature of the Josephinian Enlightenment.[62] Unlike these two writers, Tobias Gebler was quite well known in the world of Masonry and literature. This minor *philosophe* of the Crowned Hope Lodge, who also served as a Steward of the Austrian Provincial Grand Lodge, referred in his works to Enlightenment ideas. In the play "Der Minister," published in 1771, Gebler attacks some administrative officials of the crown for their abusive and corrupt practices. He further maintains that aristocrats in various lands of the Habsburg Empire should reform their ranks and should faithfully serve the crown. In other plays, Gebler applauded Joseph II for implementing administrative, legal, and religious reforms.[63] Like other Josephinians affiliated with the Craft, Gebler played an active part in helping to foster the literature of reform in Vienna and also believed that Masonry could serve as a valuable agency for its promotion.

The Vienna Charity Lodge, whose character slightly differed from that of the Crowned Hope Lodge, developed into an Enlightenment center in the Habsburg capital. The Charity Lodge, which was created in 1783, engaged, for the most part, in ritualistic activities, but did stage some cultural events; lectures concerning physics, classical philosophy, modern literature, and imperial reforms were occasionally delivered in this lodge.[64] The Charity Lodge, for a good reason, sponsored these special cultural sessions. Its administrative staff consisted of Josephinian bureaucrats and of enlighteners from the University of Vienna. Joseph J. Monsberger, who was a professor of Oriental languages in the University of Vienna, directed the affairs of the Charity Lodge between 1783 and 1784, and Johann Ellinger and Count Lazarevich, who both held positions in the *Hofkanzlei*, served as wardens of this body.[65]

The Charity Lodge consisted of various enlighteners. The astronomer Joseph von Tamerburg, the classicist Johann Bolla, the literary historian Ignatius de Luca, and the political philosopher Georg Scheidlin taught in the University of Vienna. These professors seemed to act as enlightened Masonic Catholics. They contributed to the Viennese Enlightenment by publishing a few minor works, evidently affiliated with the Charity Lodge to fill social and cultural needs, but never left the Catholic Church.[66] However, two important enlighteners of the Charity Lodge did sever ties with the Church, wrote about state reforms, and viewed the lodge as being a valuable agency for the advancement of their cause. Joseph Eybel, who denounced his vows as a Jesuit, studied law under the enlightener Riegger in the University of Vienna and in 1782 posited his views about the Catholic Church and Josephinian reforms in *Sieben Kapitel vom Klosterleben*. In this short pamphlet, Eybel defends the emperor for making decisions relating to temporal matters of the Church, inveighs against the abuses of monasticism, and lauds Joseph for closing the doors of many monasteries.[67] Like Eybel, Johann Pezzl, who served as secretary for Count Kaunitz, supports in the *Marokanische Briefe* many policies of Joseph II. In this work, which was published in 1784 and which resembled *Lettres Persanes*, Pezzl depicts Joseph as an exemplary monarch and offers praise to him for his embracing religious, educational, and judicial reforms.[68]

The Vienna St. Joseph Lodge, which was established in 1781 as a tribute to the emperor for enacting the Masonic Patent, served, like its sister lodges, as a source of the Enlightenment in the imperial capital. Besides its ritualistic operations, the St. Joseph Lodge during the early 1780s engaged in some special cultural enterprises. This lodge occasionally staged plays at the *Hoftheater* and held a few concerts. As a result of the leadership of the enlightener Johann Alxinger, who served as its Master between 1782 and 1784, the St. Joseph Lodge sponsored several lectures concerning medicine, imperial reforms, and contemporary Viennese literature.[69] This lodge donated, moreover, some funds for the publication of the *Wiener Musenalmanach* and the *Wiener Realzeitung*, and some lodge members from the literary circle of Alxinger contributed several articles to these journals.[70]

The St. Joseph Lodge was comprised of several enlighteners and of individuals from various groups in Vienna. For the Habsburg army officers Joseph Carl and Leopold Holl and for the merchants Johann Stern and Jacob Hofler, affiliation with the St. Joseph Lodge meant learning through rites about cultural and moral ideas, participating in its private social affairs, and satisfying important needs.[71] Some physicians, too, belonged to the St. Joseph Lodge; Drs. Anthony Rivolti, Max Braunn, and Joseph Werner were surgeons, taught at the University of Vienna medical school, and received from the lodge a sizeable donation for the remodeling of the university hospital.[72] The lodge also recruited to its ranks an important Viennese artist. Although not particularly active in the affairs of the lodge, Adam Braun was known for his rococo painting *Der Alte* and helped Joseph to develop the imperial collection at Schonbruun Palace.[73]

Three writers belonging to the St. Joseph Lodge were intimately involved with the cause of state reform. The careers and attitudes of Lorenz Haschka and Franz Kratter appeared to be quite similar. Haschka and Kratter were educated in Jesuit schools, but denounced this order and the Catholic Church and during the early 1780s were inducted into Masonry. As a result of their affiliation with the St. Joseph Lodge, both men received remunerative positions. Haschka was appointed to a Professorship of Aesthetics in the *Theresianum*, and Kratter worked as a writer for Prince Liechtenstein.[74] Furthermore, as a consequence of their involvement in the Masonic literary circle of Alxinger, Haschka and Kratter wrote to vindicate many policies of the crown and seemed to equate major reforms of Joseph with teachings of the Craft. Haschka, in "Ode to the Emperor," and Kratter, in *Der junge Mahler am Hofe*, advance similar views about Josephinism and offer praise to the emperor for instituting administrative and army reforms, for establishing secular schools, and for granting civil liberties to Jews and Protestants in the empire. Like Alxinger, these writers too visualized Joseph as resembling the Roman Emperor Augustus and perceived themselves as being the Vergils of the new golden age of the Habsburg Empire.[75] A literary lion in Vi-

enna during the early 1780s, Johann Alxinger, who as well received a
doctorate of law from the University of Vienna and was a man of considerable means, became a leading propagandist of Josephinism and
especially defended the emperor for recognizing the civil and religious
status of Jews in Habsburg lands. In "Lied eines alten Juden" and in
"Die Duldung," Alxinger claims that Jews would play an active role
in contributing to the political, cultural, and economic development
of the empire.[76]

Alxinger also acted and wrote as an enlightened Mason. After his
election as Master of the St. Joseph Lodge, Alxinger participated in a
Masonic literary group known as the *Wiener Freunde* and published
in several Viennese journals essays and poems about Masonry and its
relation to the Enlightenment.[77] In "Empfindungen eines Freymaur-
ers am Tage seiner Aufnahme," he maintains that the reform policies
of Josephinism and the cardinal teachings of Masonry reflected the
ideas of ancient secular humanists and contributed to the development
of Vienna as a center of the Enlightenment.[78] Masonic and Enlightenment ideas also appeared in "Prophezeihung," a poem published
in the *Wiener Musenalmanach.* In this poem, Alxinger describes the
function of the poet, stresses the importance of Nature, refers to Templarism, and seems to subscribe to the tenets of an enlightened feudal
civil religion.

> Friends, we are men and poets, writing for the young and
> old. Our travels permit us to write about the flowing of
> rivers and the beanty of mountains. Are we not fortunate
> to prophesy about and to convey the beauties of Nature in
> our poems? Dream and prophesy, for these are our duties.
> . . .
>
> Poetry serves as an avenue of learning. We have told about
> the heel of Achilles, the plight of the Romans and Gauls,
> and the heart of Macbeth. . . .
>
> We have written about the Templar Order. The ethical sys-
> tem of these knights has served as the basis of Modern Ma-
> sonry. We have learned from this medieval order, acting
> according to their teachings and imitating their splendorous
> dress. As Masons, we toast their name and believe that they
> would do the same. . . .[79]

By securing support from Alxinger and many other intellectuals,
Zinnendorf Masonry during the early 1780s played an important part

in the cultural life of Vienna. As a result of their ritualistic operations and their special cultural functions, Zinnendorf lodges in Vienna helped to foster the cause of the Enlightenment. In seeing that there was a great influx of enlighteners into these bodies, Ignatz von Born and officials of the Austrian Provincial Grand Lodge acted in 1781 to establish the True Harmony Lodge as a Viennese Masonic learned society.

C. The Origins, Structure, and Operations of the True Harmony Lodge

1. The Creation of the True Harmony Lodge

There seemed to be a genuine need for a Masonic learned society in Vienna. The imperial capital had few learned societies, and the True Harmony Lodge consequently would fill a cultural gap. As a result of the 1781 Masonic Patent, which demonstrated that the crown would support the operations of the Craft, this lodge would be able to function in several realms to promote the cause of the Enlightenment in Vienna. The True Harmony Lodge was especially intended to serve as a literary and political center; many members of this body would be given the opportunity to publish works about Josephinian reforms, about ancient and modern literature, and about Masonic doctrines. The True Harmony Lodge would also function as a musical salon. It would have its own orchestra and would sponsor special musical performances. This Viennese lodge, too, would serve as a locus of scientific research and would allocate funds for a scientific publication.

In early March of 1781, Prince Dietrichstein and other administrators of the Austrian Provincial Grand Lodge acted upon the proposal of Born concerning the creation of the True Harmony Lodge. After receiving the proposal of Born on March 1, 1781, Dietrichstein and officers of this grand lodge met that day to review it. They unanimously decided to establish the True Harmony Lodge and believed that this body would evolve into a leading center of Masonic and Enlightenment operations in Vienna and in the Habsburg Empire. Dietrichstein, on March 3rd, informed Born of the decision reached by administrators of the Austrian Provincial Grand Lodge and that day presented to him the constitution of the True Harmony Lodge.[80]

2. The Organization, Officers, and Cultural Projects of the True Harmony Lodge

The constitution of the True Harmony Lodge defined its aims. According to this document, Masons connected with this lodge were to examine the varying facets of Nature, were to promote the study of the arts and sciences, and were to investigate Enlightenment and Masonic teachings. The lodge seal, which appeared on the first page of the constitution, contained Masonic symbols related to these aims. The Sun suggested to members of the True Harmony that their efforts should be devoted to discovering the laws and powers of the universe. The globe represented the studies of lodge members to determine the operations of Nature. The symbol of the triangle was intended to induce members of the True Harmony to comply with the moral teachings of Masonry.[81]

The constitution explained how the lodge would function as a Masonic body. This document specified that the True Harmony Lodge was required to adhere to laws enacted by the Austrian Provincial Grand Lodge. According to the constitution, stated meetings would be held. During these meetings, members of the True Harmony were to hear committee reports, were permitted to voice their views about committee proposals, and in light of the majority rule principle were to make decisions about operational policies of the lodge. The constitution stipulated that members of the lodge during stated meetings were to vote upon the petitions of candidates and that a unanimous vote was required to elect candidates to the True Harmony. In complying with the provisions of the constitution, the True Harmony Lodge held some sessions devoted to the conferring of the Zinnendorf Degrees and occasionally staged banquets.[82]

The constitution of the lodge also described how this body would operate as a learned society. There was in this document a provision concerning the recruitment of members. Like those of the Nine Sisters, members of the True Harmony were required to be Masons and were permitted to be affiliated with other Masonic lodges. Active members of this lodge, who in most cases were Viennese Masonic bureaucrats, writers, musicians, and scientists, constituted the first membership category. Corresponding lodge members, who for the most part were Masonic intellectuals from other cities in the Habsburg Empire, comprised the second category and were not permitted to vote on operational matters concerning the True Harmony.[83] According to the constitution, both active and corresponding members of the True Harmony could participate in special cultural sessions sponsored by the lodge. However, this provision did not prove to be meaningful to the operation of the True Harmony, for with the exception of several musical performances, this Viennese lodge held few cultural events and thus significantly differed from its Parisian counterpart. The constitution more importantly stipulated that with the approval of its officers and its active members, the True Harmony Lodge could grant funds for its own literary and scientific publications.[84]

Ignatz von Born provided the True Harmony Lodge with capable leadership and occupied a significant place in the cultural affairs of late eighteenth century Vienna. From the inception of this lodge until its closing in 1786, Born served as its Master. As the chief administrative officer of the True Harmony Lodge, he directed its ritualistic activities and supervised its cultural affairs.[85] The contributions of Born to the Josephinian Enlightenment and to Masonry suggested why he was elected as Master of this body. Like many Viennese Masonic intellectuals, Born prepared himself for a career in the Jesuit order, but after the dissolution of this order in the Habsburg Empire, filled his cultural needs by pursuing the study of literature and science. He conducted in 1774 a major geological survey of Hungary and two years later was named the director of the Imperial Natural History Collection in Vienna.[86] Born became well known in European geological circles and during the late 1770s was elected to the Royal Society of London and to scientific academies in Padua and in Stockholm. He emerged during the early 1780s as a vocal supporter of imperial reforms and in the *Monachologia* lauded Joseph for establishing state schools in Habsburg lands and for ending the hegemony of Catholic clergymen in the realm of education.[87] Born, too, acted and wrote as an enlightened Mason. He recruited many Masonic intellectuals from Vienna and from the Habsburg Empire to the ranks of the True Harmony Lodge, participated with Alxinger, Blumauer, and Ratschky in the literary activities of the *Wiener Freunde*, and published pertinent articles about Masonic rites and their teachings.[88]

Joseph von Sonnenfels served as Deputy Master of the True Harmony Lodge, and his varying cultural roles in eighteenth century Vienna seemed to illustrate why he held this administrative position. Sonnenfels in 1782 replaced the obscure mathematician Stolzig as Deputy Master and held this position until 1786. He occasionally presided over the True Harmony in the absence of Born, helped to arrange its banquets, and served on its publication committee.[89] Sonnenfels, too, acted and wrote as a Masonic enlightener; he served as President of the Viennese *Deutsche Gesellschaft* and while heading this literary society published in 1765 *Der Mann Ohne Vorurteil*. Through Capa-Kaum, the hero of this work, Sonnenfels calls for the abolition of capital punishment and torture and for the implementation of legal and religious reforms.[90] During the early 1780s, he wrote articles to vindicate the imperial reform program and was appointed to the Chair of Political Administration and Economy.[91] In light of this position, Sonnenfels recruited the legal theorist J. A. Riegger, the philosopher Anton Kreil, and other professors from the University of Vienna to the ranks of the True Harmony Lodge.[92]

The minor Josephinian writer Jacobi served as Treasurer of the True Harmony between 1781 and 1786 and was involved with significant decisions regarding the cultural functions of the lodge. Jacobi paid the bills of the lodge and collected dues from its members. With Born and Sonnenfels, Jacobi formulated pertinent proposals presented to the lodge in 1783. These three officers recommended that the lodge sponsor a literary and a scientific journal and appoint editors to manage the affairs of each of these journals. Members of the True Harmony approved these proposals, naming Born as editor of the *Physikalische Arbeiten der Einträchtigen Freunde in Wien* and appointing Alois Blumauer as editor of the *Journal für Freymaurer*.[93] As a consequence of deciding to publish these journals, administrators and members of the True Harmony Lodge demonstrated that the cultural operations of this Viennese learned society would acutely differ from those of their Parisian counterpart.

Blumauer occupied a central place in the world of Josephinian literature and consequently was selected as editor of the literary journal of the lodge. Blumauer had been ordained into the Jesuit Order and after its dissolution was required to seek a new career. During the 1770s he held several minor posts in the imperial bureaucracy, emerged in 1780 from the Viennese *demimonde* to secure employment in the imperial library, and was provided with the opportunity to engage in research. By publishing in 1782 "A Travesty of the Aeneid," Blumauer was well received in Viennese literary circles. In this lengthy poem, he gave credit to modern Josephinians for reviving major political and philosophical ideas of the ancients and for improving secular and cultural institutions in the Habsburg Empire. After the critics favorably reviewed this poem, Blumauer in 1782 was named to other positions. He was appointed as a censor for the Educational Commission, as a co-editor of the *Wiener Musenalmanach*, and as editor of the *Wiener Realzeitung*.[94] These appointments would be helpful, moreover, to Blumauer in his role as editor of the *Journal für Freymaurer*. By serving as a censor, Blumauer could promote and protect his works and those of Masonic colleagues. He, too, could publish some works appearing in the *Wiener Musenalmanach*, in the *Wiener Realzeitung*, and in the *Journal für Freymaurer*. By serving as editor of this lodge journal, he also could demonstrate that Masonic writings were intimately related to the literature of reform.

Blumauer edited the *Journal für Freymaurer* from 1783 to 1786 and inserted varying works into its volumes. The purpose of the writings in this journal was to stimulate interest in the study of Masonic and Enlightenment ideas. Each volume was approximately two hundred pages long and contained essays, poems, biographical sketches of Masons, and a few musical pieces. Blumauer inserted into the volumes of the *Journal für Freymaurer* some essays and poems about Josephinian reforms and many articles about the doctrines and symbols of Masonry. In the first volume of this journal, Blumauer describes the fundamental functions of Masonry and explains how members of the Tree Harmony Lodge worked to advance the cause of the Enlightenment.

> Masonry is dedicated to the advancement of the arts, sciences, and humanity. The *Eintracht* has members devoted to these objectives and is issuing two journals to fulfill these aims. . . . Members of the lodge have been assigned to observe the workings of Nature, to determine her laws, and to work for the improvement of society; they are members of the cultural nobility, philosophizing about society, writing poetry, and opposing fanaticism and intolerance. . . . Dedicated to the advancement of virtue and wisdom, lodge members have probed Nature and have attempted to apply her laws for the improvement of the state. Similar to the ancients, the modern Masons of the *Eintracht* have studied the beauties of the Earth and heavens, the mysteries of the ancients, and the problems involved with the injustices of contemporary society. . . .[95]

Born directed the other major cultural project of the True Harmony Lodge, serving as editor of the *Physikalische Arbeiten der Ein-*

trächtigen Freunde in Wien. Born certainly knew that few scientific
journals were published in Vienna and that numerous active and corresponding members of the True Harmony would contribute articles to
the scientific journal of the lodge. Born also realized that many writings appearing in the *Physikalische Arbeiten der Einträchtien Freunde
in Wien* would contain significant discoveries, would be read by Masonic and non-Masonic scientists, and would enable the True Harmony
Lodge to evolve into a Central European center of Enlightenment science. Born between 1783 and 1785 published three volumes of the
Physikalische Arbeiten der Einträchtigen Freunde in Wien. Each volume of this journal consists of approximately 300 pages and contains
articles concerning mathematics, astronomy, physics, and electricity.
More importantly, the many geological articles also appearing in the
scientific journal of the True Harmony marked a distinctive contribution to Enlightenment science.

D. The Cultural Functions of Members of the True Harmony Lodge

1. Geology and the True Harmony

There were several reasons why geologists belonged to the True
Harmony Lodge. Masonic explanations of theological and scientific
theories concerning the origins, evolution, and flooding of the Earth
were of considerable interest to some geologists in the lodge. These
geologists seemed to think that their findings might help to substantiate these theories.[96] Most geologists in the True Harmony espoused,
moreover, materialistic theories; they attempted to determine the
properties of various substances, endorsed the atomistic theory, and
also believed that their findings would help to confirm significant discoveries made in chemistry. As a result of their desire to publish their
findings in the *Physikalische Arbeiten der Einträchtigen Freunde in
Wien* and as a result of their friendship with Born, numerous geologists joined the True Harmony Lodge. Many Habsburg geologists,
too, exhibited interest in the models and views of Torbern Bergman,
knew that this Swedish scientist was a corresponding member of the
True Harmony, and consequently decided to affiliate with the lodge.

Bergman was known for classifying substances according to their
properties and their strata. In *Physical Description of the Earth*, first
published in 1766 and then reprinted during the early 1780s, Bergman
explains that rock strata could be classified according to age and to
water content and proposed that granite, limestone, sandstone, and
coal could serve as major stratigraphic categories.[97] He expanded

upon his stratigraphic views in *Outlines of Mineralogy*. Bergman emphasizes that observations and inductive reasoning procedures enabled those involved in the geological sciences to determine the density, size, and shape of different substances.

> Let us well note external characteristics. They permit the accustomed eye without troublesome trials to acquire a degree of certainty. External properties are observed by our senses. We see the hardness and color of scientific substances; we can classify substances into classes, genra, and species. In methodizing substances, we know that compounds are most abundant, that properties of minerals are not of the same intensity, and that mineral substances should be ranked according to their value. . . .[98]

Bergman then proposes four categories into which matter could be classified. Salts constituted the first category, are frequently found in iron, nickel, and copper ores, and often glow radiantly. His second category consisted of acids; Bergman explains that pure acids have neither colors nor odors, emit vapors, and are corrosive. He maintains that acids should be tested to determine their weights and phlogiston content. Inflammable substances constituted the third category and are known for easily burning and for emitting phlogiston. Metals comprised the fourth category. Bergman believes that metals should be observed in light of tests with fire and water and that their properties, weight, and phlogiston content then should be ascertained.[99] This stratigraphic scheme was of considerable importance to some chemists involved with the study of the phlogiston theory and to numerous geologists connected with the True Harmony.

The correspondence between Bergman and Born revealed the interest of this Viennese enlightener in the geological ideas and models of Bergman. This correspondence between 1778 and 1781 also illustrated the international character of eighteenth century geology and Freemasonry. Born in July 1778 wrote Bergman about the discovery of tourmaline in the Tyrol and believed that after receiving this silicate, Bergman could test and classify it.

> Baron Gagnek [the Danish envoy to Vienna] has given a box to me which I am forwarding to you. This box contains pieces of tourmaline discovered in the Tyrol. You can experiment with these rocks to determine the content and features of this mineral. . . .[100]

Two years later, Born wrote to Bergman, wishing to know about the results of the experiments of the Swedish scientist concerning tourmaline. Born also informed Bergman about his discovery of quartz in the Schemnitz mines. Born sent to Bergman quartz samplings from these mines, believing them to be of geological significance.

> I thank you for the books which you recently sent to me. .
> . . I am interested to know about your experiments with
> tourmaline and about its value. . . . I am sending to you
> zinc crystals to be examined. . . . I should mention that
> chalcedony [or quartz] in crystalline form has been discov-
> ered in the Hungarian mines in Schemnitz and that samples
> of this mineral will be forwarded to you. . . .[101]

Like Bergman, Peter Pallas was a major geologist and a significant contributor to the True Harmony Lodge. Pallas in 1768 consented to the request of Czarina Catherine II to head a survey team established to investigate the geological features of regions in Russia. His important geological accounts about Siberia were published in 1783 in the scientific journal of the lodge. In "Schreiben aus St. Petersburg," Pallas classifies minerals discovered in Siberia according to their properties; he demonstrates that water and soil erosion precipitated great changes in Siberian rock strata and were responsible for the formation of primary, secondary, and tertiary mountains in this region. Pallas also claims that water and soil erosion led to the formation of vast deposits of quartz, granite, copper, and glass.[102]

Other geologists, too, were affiliated with the True Harmony and engaged in stratigraphic studies. Peter Jordan served with Born in the Imperial Natural History Department, published geological surveys of the Tyrol, and investigated salt compounds in this region.[103] A member of the Born circle and a professor in the University of Vienna, Joseph Raab in 1782 conducted a geological survey of Galicia and two years later published in the scientific journal of the lodge his findings concerning salts examined in this region. He melted salts, attempting to determine how much heat they emitted and how much weight they lost. In light of his experiments, Raab discovered that when exposed to fire, salts generated considerable heat and lost much weight. He further proposed that salts could be effectively used as bleaching agents.

> During my 1782 expedition to Galicia, I collected, observed,
> and tested salts. I mixed them with solutions, exposed them

to acids, and burned them. . . . My objective was to
determine their weights and their heat levels. . . . I melted
salts and used a thermometer to determine how much heat
salts were to emit. . . .[104]

Karl Haidinger, who also taught geology in the University of
Vienna and was a director of the Imperial Natural History Department, accompanied Raab in 1782 to Galicia. Haidinger conducted
experiments with salts discovered in this region. He classified and
experimented with salt crystals extracted from alabaster, ammonia,
and other Galician minerals. Haidinger also heated salt crystals to
determine their weight loss and mixed these crystals with acids to
ascertain their reaction. He discovered that upon exposure to fire,
salt crystals turned different colors and that when mixed with acids,
new compounds were not formed. These experiments revealed that
Haidinger was working within the geological framework of Bergman
and was attempting to illustrate the importance of geological findings
to chemical theories.

There are many salts in Galicia. I extracted salts from ores
found in mines and on mountains in Galicia. . . . Because of
changes in weather, salts are not always white and in some
cases are a brownish color. . . . Salt can be extracted from
ammonia, from alabaster, and even from sandstone. . . .
When heated, salts from Galicia became either a black or a
blue shade. . . .[105]

Andreas Stütz, who was a minor geologist connected with the
circle of Born, conducted geological surveys of regions in Austria.
Influenced by the views of Bergman, Stütz collected, classified, and
experimented with salt, granite, limestone, quartz, and other minerals
found in Austria. In light of his work, Stütz proposed that granite
and limestone could be utilized for industrial purposes.

Austria is endowed with many minerals. Granite and quartz
are found in great quantity near Donau and Vienna. Exposed to fire, these two minerals do not melt and retain
their color and firmness. Found near Vienna, sandstone,
when heated, does not burn or decompose. . . . Pure
quartz from Annenberg and granite from Schadwien, when
heated, retain their original properties. . . . In Rothenberg,
salt and quartz are mined and sold in large quantities for
commercial purposes. . . .[106]

Johann B. Ruprecht examined metals and minerals in Hungary. This geologist and chemist, who also belonged to the Schemnitz Academy, made comprehensive reports to Born about the properties of and his experiments with antimony, bismuth, quartz, and silver. During his experiments, Ruprecht applied heat and acids to minerals and metals to determine their chemical components and phlogiston levels.

> I conducted experiments with antimony and bismuth. Antimony and bismuth do not dissolve easily in mineral water. . . . When mixed with saltpeter, antimony and bismuth resist combining with this substance. . . . When antimony and bismuth are hammered, difficulties are encountered in breaking both metals into pieces. . . .[107]

Ruprecht, too, investigated the properties of gold. To this geologist, the study of gold was significant for an understanding of the natural and occult sciences; Ruprecht viewed gold as the king of the metals and performed experiments with heat, acids, and saline solutions to determine its chemical and geological features. He also believed that gold possessed occult powers and that after determining these powers, scientists would be able to discover the principle associated with the transmutation of common metals into gold. Ruprecht conducted valuable experiments to explain the properties of gold, but unfortunately failed to discover the principle pertaining to transmutation.

> I experimented with and wrote numerous reports about gold found near Nagyág. I used fire, acid, and water to test gold ores. . . . Upon exposure to fire, gold emits a brown vapor. . . . When submersed in a vessel containing acid, most gold ores gradually dissolve and become a reddish shade. . . . When gold is mixed with a saline solution, there is no reaction. . . . When gold is mixed with arsenic and with quicksilver, no new compounds are produced. . . . When being hammered, gold does not easily shatter. . . .[108]

Johann Müller conducted geological surveys in Transylvania and discovered large deposits of antimony and bismuth in this region. In his experiments with these two metals found in the Faczebay region, Müller utilized fire, acids, and distilled water to determine their properties. He also believed that antimony and bismuth could be used for industrial purposes.

When submersed in water, antimony neither mixes nor dissolves well. After being lifted from water and being weighed, this metal slightly increases in weight and does not lose its original color. Upon exposure to a flame, antimony changes color and becomes a light brown shade. When heated antimony is mixed with salt, a brittle and sticky compound is produced. When observed through a prism, this compound reflects colorful rays. . . . Antimony is found in great supply in Transylvania, is durable, and can be mined for industrial purposes. . . .[109]

When exposed to sulfuric acid, bismuth turns into a brilliant red color. Bismuth is also corroded by this acid. . . . When placed in a glass of distilled water, bismuth does not react. . . . When mixed with sulfuric acid and exposed to heat, bismuth forms a new compound. When placed on a piece of cloth, this compound burns a hole in it. . . . This compound seems to be powerful and to emit phlogiston. . . .[110]

The True Harmony Lodge consequently was identified with major breakthroughs in the realm of geology. The writings of lodge geologists contain valuable classification schemes concerning substances found in Central and Eastern Europe, and their observations and experiments helped to support atomistic theories. The geological articles, too, appearing in the scientific journal of the True Harmony undoubtedly were read by scientists throughout Europe and enabled this lodge to serve as an international center for the study of geology.

2. The Mechanists of the True Harmony

Although the True Harmony Lodge primarily consisted of materialists, a few mechanists did belong to this body. As a result of the interest during the early 1780s in sciences revolving around materialistic theories, mechanistic ideas especially in Vienna at this time were not extensively investigated. To a great extent, this pattern was applicable to the True Harmony Lodge, which consisted of no astronomers or of no physicists. There were, however, two minor members of the True Harmony involved with the study of electricity. In their works, these two lodge members merely summarized important concepts of electrical theorists and failed to offer new theories concerning the study of electricity. More importantly, the major group of mechanists in the True Harmony consisted of physicians. Indebted to the views of Dutch Newtonian medicine, these physicians employed inductive techniques to make their clinical observations and believed that mechanistic laws could be discovered to explain the operations of the body. They, too, improved the facilities of the University of Vienna Medical School and assisted in transforming this institution into a leading European medical center.

Dr. Johann Hoffinger evidently viewed affiliation with the True Harmony as being important to his career. He practiced medicine in Budapest until 1780, came that year to Vienna to resume his practice, and three years later was admitted to the lodge. As a result of his association with the lodge, Hoffinger participated in the circle of Masonic physicians from the University of Vienna and published several works. Published in 1784, *Vermischte medicinische* was his most important contribution to Viennese medical literature. In this work, Hoffinger discusses the functions of the heart, veins, and arteries and also presented important clinical findings.[111]

Two doctors affiliated with the True Harmony embraced the cause of medical and state reforms. After studying under Dr. Lind in London and the *ideologue* Dr. Louis in Paris, Dr. Johann Hunczovsky in 1781 returned to Vienna and in 1783 published his views about English and French medicine in *Medicinisch Chirurgische*. In this work, he comments on hospital life in both states; he maintains that St. Thomas in London, *Charité* in Paris, and other major hospitals in England and France treated both wealthy and poor patients. Hunczovsky proposes that Viennese hospitals should initiate measures to provide attention to the wealthy and the poor. He further discusses surgical problems, claiming that like English and French physicians, those in Vienna should become familiar with new techniques regarding arm and leg amputations.[112] Dr. Ferdinand Leber expressed interest in learning about surgical techniques practiced by English, French, and Dutch doctors. While known for his textbook on surgery, this physician, who chaired the Department of Anatomy and Physiology in the University of Vienna Medical School, became a spokesman of imperial reform. Leber served with Sonnenfels on the committee studying criminal and legal reforms in the empire and in several short works proposed the abolition of capital punishment and torture.[113] Leber and Hunczovsky consequently seemed to perceive the True Harmony Lodge as being a significant institution for the promotion of research and reform.

The lodge members Abbé Jacquet and Joseph von Retzer wrote about electricity. Both Masons explained concepts discussed in the electrical experiments of Franklin. In *Précis de L'Electricité*, published in 1775, Jacquet provides his readers with a summary of electrical terms defined by Franklin. Jacquet maintains that electricity operates as an invisible force capable of penetrating objects in Nature. Electricity, he explains, possesses the powers of attraction and repulsion. Jacquet as well defines other terms associated with electricity and explains the importance of the lightning rod. He shows that this invention protects buildings from fires which result from electrical storms.[114] In *Physikalische Abhandlung von den Eigenschasten des Donners*, published in 1772, Retzer explains how electrical charges are emitted during thunderstorms. He also comments on properties and reactions of electrical and non-electrical charges.

> Electrical substances retain their electrical virtues. Electrical virtues cannot be communicated to such non-electrics as glass, porcelain, and sand. When applied to such electrics as paper and wood, electricity will cause heat and in many cases fire. . . . When metals receive virtues, heat in many cases will be generated. . . . Dr. Franklin has demonstrated that iron rods, nails, and pins serve as excellent receivers of electrical virtues. . . . Nollet and Monnier have performed similar experiments and have confirmed the findings and theories of Franklin. . . .[115]

Jacquet and Retzer during the early 1780s continued to write about electricity, but their works proved to be of minimal importance. Unlike the physicians of the lodge, whose contributions to Viennese medical life were quite impressive, Jacquet and Retzer did little to advance the cause of mechanism in the Habsburg capital. By failing to offer speculations about the application of electricity to other sciences, Jacquet and Retzer seemed to be unimaginative.[116] These two minor mechanists consequently differed from members of the True Harmony Lodge who were significant contributors to the science and literature of the Josephinian Enlightenment.

3. Lodge Proponents of State Reform

The True Harmony Lodge also served as a haven for Masons involved with the literature of reform. As a result of its functions as a learned society, the True Harmony Lodge provided its literary members with the opportunity to publish their works concerning reform in the *Journal für Freymaurer* and thus filled a major cultural need.

Numerous Viennese imperial administrators and writers from the circles of Born and Blumauer were recruited to the True Harmony and as suggested by their writings, viewed the lodge as an essential urban literary agency for the promotion of their Enlightenment and Masonic concepts concerning reform.

In an article in the *Journal für Freymaurer*, Blumauer describes the modern enlightener Joseph II in terms of ancient concepts. In "Gesundheit auf den Kaiser," Blumauer visualizes Joseph as possessing qualities resembling those of Solomon. Like the ancient Jewish monarch, Joseph was judicious, virtuous, and wise.

> Similar to birds in a nest, Masons live as brothers in the House of Joseph. We are indebted to the emperor for his benevolent acts. Fire is in our hearts and has been ignited to guide us in our search for light. . . . In our efforts to achieve this end, we recognize that a virtuous king is serving and deserves our support. . . .[117]

Blumauer in several articles appearing in the literary journal of the lodge presented his views about the religious policies of the emperor. To Blumauer, these policies helped to reduce the possibilities of religious conflict in the empire, to weaken the status of the Catholic Church, and to strengthen imperial institutions. He also believed that Habsburg Masons wished to cooperate with the emperor to end religious prejudice and fanaticism and in Masonic terms explained that religious toleration permitted Joseph to cement the blocks of his empire firmly.

> The operations of our venerable fraternity must never cease, and Masons must never separate. Religious toleration has been granted, and this accomplishment has been our hope.
>
> Our lodges have praised Joseph, for his policies have been comforting and humane. Let us hope that the *Eintracht* and sister lodges will revere his name. . . .[118]
>
> My brothers, unite as virtuous men and act to end suffering in society. Work with state authorities to help the oppressed. Let reason and virtue serve as your guide in working for the reform of society and for the welfare of humanity. . . .[119]

Heinrich Watteroth, who was a member of the True Harmony Lodge and was a professor of history in the University of Vienna, published works about religious toleration. In *Für Toleranz uberhaupt und Burgerrechte der Protestanten in katholischen Staaten*, published in 1781, Watteroth advances his views about the place of religion in the state and about religious toleration. To Watteroth, religion is identified with natural morality and is intended to make citizens loyal to the state.[120] He speaks of religion in Masonic terms, claiming that the major religions of the world share in common such principles as brotherly love and benevolence. Watteroth also argues that each state should recognize religions within its realm; he believes that by granting toleration to religious groups, the monarch would strengthen his state and thus would receive cooperation from clergymen who would instill their practitioners with the tenets of natural morality. Watteroth, too, thinks that religion could be a constructive institution in the state and suggests that Masonry succeeded in uniting men of various faiths and in diffusing the doctrines of a public morality.[121]

Karl Reinhold, who was admitted to the True Harmony Lodge in 1782, was another spokesman of Josephinian religious reforms. In his poems and essays published in Viennese literary journals, Reinhold defends the emperor for granting religious toleration to Jews and Protestants, criticizes the corrupt practices of some Catholic clergymen, and pays tribute to Joseph for instituting church reforms.[122] In an article appearing in the *Journal für Freymaurer*, he explains that moral teachings of the Craft induced Masons to oppose religious intolerance and to work for the reform of educational institutions in the Habsburg Empire.

> Masonry is an institution dedicated to teaching its members the tenets of a universal moral system and to improving society. Throughout Europe, Masonic lodges have been recognized for their efforts to reform the state. . . . Masonry is an international order of virtuous men dedicated to the principles of the Enlightenment, to the improvement of education, and to the promotion of benevolent projects. Masonry aspires to shape the character of men and to enlighten humanity. . . . Reason, virtue, and compassion will enable our fraternity to accomplish its aims.[123]

As a result of his vitriolic attacks against the Catholic Church, Reinhold in 1784 was forced to leave Vienna. Disguised as a woman and with financial support from members of the *Wiener Freunde*, he left the imperial capital, first going to Leipzig and then to Weimar.

Reinhold was well received in Weimar, was housed by Wieland, and in 1785 married one of his daughters. After his marriage, Reinhold received an appointment as a professor of literature and philosophy in the University of Jena. He also continued during the middle years of the 1780s to espouse the cause of state reform and to correspond with Ratschky and with other members of the *Wiener Freunde*.[124]

Another Josephinian propagandist affiliated with the True Harmony was Josef F. Ratschky. In *Melchior Striegel*, Ratschky depicts Joseph as being the archetype of an enlightened monarch; he pays tribute to the emperor for recognizing the civil and religious liberties of Jews and Protestants in the empire and for enacting measures to improve imperial schools and courts.[125] Ratschky, too, in his poetry frequently refers to the importance of Masonry to the Josephinian Enlightenment. In "Ermunterung zur Arbeit," published in 1783, he comments upon the Masonic symbols of the level and square, perceives Masonry as being a community of enlighteners, and implores members of the Craft to continue to work for the amelioration of Habsburg institutions.

> Brothers, uplift your spirits and perform your work. Sing with joy and work with the zeal of a Mason. . . .
>
> Work conscientiously through the day to build your spiritual temple and strive with your brothers to promote harmony within the state. . . . Work to elevate your status in life and to eliminate civil strife. . . .[126]

Proponents of reform from the True Harmony Lodge were significant contributors to the Enlightenment in Vienna. These writers served as a moderate faction in the Josephinian Party and utilized the True Harmony Lodge as a propagandistic institution to disseminate their views of reform. What the writers of the True Harmony Lodge shared in common was their admiration for the Enlightenment and Masonic doctrine of religious toleration. They also seemed to be enlightened Masons, explaining and substantiating their ideas of reform in light of Masonic concepts and symbols.

4. Members of the True Harmony and A Masonic Philosophy of the Enlightenment

There was another important dimension to the literary operations of the True Harmony. Numerous writers connected with the lodge published in the *Journal für Freymaurer* articles and poems about topics relating to Masonry. These writers, who were associated with the literary circles of Blumauer and Born, described Masonic teachings and symbols and especially illustrated the importance of ancient ideologies to Masonic thought. They also attempted to demonstrate that salient ancient and modern concepts of Masonry were intimately related to major tenets of the Enlightenment and constituted the basis of civil morality.

Ignatz von Born wrote several lengthy articles concerning the ancient mystery cults in the *Journal für Freymaurer.* Like Court de Gébelin, he believed that these cults offered a synthesis of major ancient ideologies and that the teachings of these ancient cults were important to Speculative Freemasonry and to the Enlightenment. Born emphasized that the ancient mysteries contained explanations concerning the Attributes of the Supreme Creator and concerning the operations of objects in the heavens and in Nature. To Born, these mysteries also stressed the importance of the arts and sciences and contained the teachings of a universal ethical system. He believed that in attempting to revive the ideas of the ancients, Masons and enlighteners should study the teachings of the mysteries.[127]

Born wrote about the Osiris Cult and well described the ritualistic behavior of its members. He maintained that this cult was the first in history to reveal the teachings of the ancient mysteries. To be received into the Shrine of Osiris, a candidate, Born explained, was required to have made noted contributions to the culture of ancient Egypt. Born proceeded to describe the ceremonies of the Osiris Cult. The candidate was blindfolded, led into the inner chamber of the shrine, and then took an oath of allegiance to Osiris. He was informed that this god possessed the mysterious powers of the Sun and was depicted as a symbol of omnipotence and perfection. The candidate was told that Isis was the earth goddess and possessed powers relating to the raising of crops. Priests of the cult then explained to the candidate that Hermes was capable of transforming common metals into rare ones and that an understanding of mathematical principles would enable the initiate to discover the secrets of Nature. During the final ceremonies of the initiation, priests described to the candidate the attributes of man. They explained that man was endowed with reasoning powers, was capable of understanding the operations of Nature, was benevolent and virtuous, and possessed an immortal soul.[128] Born believed that by utilizing ritualism to explain the powers of Deity, Nature, and man, priests of the Osiris Cult significantly contributed to ancient thought.

As Born explained, the teachings of the ancient mysteries were passed from the Egyptians to the Jews and in some respects were modified. He maintained that Jewish priests conferring the ancient mysteries perceived Yahweh as an Omnipotent, Omniscient, and Benevolent God. Born emphasized that the Temple of Solomon was built as a symbol of the covenant established between Yahweh and the Jews and represented architectural and spiritual perfection.

The temple, too, was related to Jewish views concerning the powers of Nature. Born maintained that in staging the rites of the ancient mysteries, Jewish priests referred to symbols in the temple to illustrate the qualities of the sun, moon, planets, and stars. Jewish priests also taught that as the principles of mathematics and architecture had been applied to build the Temple of Solomon, man should use mathematics and reason to determine the laws of Nature.

> Ceremonies in the Temple of Solomon center on themes of the ancient mysteries. Allegories are presented concerning the movements of the stars, planets, and moon. Rituals concerning the powers of water are performed and are related to the legend of Noah and the Great Flood. . . .[129]

As Born showed, tools used for the building of the temple symbolized the moral conduct of ancient Jewish Masons. The gavel was used for the fitting of stones and represented the education needed by a builder of the temple to pursue his work. Used in the dressing of a stone, the chisel referred to the advanced training received by a Mason. The square was essential for measuring purposes and alluded to the honesty of Masons, while the level was required for the drawing of lines and illustrated the doctrine of equality among Masons. Used for the accurate construction of buildings, the plumb represented the humane actions of members of the Craft.[130]

Born stressed the role of the Pythagorean Brotherhood in disseminating the tenets of the ancient mysteries in Greece. The members of this brotherhood worshipped the Supreme Creator. They also believed that the principles of geometry could be applied to determine the operations of Nature and the heavens and to understand the grand design of the Supreme Architect. The Pythagoreans even attempted to apply mathematical principles to the study of morality. They used mathematical principles and symbols to explain the moral tenets of charity, prudence, temperance, and virtue.

Pythagoras established his own school of philosophy and emphasized the study of mathematics. He postulated a famous theorem to explain the attributes of a triangle and to reveal the precision of geometry. . . . He thought that the principles of geometry could be used to study Nature and morality. . . . Symbols of geometry could serve as symbols of beauty, benevolence, and virtue. . . .[131]

Born maintained that during the reign of Darius, mystery cults in the Persian Empire conferred rites to explain the teachings of Pythagoras and that priests of these cults made contributions to science; these priests studied geometry, made observations of the planets and stars, and wrote about the properties of objects in Nature. To Born, the mystery cults in Persia functioned as a valuable institution. They helped to diffuse in the empire the concepts of a cultural and moral system which had been prevalent in three ancient civilizations in the west.[132]

Minor writers of the True Harmony published articles in the *Journal für Freymaurer* about the practices and teachings of Masonry. Count Schittelsberg wrote about the importance of Masonic ceremonies. This obscure Viennese aristocrat maintained that ceremonies were performed in Masonry to explain the attributes of a Universal God and to illustrate major teachings concerning morality and Nature. Schittelsberg explained that lodge ceremonies centered on the signs, passwords, and oaths of Masonic degrees and were intended to bind the candidate to the Masonic community.[133] He also maintained that Masonic ceremonies revealed a pertinent educational function of the order. Through ceremonies, the candidate learned about the tenets of brotherly love, benevolence, prudence, and virtue. The candidate, too, was encouraged to promote the arts and sciences and to engage in projects for the advancement of the state.

Masonry teaches its candidates universal moral tenets. Our institution encourages members to respect the powers of the Supreme Creator and to seek the knowledge of the arts and sciences. . . . Masonry is not a religion, but wishes to instill its members with ethical tenets recognized by major religions of the world. The moral teachings of the order should serve as the guiding light in their lives. . . . By taking their vows at the altar of the Temple of Solomon, Masons will be exposed to the teachings of God and to the ethical tenets recognized by mankind. . . .[134]

The minor Viennese writer Andreas Stütz explained the Masonic concept of traveling or circumambulation in terms of ritualistic behavior. The journeys of the candidate around the lodge illustrated the importance of the four points or directions of Masonry. According to Stütz, the east represented wisdom, the west strength, the north darkness, and the south beauty.[135] To Stütz, traveling also helped to explain concepts of science. In traveling to the east, the candidate attempted to discover enlightenment and more precisely endeavored to find those laws governing Nature. The activities of the lodge Master were representative of the powers of the Sun. As the Sun is the fixed center of the planetary system and emits light rays to permit the orderly operations of Nature, the Master is the nucleus of Masonry and is empowered to confer rites regarding natural laws. Through his travels in the lodge, the candidate learned from the Master about the movements of celestial objects and about the cycles of Nature.[136]

Several members of the True Harmony wrote about the Masonic concept of charity. The minor writer and scientist Joseph von Retzer explained that by engaging in charitable activities to assist members of the Craft and those not affiliated with it, Masons were fulfilling a significant function of the order, were exemplifying virtuous conduct, and were working for the welfare of the state.[137] Blumauer, too, regarded charity as one of the major objectives of Masonry; he lauded Prague Masons for exhibiting the spirit of philanthropy and implored Viennese Masons to engage in charitable enterprises. Blumauer claimed that under the capable direction of Count Kinigl, the Prague Masonic Orphanage successfully functioned. This institution succeeded in educating orphans, in providing funds for their medical care, and in assisting them in securing jobs.[138]

Retzer and Blumauer published articles concerning the relationship of Masonry to the Enlightenment. Retzer believed that Viennese Masons acted in light of the Masonic concept of harmony to advance the arts and sciences and to promote the cause of state reform.

Harmony should characterize the operations of Masonic lodges. Harmony was emphasized by the priests of the Osiris Cult and by those of the Temple of Solomon. Harmony applies to activities governing Masons in and outside of the lodge, to the efforts of brothers to provide assistance to the distressed, and to the attempts of Masons throughout the world to work for the improvement of humanity. . . . Harmony applies to the operations of the state and induces citizens to obey moral and secular laws. . . .[139]

Blumauer perceived Masonry as being a cosmopolitan institution devoted to the diffusion of Enlightenment tenets throughout the world. He maintained that as a result of its international character, Masonry served as a valuable vehicle for the promotion of Enlightenment activities. Blumauer thought that the Enlightenment and Masonry shared common objectives: Masons and enlighteners acknowledged deistic ideas, subscribed to the moral and philosophical teachings of the ancients, advocated secular reforms, worked to promote the arts and sciences, and most importantly probed Nature to seek her laws. Blumauer speculated that the mission of enlighteners and Masons would culminate in the achievement of material progress.

Masonry is a cosmopolitan institution. Her members investigate Nature and strive to contribute to the sciences. . . . Masons are taught the tenets of an ancient and a universal morality and are benevolent, honest, and just in their pursuits. . . . Masonry is an institution devoted to ending religious fanaticism, to reforming the state, and to achieving material progress. . . .[140]

Writers of the True Harmony Lodge in several respects contributed to Masonry and to the Enlightenment in Vienna. These writers were the first to publish works about the teachings of the Craft and succeeded in developing a Masonic philosophy of the Enlightenment. In light of Masonic concepts and symbols, they explained the deistic Attributes of the Supreme Architect, the mechanistic operations of Nature, and the intellectual and moral qualities of man. Another distinctive achievement of writers of the True Harmony concerned their accounts about Masonic humanism and civil morality. What these writers succeeded in showing was that the concepts of benevolence, social justice, and virtue were postulated by ancient philosophers and by Enlightenment theorists and constituted the core of Masonic civil and moral thought.

5. Masonic Musicians and the True Harmony Lodge

Like lodge members involved with literature and with moral philosophy, those engaged in music occupied an important place in the True Harmony. Musicians of the True Harmony perceived the lodge as a center of Viennese music and actively engaged in its cultural and organizational operations. Musicians of the lodge composed works about various facets of Masonry and published them in the *Journal für Freymaurer*. Some musicians of the True Harmony also played in the orchestra of the lodge and gave performances during its special sessions.

The orchestra of the True Harmony consisted of numerous minor musicians. When the lodge held sessions to confer degrees and staged banquets, Paul Wranitzsky directed the lodge orchestra. Wranitzsky also composed special hymns and songs for these occasions and re-cruited musicians to the lodge. Valentin Adamberger sang during banquets staged by the True Harmony. After his admittance to the lodge, Johann Holzer composed approximately a dozen songs about Masonry for the *Journal für Freymaurer* and attempted to illustrate the ethical importance of such symbols as the Sun, square, level, and plumb. His friend Joseph von Holzmeister played the violin in the or-chestra of the lodge and wrote a song to commemorate the initiation of Haydn into the True Harmony.[141]

As a result of his desire to associate with "men of high culture," Joseph Haydn became a member of the True Harmony Lodge.[142] He was admitted to the lodge on February 11, 1785, but after his induction, exhibited minimal interest in Masonry. Haydn composed no music for the lodge and in 1786 resigned from it.[143]

Unlike his friend Haydn, Mozart developed astute interest in Vi-ennese Masonry. He was inducted into the Charity Lodge on January 7, 1785. Although a Catholic, Mozart believed that the teachings of Masonry were compatible with those of the Church and that both institutions helped their members to achieve moral purification, pro-vided them with an understanding of Deity, and worked for the ame-lioration of society.[144] Mozart in April 1785 witnessed the initiation of his father Leopold into the Charity Lodge, became friendly with Born, and that same year paid frequent visits to the True Harmony Lodge.[145] Mozart in 1785 also composed several Masonic works.

The Masonic music of Mozart reflected important themes and symbols of the order. In K. 483, a poem set to music, Mozart praises Joseph for legalizing the operations of Masonry in the empire and explains that "Joseph's benevolence has crowned anew Masonic hope."[146] The symbols and moving rites involved with the closing of a lodge inspired Mozart in 1785 to compose K. 484. In this hymn, Mozart alludes to the symbolism pertaining to the mysterious number three and implores Masons "to follow the path of virtue, to strive for the perfection of the Great Temple, and to move towards the Throne of Wisdom."[147] *Masonic Funeral Music* or K. 477 was considered as one of the most important Masonic compositions by Mozart. Written in 1785, this work was played that year during the Lodge of Mourning held for Count Esterházy and the Duke of Mecklenberg. In this composition, Mozart masterfully conveyed themes and symbols involved with life and death, placing emphasis on the threatening notes of the winds to depict the fear that Masons had for God. He juxtaposed winds and strings to demonstrate the struggle between the forces of life and death and made frequent usage of the string quartet to convey the moods of man prior to death.[148] Mozart also wished to write an opera to explicate major doctrines of Masonry. As a result of his familiarity with the opera *Osiris* by the Mason John Naumann and with the articles of Born about the ancient mysteries, Mozart in approximately 1786 began to compose the lyrics to *The Magic Flute*.[149]

The Magic Flute alludes to mysteries concerning life and death, stresses the Enlightenment theme concerning the beauties and powers of Nature, and accentuates the Masonic tenets of virtue and wisdom. Entrusted in Act One with a magic flute, a symbol of wisdom, the adventurous Prince Tamino enters the Temple of Nature, Reason, and Wisdom and meets Sarastro. Sarastro proves his allegiance to the prince, punishing an evil Moor who held the beautiful maiden Pamina in captivity.[150] As the first act draws to a conclusion, Tamino and Pamina, in the presence of the virtuous Sarastro, are married and then are required to encounter further hardships to demonstrate their allegiance to each other.

In Act Two, Mozart subjects Pamina and Tamino to numerous trials to reveal their character traits. As a symbol of virility, Tamino enters the Cabinet of Reflection in the temple and, like a Masonic candidate, is divested of metallic substances prior to receiving his initiatory rites symbolic of the trials of life and Nature.[151] After Tamino receives these rites and is provided with insight into the operations of Nature, Pamina intervenes to protect Sarastro from being stabbed by the Moor. In the final scenes of the opera, Pamina is reunited with Tamino in the caverns of the temple. By successfully confronting the trials of air, earth, fire, and water, Pamina and Tamino strengthen their marriage and demonstrate their abilities to resolve problems encountered in life and in Nature. Significance was attached to this Masonic opera, since Mozart, as numerous critics have claimed, portrayed Tamino as a symbol of the wise and virtuous Joseph II and endowed Sarastro with the qualities of the enlightener Ignatz von Born.[152]

Several patterns consequently characterized the musical operations of the True Harmony. Like their counterparts in the Lodge of the Nine Sisters, musicians in the True Harmony Lodge participated in the lodge orchestra and contributed to the ritualistic operations of the lodge. Music, however, played a more important role in the True Harmony Lodge than in the Lodge of the Nine Sisters, and the musicians in this Viennese lodge seemed to behave as enlightened Masons. Through their songs, poems, and concerts, musical composers involved with the True Harmony Lodge explained Enlightenment concepts, vividly described Masonic doctrines and symbols, and thus significantly contributed to the cultural life of Josephinian Vienna.

E. Revolutionary Threats and the Closing of the True Harmony Lodge

The fortunes of Masonry in Vienna radically changed after 1785. Joseph by that year instituted most of his major reforms, began to heed the advice of conservative and anti-Masonic ministers, and upon their suggestion, established a secret police force to suppress political opponents of the empire and to investigate the operations of Masonry and other secret societies.[153] The emperor, too, wished to improve relations with the Catholic Church and seemed to be quite concerned about the anticlerical views of Viennese Masons.[154] What also led to the demise of Masonry was the prolific circulation of anti-Masonic literature in the Habsburg capital. Leopold Hoffmann, who was a former member of the Charity Lodge, emerged as the chief spokesman of anti-Masonry, in Vienna. In his articles published in the *Wiener Zeitschrift*, Hoffmann criticized Viennese Masons for attacking the Catholic Church and perceived them as constituting a threat to the monarchy. Hoffman claimed, moreover, that the Illuminati Order was even more dangerous than Masonry and through its international network of lodges was preparing to destroy conservative institutions in Europe.[155]

The perceptions of Hoffmann about the Illuminati, to a great extent, were quite correct. Established in Bavaria in 1776 by Adam Weishaupt, a former Jesuit and a professor of law from the University of Ingolstadt, the Illuminati was pledged to engage in unremitting warfare against royal absolutism, feudal exploitation, and organized religion.[156] After the destruction of these depravic forces, members of the Illuminati wished to establish democratic states throughout Europe. The structure and ritual of the Illuminati resembled in some respects those of Freemasonry. The Illuminati operated in secrecy and conferred the Blue and Strict Observance Degrees. Unlike those of Masonry, lodges of the Illuminati conferred the Degrees of the Mysterious Class and encouraged its members to engage in revolutionary activities against European monarchs.[157] An Illuminati lodge by 1785 operated in Vienna. Although this body recruited very few Masons to its ranks, its subversive operations greatly disturbed Joseph II.[158]

The emperor in late 1785 took action against secret societies in the empire and evidently believed that the aims and operations of Masonry were the same as those of the Illuminati.

> The so-called Freemason societies are increasing and spreading even to the small towns; left alone, without supervision, they might become dangerous in their excess to religion, order, and morals. . . .[159]

On December 1, 1785, Joseph instituted the *Freimaurerpatent;* this edict stipulated that only one lodge was to function in the capital city of each province and that all other lodges were to be dissolved. This patent further provided that each lodge was required every three months to submit its roster to the secret police and that the secret police could inspect the activities of lodges in the empire.[160]

Some members of the True Harmony were disappointed about the attacks of the anti-Masons and about the restrictive imperial decree. In "Ueber Maurerintoleranz," published in 1785 in the *Journal für Freymaurer*, Alxinger claims that anti-Masonic advisers would succeed in convincing the emperor to curb the operations of Habsburg Masonry. He maintains that Viennese Masons should continue to support the ideals and activities of the Craft and should respond to their critics.

> Despite opposition to our cause, my brothers, we must try to preserve the lights of Masonry. As the Sun rises in the east and sets in the west, the spirit of Masonry must endure. . . . Our art must be practiced, our principles must be taught, and our energies must be directed to the improvement of civil society. . . .[161]

In a letter sent to Reinhold in August 1786, Gottlieb Leon claimed that Joseph envisioned the operations of Masonry and the Illuminati as being similar and thus decreed the 1785 Masonic Patent. Leon explained to his friend that the radical intentions of the Illuminati had led to the destruction of the world of the secret societies in the Habsburg Empire and predicted that the emperor would never restore the privileged status of Masonry.[162]

The 1785 Masonic Patent produced significant effects upon the Craft in Prague and in Vienna. As a result of the pressure from the imperial police, Strict Observance administrators in Prague dissolved in 1787 the Lodge of the Three Crowned Stars.[163] After the closing of this lodge, former Prague Masons neither affiliated with the Illuminati nor became involved in revolutionary activities. As a result of the promulgation of the Masonic Patent, the cultural operations of the True Harmony Lodge in 1786 came to an abrupt end. The Lodge of Truth was established in 1786, functioned as the only Masonic body in the imperial capital, and attracted a few former members of the True Harmony to its ranks. The Lodge of Truth for approximately two years performed routine ritualistic functions. In recognizing that members of the secret police were carefully observing the activities of this lodge and that meetings of this body were poorly attended, Prince Dietrichstein in 1788 decided to close its doors.[164] Although a small group of Jacobins emerged in Vienna in 1794 and was easily suppressed by imperial authorities, no former Masonic enlighteners of the True Harmony Lodge were involved with these obscure revolutionaries.[165]

Prior to the dissolution of the special relationship between Masonry and the Habsburg Monarchy, the True Harmony Lodge functioned as an important cultural institution in Josephinian Vienna. The True Harmony Lodge especially distinguished itself in its role as a learned society, and the cultural operations of this body seemed to be more wide ranging than those of the Lodge of the Nine Sisters. As suggested by the varying works appearing in its journals, the True Harmony Lodge especially evolved into a center of reform and music, served as a hub of geological research, and fostered the study of ancient and modern ideologies relating to the Enlightenment and to Masonry. There, too, were important implications of holding membership in the True Harmony. Members of this lodge seemed to be quite cognizant of their roles as enlighteners and as Masons. They felt committed to the cause of imperial reform and attempted to describe and to classify the materialistic properties of objects in Nature. As enlightened Masons, members of the True Harmony succeeded in their mission of showing how the teachings and symbols of Masonry were related to salient concepts of the Enlightenment.

Like Masons in London and in Paris, those in Prague and in Vienna performed significant cultural functions to advance the Enlightenment. The environment of Masonry and the ideologies motivating Masons differed, however, in each of these four cities. In the conclusion, varying topics concerning Masonry in and Masons from these urban centers will be examined.

V. CONCLUSION: AN EVALUATION OF EIGHTEENTH CENTURY SPECULATIVE FREEMASONRY IN LONDON, PARIS, PRAGUE, AND VIENNA

A. Introduction

As shown in this study, Masonry operated as a multi-faceted institution in varying urban environments. This chapter, then, will attempt to provide a perspective of eighteenth century Masonry in London, Paris, Prague, and Vienna and to demonstrate the connections between Masonry and the Enlightenment in these cities. What will be investigated in this chapter are the organization and rites of Masonry, the social composition of the Craft, the impact of Enlightenment ideologies upon Masonic intellectuals, and the participation of Masons in eighteenth century cultural institutions.

B. The Organization of Speculative Freemasonry

The organizational functions of grand lodges in London, Paris, Prague, and Vienna, for the most part, resembled each other and were of importance to the Enlightenment in several respects. The operations of grand lodges in these cities, generally speaking, conformed to regulations specified in the *Constitutions* of Anderson and revolved around Enlightenment concepts.[1] The executive, parliamentary, and judicial operations of these bodies reflected significant Whiggish doctrines and especially provided grand lodge administrators in Paris, Prague, and Vienna with political training. There was another important facet of grand lodge leadership; grand lodge administrators were aristocratic or bourgeois enlighteners. Titled nobles holding positions in the Grand Lodge of London approximately amounted to 70 percent of its leadership corps, while members of enlightened aristocratic elites exclusively directed the operations of grand lodges in Paris, Prague, and Vienna. This predominance of aristocratic leadership significantly contributed to the evolution of Masonry as an Enlightenment institution in these cities and marked a major pattern of French and Habsburg grand lodges.

French and Habsburg grand lodge officials experienced some opposition from political authorities and from the papacy. The attitudes of Bourbon and Habsburg officials towards Masonry, in some instances, were quite similar; they were suspicious of the secret operations of grand lodges in Paris, Prague, and Vienna and viewed some leaders of these bodies as being conspirators. Despite the investigations of royal administrators of the operations of Masonry, grand lodge leaders in these three cities succeeded in exonerating themselves and other Masons of seditious allegations. Until the late 1780s, grand lodge authorities in these cities exercised considerable influence in government circles and successfully resisted anti-Masonic attacks.[2] When papal bulls were promulgated against the Craft and were not stringently enforced, grand lodge officials in Paris, Prague, and Vienna were also able to resist assaults from the Church. What emerged was a distinctive pattern concerning religious and political anti-Masonry. Anti-Masonry between approximately 1755 and 1787 did not constitute a serious threat to grand lodge authorities in Paris and in the Habsburg Empire and, instead, proved to be a rather weak force. Even in London during the first half of the eighteenth century, few anti-Masonic attacks were directed against officials of the Modern Grand Lodge and indicated that the crown and varying Protestant denominations were sympathetic towards the aims and operations of the Craft.

The status of the Modern Grand Lodge of London was not seriously challenged until after 1750. With the exception of the Rosicrucians, few other fraternal organizations functioned in London prior to 1750, and the Modern Grand Lodge thus dominated the world of secret societies in the British capital. As a consequence of its predominant position, the Modern Grand Lodge received capable leadership and support from enlighteners in London and, through its centralized network of local lodges in this city and elsewhere, supervised the cultural and social operations of the Craft. As has been seen, the Antient Grand Lodge ended the virtual monopoly of the Modern Grand Lodge. By establishing their base of operations in London and by conferring the Royal Arch Mason Degree, the Antients, to a certain extent, successfully competed against the Moderns in the British capital. Antient Masonry primarily developed, however, into a lower middle class town movement and produced its greatest impact upon towns in Scotland, Ireland, and America. As opposed to those of the Moderns, the leadership, membership, and lodge operations of the Antients did little, moreover, to advance the cause of the Enlightenment in London.[3]

Rivaling Masonic bodies were much more common in the three European cities examined in this study than in London. The proliferation of Masonic degrees, differing views of Masonic ideologies, and frequent disputes among members of Masonic elites served as the fundamental causes of grand lodge rivalries and in some cases posed a threat to the functioning of Masonic communities in Paris, Prague, and Vienna. Ritualistic problems in Paris revolved around the acceptance of the Scottish Degrees, while those in Prague and in Vienna centered on interpretations of the Templar Degrees, appearing first in the Strict Observance System and then in the Zinnendorf Rite. The resolution of these disputes was significant for the survival of the Craft in France and in the Habsburg Empire. Masonic grand lodge authorities in Paris, Prague, and Vienna succeeded in terminating ritualistic feuds, in integrating rivaling aristocratic elites into Masonry, and in establishing new and viable grand lodge bodies.[4] Very few secret societies functioned, moreover, in Paris, in Prague, and in Vienna. With the exception of the operations of the Illuminati in Vienna, other secret societies did not pose a serious challenge to Masonic grand lodges in these three cities. This fact suggests that the success of the social and cultural activities conducted in lodges of the Craft enabled Masonry to dominate the world of the secret societies in each of these European cities.

The organizational functions of local lodges in the cities examined in this study for the most part were quite similar. Moreover, the functions of local lodges in Paris, Prague, and Vienna closely resembled those of Modern lodges in London. The constitutional and administrative operations of lodges in the three European cities especially seemed to parallel those of lodges in the British capital. Parisian, Prague, and Viennese lodges, like their London counterparts, elected their members and officers and thus functioned as voluntary associations. The duties of lodge executives, the parliamentary operations of lodges, the functioning of special committees, and the recognition of the natural liberties of lodge members reflected salient principles of Whiggism and major doctrines of other Enlightenment legal and political ideologies. Consequently, lodges especially in Paris, Prague, and Vienna taught their leaders administrative skills and provided their members with new political experiences. A few lodges even directly engaged in political operations, supporting in Paris the cause of the American Revolution and in Vienna that of state reform.

Local lodges, too, served other purposes. These bodies functioned as philanthropical agencies, providing financial assistance to lodge members and their families. The Enlightenment concept of philanthropy was especially important to lodges in Habsburg cities. Lodges in the imperial capital donated funds to the University of Vienna Medical School, and those in Prague contributed financial assistance to hospitals, schools, and orphanages. Lodges, more importantly, operated as centers of social and cultural activities; lodges in London played a central part in its tavern, coffeehouse, and club life, while those in Paris, Prague, and Vienna functioned in some respects as salons. In both Habsburg urban centers, which had few social and cultural agencies, lodges especially tended to be centers of activism. Like those in London and Paris, lodges in Prague and Vienna sponsored banquets and special lectures, but unlike their West European counterparts, these Habsburg lodges staged musical performances. Another significant cultural function of lodges in each of the cities examined concerned their role as ritualistic centers. Lodges psychologically provided their members with the secrecy and privacy in which the drama of ritualism could be staged. These bodies consequently bound their members to an exclusive community and were involved with the process of acculturating them to the norms of Masonry and the Enlightenment.

C. The Cultural Functions of Masonic Rites

Ritualism, in many respects, served as the core of Speculative Freemasonry. Desaguliers and other founding fathers of the Modern London Grand Lodge invented the Blue Degree System to achieve several purposes. These leaders developed a distinctive Masonic language to explain the tenets of a moral system prevalent in the ancient and modern worlds. The founding fathers of the Craft also used the teachings of ancient Masonry and the symbols of architecture and mathematics to explain in simplified terms pertinent political, philosophical, and scientific concepts circulating in early Hanoverian London. Unlike the rites of other secret societies either in London or in other European cities, the degrees of Modern Masonry offered a ritualistic synthesis of significant Enlightenment ideologies.[5] The Blue Degrees, then, served in London as an effective socializing agency of Augustan culture and affected the attitudes of British Masons towards society. As has been seen, the British Masonic civil religion revolved around the beliefs that members of the Craft should obey the ancient ethical teachings of the Supreme Architect, should work to protect English natural liberties, should support Parliamentary government, and should attempt to improve British society through the application of mechanistic concepts to technology and to other realms.

The ritualism of Masonry, too, assisted in the diffusion of major eighteenth century cultural concepts in Paris, Prague, and Vienna. In these European cities, the Blue Degrees served as a source of Anglophile and Enlightenment ideas. The teachings and symbols of these degrees provided Masons in these cities with explanations regarding concepts of classicism, deism, mechanism, constitutional government, and civil liberties. As has been seen, the evolution of other Masonic ritualistic systems suggested that members of the order in the European cities studied developed new Masonic interpretations of Enlightenment ideas. Like the Scottish Rite in Paris, the Strict Observance System in Prague illustrated the importance of education and ancient ideologies, and the Zinnendorf Rite in Vienna especially demonstrated the significance of natural liberties. These Masonic systems, too, emphasized fundamental principles of civil liberties and state reform and consequently affected the ethical behavior of members of the Craft. French and Habsburg Masons perceived the Supreme Architect as being the Moral Governor of Humanity and as being the Source of Secular Salvation. Masons in Paris consequently worked to improve educational and legal institutions, and those in Prague, who were especially motivated by the concept of philanthropy, funded hospitals, orphanages, and schools. Symbols and ethical teachings of the Zinnendorf Rite especially made Masons in Vienna self-conscious of their roles as reformers. These Masons acted and wrote to defend the causes of religious toleration, public education, and criminal justice.

D. The Social Composition of Masonry

The social composition of Masonry in the urban centers studied reflected an aristocratic and middle class character. In the four cities, aristocratic patronage of the Craft was especially extensive; aristocratic membership in London and Parisian lodges was about 50 percent, and that in Prague and Viennese lodges amounted to approximately 80 percent. Bourgeois affiliation with lodges in the two Habsburg cities was minimal, reflecting the fact that the Prague and Viennese middle classes were quite small in comparison to those in

London and in Paris. The social composition of Masonry, too, can be explained in light of how aristocratic and bourgeois individuals viewed the order. Masons of both classes looked upon the Craft as an important urban institution. They were given opportunities to participate in ritualistic, cultural, social, and philanthropical activities and thus perceived the Craft as being a major agency of the Enlightenment. The social composition of the order revealed that Masonry possessed cross-class appeal, functioning as an institution in which members of aristocratic and bourgeois elites could interact with each other.

Individuals of various religions held membership in Masonry in the cities examined. Masons in London, for the most part, were Protestants, either affiliating with the Anglican Church or with one of the dissenting churches. Masonry provided a neutral setting where Protestants in London could attempt to reconcile their religious differences and could support the cause of those Protestant groups whose religious and civil liberties were not recognized by the state. Several Catholics and Jews in London participated in Modern Masonry, but few Masons in the British capital spoke in defense of the rights of members of these two religious groups. Many Calvinists and Catholics and a few Jews were also involved in Masonry in Paris, Prague, and Vienna. The nonsectarian environment of the Craft in these European cities produced significant effects upon its members. Protestant, Catholic, and Jewish Masons in these cities viewed Masonry as playing a central role in facilitating social and political integration. They developed secular attitudes, calling for the extension of civil and religious liberties to Jews and Protestants and for the separation of church and state in matters of education. There were, however, a few Masons in London, Paris, Prague, and Vienna who had no religious affiliation. Yet these Masons were inspired by the universal moral principles of the Craft and viewed them as being intimately connected to major ideologies of the Enlightenment.

Varying groups from the English aristocracy participated in London Masonry. Nobles holding ranking positions in the British armed services were admitted to and envisioned Masonry as being committed to moral, patriotic, and Enlightenment principles. Noble statesmen and Parliamentary ministers were involved with Masonry; most were Whigs and visualized the political doctrines in Masonic ritualism as being compatible with those of their party. They, too, believed that Masonry could serve as a valuable agency for the promotion of their political programs and commercial enterprises. A few Tories were Masons and, like their Whig opponents, worked through coffeehouses and taverns in London to secure the support of members of the Craft for the policies of their party.[6] London Masons actively participated in party politics and thus differed from those in Paris and in Habsburg cities. Despite party affiliation, many London aristocrats generated common interest in the arts and sciences, recognized the importance of the cultural functions of Masonry, and thus behaved as Masonic enlighteners.

Nobles in Paris assumed an active part in Masonry. The order provided Catholic and Protestant nobles in the French capital with the opportunity to meet and to intermingle with each other in an urban environment where political and social gatherings were restricted. Masonry, too, induced French nobles to participate in cultural institutions in Paris and especially served for these nobles as a source of secular and ethical ideologies of the Enlightenment. The fraternity resembled a cult of honor.[7] By stressing military legends and by conferring to its members awards and titles, Scottish Rite Masonry in Paris drew support from many nobles of the sword. Political and legal doctrines explained in this rite were also compatible with those advocated by Parisian nobles of the robe and corroborated their views concerning the *Thèse Nobiliaire.*

The titled nobility also dominated the affairs of Masonry in Prague and in Vienna. In these cities, aristocrats looked to Masonry to achieve cultural integration, were both Protestants and Catholics, but came from varying ethnic groups. Most Masonic aristocrats in Prague were of Czech and German Bohemian lineage, while those in Vienna were Austrian, Hungarian, Romanian, and Italian. Many Habsburg nobles, too, either served in the armed forces or in the imperial bureaucracy. Most wished to acquire an understanding of major concepts connected with eighteenth century English and French culture and thus affiliated with Masonry to accomplish this objective. Many aristocratic enlighteners in Prague and in Vienna utilized the Craft as a cultural agency to sponsor libraries, museums, and schools and to vindicate the cause of imperial reforms. Consequently, Masonry in both cities enabled aristocrats to foster the process of assimilation and to occupy new institutional roles.

Along with the support of the aristocracy, the patronage of the middle class was important to Masonry in London and in Paris. The Craft provided middle class individuals in both cities with opportunities to acquire an understanding of Enlightenment ideologies, to engage in social and cultural activities, to promote their economic and professional interests, and to secure recognition. London and Parisian lawyers assumed leadership roles in Masonry, generating interest in the legal doctrines embodied in its rites and becoming involved in its judicial proceedings. As opposed to their counterparts in the British capital, Masonic lawyers in Paris emerged as proponents of criminal and legal reforms. Yet many merchants and industrialists in London belonged to Masonry and in light of its extensive patronage by the Whigs envisioned the order as being important for the promotion of their business interests. Many, too, expressed interest in architecture and built Palladian styled mansions in London to imitate their aristocratic friends. In attempting to make business contacts and in endorsing Masonic and Enlightenment concepts concerning natural liberties and the work ethic, London and Parisian merchants became involved in the operations of the Craft. Catholic merchants and professional men especially played an active part in Parisian Masonry. The teachings of the order provided Catholic middle class Masons with moral and religious concepts to justify their positions in the *ancien régime*.

There were also some middle class Masons in Prague and in Vienna. Although less numerous than those in the French and British capitals, middle class Masons in the Habsburg cities envisioned the principles of the order as serving as an alternative to those of Christianity. Protestant and Catholic Masonic merchants and industrialists in Prague and in Vienna gave maximum support to the Craft. They subscribed to Enlightenment moral secular ideologies and utilized the order as a means for advocating their political and economic reform proposals.

E. Masonic Intellectuals and Enlightenment Ideologies

As has been argued, Masonic intellectuals for the most part were urban enlighteners. These aristocratic and bourgeois Masons were affiliated with progressive cultural elites and were predominantly involved with the study of the natural sciences, medicine, political thought, literature, and the fine arts. Many Masonic intellectuals belonged to learned societies, participated in urban social institutions, and thus behaved as Masonic enlighteners. Some of these intellectuals were cognizant of their roles as Masons and as enlighteners. They utilized some lodges of the Craft to disseminate their concepts of Masonry and the Enlightenment. The interest of Masonic intellectuals in different ideologies suggested, however, the variations of the Enlightenment in London, Paris, Prague, and Vienna.

Newtonian mechanistic ideas, which were explained in the Blue Degrees, were of central importance to London and Parisian Masons. They gave frequent demonstrations and published works concerning the laws of motion and gravity. Some English and French Masonic mechanists were astronomers; others were physicists, devoting their attention to the study of primary and secondary qualities and to that of the concepts of attraction and repulsion.[8] A few English and French mechanists pursued electrical studies, attempting to explain the operations of electrical bodies in terms of the concepts of attraction and repulsion. Many French Masonic mechanists denounced the physical theories of the Cartesians and attempted to develop a precise scientific language to explicate Newtonian concepts. In comparison to scientists in London and in Paris, those in Prague and in Vienna, who were primarily concerned with the study of materialistic theories, displayed minimal interest in mechanistic concepts.

Mechanistic views influenced London, Parisian, Prague, and Viennese doctors. Masonic physicians in these cities were familiar with the medical procedures and teachings of the mechanist Hermann Boerhaave. They used inductive procedures to develop their taxonomies concerning diseases and believed that mechanical principles could be evolved to explain the operations of the body.[9] In light of the medical thought of this Dutch Newtonian, Dr. Cabanis and other Parisian Masonic physicians became *ideologues*, advocating in many cases positivistic medical philosophies and working for the amelioration of hospitals in the French capital. Under the influence of the Newtonian Gerard van Swieten, Masonic doctors in Prague and in Vienna played a central role in improving hospitals in these two urban centers. Moreover, Masonic physicians in the imperial capital actively worked to transform the University of Vienna Medical School into the leading medical institution in Central Europe.[10]

Some Parisian and Viennese scientists during the last half of the eighteenth century were proponents of Newtonian materialistic views. In light of their examination of notions advanced in the *Opticks*, they worked to determine and to classify the constituent ingredients of matter and to evolve a workable atomistic theory. The studies regarding heat, oxidizing agents, gases, and compounds by Parisian Masonic scientists led to the transformation of chemistry into a Newtonian science.[11] The stratigraphic findings of Viennese Masonic geologists concerning the properties and uses of minerals contributed to Newtonian materialistic studies and confirmed many chemical views. With an interest in the legends and teachings of the Craft, these geologists probed Nature to explain theories concerning the origins, evolution, and flooding of the Earth.

Influenced by Masonic and Enlightenment tenets, many intellectuals of the Craft subscribed to various doctrines of deism. To English Masons, the teachings of deism reflected significant moral concepts of the ancients and moderns and constituted the basis of a scientific religion. Many French Masonic intellectuals associated deistic doctrines with Newtonian concepts, with Anglophile ideas, with ancient moral teachings, and with state reform arguments.[12] Habsburg Masonic intellectuals, especially former Catholic clergymen, integrated concepts of deism into their proposals concerning imperial reforms and attempted to evolve a Masonic deistic philosophy in light of their studies of important ancient writers.

In addition to their interest in deism, many Masonic intellectuals in Paris and in Vienna were proponents of state reforms. Masonic spokesmen of reform in Paris were lawyers and minor *philosophes* and were affiliated with various cultural elites in the French capital. They occasionally used Parisian lodges to espouse their ideas about reforms. Parisian Masonic advocates of reform sometimes were critical of the policies of the Bourbon Monarchy, in many cases found their works censored, and in some instances were constrained to leave France. In contrast to those in Paris, Masonic proponents of reform in Vienna adamantly wrote to support the reform program of Joseph II. Generally speaking, they occupied positions in the Josephinian bureaucracy and were quite conscious of their roles as reformers. These Viennese Masons, in many cases, behaved as enlightened Masons, frequently utilizing lodges in the imperial capital to popularize their views concerning reforms.[13]

Many Parisian and Viennese Masonic intellectuals favored the implementation of educational and legal reforms. These advocates of reform wrote to vindicate the principle of the separation of church and state as applied to education. They applauded their monarchs for reducing the influence of Catholic clergymen in schools and in universities. Educational reforms enacted in France were minimal in comparison to those enacted in the Habsburg Empire. However, Masons in Paris established and operated special *lycées* and *musées*,

while those in Vienna gave donations to newly created state schools
and to the university in the imperial capital. Parisian and Viennese
Masonic writers advocated similar criminal and legal reforms. Yet,
the Masonic campaign concerning these reforms was more successful in the Habsburg Empire than in France. Educational and legal
problems resembling those in France and in the Habsburg Empire did
not arise in England and consequently were of minimal importance
to Masonic writers in London.

Masonic intellectuals in London gave limited support to the cause
of religious toleration in England. The reason for this lack of support
was that London Masons were predominantly Whigs and, generally
speaking, were satisfied with the religious and political statuses of
most Protestant sects. However, a few Masonic ministers, writers, and
parliamentary representatives defended the cause of Protestant dissenting groups. Yet, no Masonic intellectuals in London campaigned
for the termination of disabilities imposed upon Catholics and Jews
in England.

Masonic intellectuals in Paris and in Vienna conversely took firm
positions in defending the cause of religious reforms. Many minor
Masonic *philosophes* in Paris pamphleteered in support of religious
reforms for the Huguenots and exercised some influence upon Louis
XVI to promulgate the 1787 Edict of Toleration. Viennese Masonic
writers, many of whom had been former Catholic clergymen, were
anticlerical and proponents of religious reforms. The many works of
these writers defended Joseph for his clerical and monastic reforms,
praised him for his recognition of Jews and Protestants, and marked
a significant variation of the Enlightenment in the Habsburg Empire.

Many Masonic intellectuals, too, were involved with the promotion of the Neoclassical Movement. These Masonic enlighteners were
trained in the classics and realized that the rites of the Craft provided
interpretations of important concepts advanced by the ancients. They
favored the formulation of precise literary and artistic standards and
insisted upon an accurate depiction of Nature and of the role of man
in it.

In the cities examined in this study, Masonic writers demonstrated great interest in ancient ideologies and contributed to the
development of the cult of antiquity. Masonic writers in London envisioned themselves as being Augustans and believed that their status
was similar to that of writers in ancient Rome. Some Masonic writers
in the British capital published translations of ancient poems; oth-

ers in their works referred to concepts espoused by the ancients to justify their modern views of deism and Whiggism. Many London Masonic writers cultivated interest in modern science but alluded to the importance of ancient scientific theories in their works about the discoveries of Newton.[14] However, London Masonic writers, who devoted extensive attention to major topics regarding literature and science, and who for the most part did not hold positions of leadership in the Craft, felt little need to publish works about ancient teachings in Masonic ritualism and thus significantly differed from their Habsburg counterparts.

French and Habsburg Masonic writers also contributed to Neoclassical Literature. Many of these writers in Paris, Prague, and Vienna imitated English authors, issuing translations of ancient literary masterpieces and subscribing to deistic tenets in light of their studies of ancient philosophies. Masonic Neoclassical writers in Paris played, however, a more significant role in disseminating scientific concepts than those in the Habsburg cities. By staging ancient comedies and tragedies, some Parisian and Viennese Masonic playwrights contributed to the Neoclassical Movement and through their characters revealed the importance of state reforms to the ancients and the moderns.[15] Furthermore, many Neoclassical writers in these two cities were proponents of state reforms and utilized literary devices and pertinent teachings of the ancients to substantiate their views. As a consequence of the publication of the *Journal für Freymaurer*, Masonic spokesmen of Neoclassicism in Vienna differed from those in Paris and were given the opportunity to explain how Masonic and ancient teachings were compatible with reform doctrines espoused by Joseph II.

Masonic enlighteners involved with the fine arts also emphasized themes of the ancients. Paintings of Nature and portraits, busts, and statues of significant ancient and modern men appeared in London, Paris, Prague, and Vienna; these works suggested that Masonic painters and sculptors shared similar artistic views. Moreover, there were more Masonic artists and sculptors from Paris than either from London or from the Habsburg cities. This fact confirmed the belief that Paris during the late eighteenth century developed into a major center of the Neoclassical Movement in the arts. However, Masons in London did more to promote ancient principles of architecture than those either in Paris or in the Habsburg cities. Emphasized in the Blue Degrees, the principles of the ancient Roman architect Vitruvius were reflected in mansions and temples built in early Hanoverian London. What appeared to be unusual was that Palladianism, unlike Masonry, met with ephemeral success in Paris, Prague, and Vienna.

Music during the eighteenth century embodied important themes of antiquity and was promoted and patronized by many Masonic enlighteners. The ancient myths and stories conveyed through opera and the classical themes appearing in the sonata-symphony enabled music to perform valuable cultural functions.[16] In London and in Paris, some Masons were musicians, orchestra directors, and minor composers; a few Masonic orchestras were established in these cities and were sponsored either by lodges or by aristocratic patrons. English and French Masons composed, however, few musical pieces concerning the principles and symbols of the Craft. The status of the Masonic musician in Vienna differed from that of Masonic musicians in London and in Paris. By receiving extensive financial support from lodges and from aristocrats affiliated with the Craft, Masonic musicians, composers, and orchestras played a prominent role in the imperial capital during the Josephinian Enlightenment. Numerous operas, symphonies, and songs either were written about Masonry or referred to its ritualism. Mozart and other Masonic composers in Vienna utilized music as an effective device to reveal the doctrines and symbols of Masonry and to demonstrate that the ancient teachings of the Craft were intimately related to cardinal tenets of the Enlightenment. Prior to and during the French Revolution, a few former Masons affiliated with the Illuminati in Vienna and with radical secret societies in Paris and relied upon music as a vehicle for explicating revolutionary symbols and for inspiring members of these organizations to engage in seditious activities.[17]

F. Involvement of Masons in Eighteenth Century Cultural Institutions

However, most Masons did not affiliate with subversive secret societies but rather gravitated to cultural institutions involved with the promotion of Enlightenment ideologies. Some Masons occupied administrative positions and actively participated in major eighteenth century learned societies. A few Masons connected with these urban cultural institutions were important enlighteners, looking for disciples to disseminate their views. But most Masons belonging to urban learned societies were minor intellectuals who made some important contributions to the Enlightenment.

Some Masonic intellectuals held positions in universities. Numerous Masonic scientists and mathematicians in London and in Paris taught in universities and assisted in diffusing concepts of modern experimental science. More numerous than those in the British and French capitals, Masonic professors in Vienna, in many cases, imported cultural concepts from Western Europe into the Habsburg Empire. As a result of educational reforms instituted by Joseph, these professors especially played an active part in circulating medical, legal, and political ideologies of the Enlightenment in Vienna and throughout the empire.

Masonic intellectuals, too, were associated with other urban cultural agencies. Coffeehouses and taverns in London and salons in Paris attracted to their ranks aristocratic and bourgeois intellectuals and performed significant cultural functions. Participation in these institutions meant that London and Parisian Masons could stage displays, demonstrations, and lectures and thus could contribute to the spread of Enlightenment concepts. As a result of the lack of salons and comparable institutions, Habsburg Masonic intellectuals, especially in Vienna, utilized lodges for the sponsoring of Enlightenment projects.

Many Masonic intellectuals held membership in London learned societies. Many Masons in the British capital were elected to and held administrative positions in the Royal Society of London, thus exhibiting their philosophical commitment to Newtonianism. Most in this society were mechanists, but a few were materialists. Most London Masons belonging to this society were intellectuals, but some were gentlemen who served as patrons of the arts and sciences.[18] The Royal Society did not restrict its members to Englishmen and admitted to its ranks some French Masonic enlighteners and a few from the Habsburg Empire. The involvement of London Masons in the College of Physicians was considerable and suggested that, similar to the physical sciences, medicine was important to the Enlightenment in the British capital.[19] By affiliating with and contributing to the Society of Antiquaries, the Academy of Art, and the Academy of Ancient Music, London Masonic intellectuals demonstrated the importance of the humanities to the Enlightenment during the Augustan Era. Most London Masonic intellectuals belonged to learned societies in the British capital, but some held membership in academies in other English and European cities. Their involvement in these academies meant that Masonry served as an important channel through which the Enlightenment could develop in other places.

As has been shown, French Masons during the *ancien régime* were active in Parisian learned societies. The Paris Academy of Sciences developed into an important institution for the diffusion of Newtonian concepts and elected numerous Masons to its ranks. A few were astronomers and physicists, but most devoted their efforts to the study of chemistry, thus revealing the importance of Newtonian materialistic theories to the French Enlightenment. Parisian Masonic intellectuals, too, were elected to and were active in the *Académie de Peintre et de Sculpture*, the *Académie des Inscriptions et Belles-Lettres*, and the *Académie Française*. The participation of Parisian Masons in these learned societies demonstrated that major themes of the ancients were viewed as being important to the moderns of the French Enlightenment. Those Masons belonging to the *Académie Française* used drama and literature as propagandistic instruments to convey to the public their proposals regarding state reforms. Most Masons elected to Parisian learned societies were from the French capital. However, some had lived either in cities or in towns in France prior to coming to Paris and had distinguished themselves for their contributions to provincial academies. Eminent and less important Masonic intellectuals in the French capital also participated in minor Parisian learned societies and thus differed from their counterparts in Vienna who had few learned societies in which they could become involved.

In light of their affiliation with the Parisian Lodge of the Nine Sisters and with the Viennese True Harmony Lodge, Masonic intellectuals were given opportunities to promote the tenets and teachings of the Enlightenment and Freemasonry. Both societies were intended to give Masonry additional cultural stature and consisted of a few major and of many minor intellectuals; members of both societies became involved in activities indicative of the Enlightenment in Paris and in Vienna. Enlighteners of the Nine Sisters were mechanists and materialists, exemplars of the Neoclassical Movement in the fine arts, and proponents of state reforms. Yet, the most significant contributions of the personnel of the Nine Sisters centered on their sponsorship of schools open to the public and on their support of republican principles of the American Revolution. While occasionally conferring Masonic rites and holding special banquets, members of the Nine Sisters, unlike their colleagues in the True Harmony, expressed little interest in studying Masonic ritualism and were able to utilize other Parisian learned societies as well as this French lodge for the staging of their cultural activities.

In contrast to the Lodge of the Nine Sisters, the True Harmony Lodge satisfied a great cultural need and functioned as one of the very few learned societies in Josephinian Vienna. The True Harmony, unlike the Nine Sisters, issued literary and scientific proceedings, thus resembling a learned society and providing accounts of its cultural functions. Geological papers appearing in the scientific journal of the lodge marked a distinctive contribution to and a variation of Newtonian materialistic science. Articles, too, concerning ancient philosophies, deism, state reforms, and anticlericalism were published by Masonic enlighteners in the literary journal of the lodge and revealed significant features of the Enlightenment in Josephinian Vienna. While the True Harmony Lodge infrequently staged rites, its members published articles and musical compositions about Masonic ritualism, attempting to relate the principles of Masonry to those of the Enlightenment and demonstrating their roles as enlightened Masons.

The operations of Masonic grand lodges, lodges, and learned societies might be viewed from another context. Masonry during the eighteenth century seemed to function as a cultural movement; this movement had considerable cohesion, endorsed specific principles, and developed institutions to implement its ideologies. Moreover, its organization, rites, cultural operations, and personnel enabled the encompassing Masonic movement to play a central role in fostering the Enlightenment in specific regions of Europe. While this comparative study has focused on the organizational and cultural functions of the Craft in four major European cities, future works might emphasize the impact of Masonry as an international cultural movement upon eighteenth century Europe.

APPENDIX

A Listing of Lodges

Dates	Lodge	City	Jurisdiction
1717 to ca. 1745	The Apple-Tree Tavern Lodge	London	The Modern London Grand Lodge
1717 to ca. 1762	The Crown and Anchor Lodge	London	The Modern London Grand Lodge
1717 to ca. 1741	The Goose and Gridiron Lodge	London	The Modern London Grand Lodge
1717 to ca. 1745	The Rummer-and-Grapes Tavern Lodge	London	The Modern London Grand Lodge
1720 to ca. 1746	The Blew Boar Lodge	London	The Modern London Grand Lodge
1720 to ca. 1745	The Freemason's Coffeehouse Lodge	London	The Modern London Grand Lodge
1720 to ca. 1755	The Salutation Lodge	London	The Modern London Grand Lodge
1721 to ca. 1741	The Horn Lodge	London	The Modern London Grand Lodge
1722 to ca. 1746	The Swan Lodge	London	The Modern London Grand Lodge
1723 to ca. 1742	The Bedford Head Lodge	London	The Modern London Grand Lodge
1723 to ca. 1744	The Cross Keys Lodge	London	The Modern London Grand Lodge
1723 to ca. 1742	The Foot Lodge	London	The Modern London Grand Lodge

Dates	Lodge	City	Jurisdiction
1724 to ?	The Bear and Harrow Lodge	London	The Modern London Grand Lodge
1724 to ?	The Cock and Bottle Lodge	London	The Modern London Grand Lodge
1724 to ca. 1743	The Sun Lodge	London	The Modern London Grand Lodge
1724 to ca. 1739	The Three Kings Lodge	London	The Modern London Grand Lodge
1724 to ca. 1742	The Vine Tavern Lodge	London	The Modern London Grand Lodge
1725 to ca. 1743	The Queen's Head Tavern Lodge	London	The Modern London Grand Lodge
1725 to ?	The Rose Tavern Lodge	London	The Modern London Grand Lodge
1726 to ?	The Bell Tavern Lodge	London	The Modern London Grand Lodge
1726 to ca. 1742	Dick's at the Strand Lodge	London	The Modern London Grand Lodge
1726 to 1743	The Three Stars Lodge	Prague	The Modern London Grand Lodge
1727 to ca. 1744	The Green Lettice Lodge	London	The Modern London Grand Lodge
1727 to ca. 1742	The Old Devill Lodge	London	The Modern London Grand Lodge
1727 to ca. 1744	The *Louis d'Argent* Lodge	Paris	The French Grand Lodge
1728 to ca. 1747	The Busy Body Lodge	London	The Modern London Grand Lodge
1728 to ca. 1741	The Ship without Temple Bar Lodge	London	The Modern London Grand Lodge
1736 to ca. 1744	The *Bussi-Aumont* Lodge	Paris	The French Grand Lodge

Dates	Lodge	City	Jurisdiction
1736 to ca. 1744	The *Coustos-Villeroy* Lodge	Paris	The French Grand Lodge
1737 to ca. 1745	The Lodge *du Roy*	Paris	The French Grand Lodge
1742 to ca. 1765	The Three Cannons Lodge	Vienna	The Modern London Grand Lodge
1743 to ca. 1782	The Three Crowned Stars Lodge	Prague	The Strict Observance Rite
1754 to ?	The Three Hearts Lodge	Vienna	The Modern Grand Lodge of Hamburg
1762 to ca. 1781	The Generosity Lodge	Vienna	The Strict Observance Rite
1766 to 1786	The Three Eagles Lodge	Vienna	The Strict Observance and Zinnendorf Rites
1766 to ?	The Lodge of Science	Paris	The French Grand Lodge
1773 to 1786	The Crowned Hope Lodge	Vienna	The Strict Observance and Zinnendorf Rites
1776 to 1792; and 1805 to 1848	The Lodge of the Nine Sisters	Paris	The Grand Orient
1781 to 1786	The St. Joseph Lodge	Vienna	The Strict Observance and Zinnendorf Rites
1781 to 1786	The True Harmony Lodge	Vienna	The Zinnendorf Rite
1783 to 1786	The Charity Lodge	Vienna	The Zinnendorf Rite

NOTES

Notes to Chapter I

1. J. G. Findel, *History of Freemasonry*, trans. Murray Lyon (London: Asher, 1869), pp. 3–5, p. 136, p. 200, and p. 241. In this study Masonic terms are frequently used. Craft is another term for the Masonic order. Grand lodges function as the governing bodies of the order. Lodges are the institutions in which the activities of Masonry are conducted. Degrees or rites are conferred in lodges and contain the principles and teachings of Masonry.

2. A term first coined by Voltaire, the Enlightenment refers to a cultural movement preponderantly influencing Europe between 1689 and 1789. See Robert Anchor, *The Enlightenment Tradition* (New York: Harper and Row, 1967).

3. William Muraskin, *Middle-Class Blacks in a White Society* (Berkeley: California University Press, 1975), pp. 123–132.

4. Murray Hausknecht, *The Joiners: A Sociological Description of Voluntary Association Membership in the United States* (New York: Bedminster Press, 1962), pp. 9–13; and Jack C. Ross, *An Assembly of Good Fellows: Voluntary Associations in History* (Westport: Greenwood Press, 1976), pp. 5–14, and pp. 243–244.

5. William G. McLoughlin and Robert N. Bellah (eds.), *Religion in America* (New York: Houghton Mifflin, 1968), pp. 7–10; and Robert N. Bellah, *Beyond Belief: Essays on Religion in a Post-Traditional World* (New York: Harper and Row, 1970), pp. 168–186.

6. There were, however, eighteenth century groups not involved in the cultural activities of Masonry. Many prominent intellectuals not affiliated with the order had little time to participate in Masonry and evidently were not interested in its secrecy and ritualistic activities. In England, France, and the Habsburg Empire, craftsmen, guildsmen, and peasants for the most part did not hold membership in Masonry and concomitantly performed few cultural functions to foster the Enlightenment.

7. Gaston, Martin, *La Franc-Maçonnerie Française et La Prépar-ation de la Revolution* (Paris, 1926), pp. 1–2.

8. E. J. Hobsbawm, *Primitive Rebels: Studies in Archaic Forms of Social Movements in the 19th and 20th Centuries* (New York: Nor-ton, 1959), pp. 150–153.

9. Edward Tiryakian (ed.), *On the Margin of the Visible: Soci-ology, the Visible, and the Occult* (New York: Wiley and Sons, 1974), pp. 82–86 and pp. 118–120.

10. This Parisian lodge is named for the ancient muses in Greek mythology, is known in French as *Les Neuf Soeurs*, and is referred to in this study as the Nine Sisters.

11. Bernard Fay, *Revolution and Freemasonry* (Boston: Little Brown and Company, 1935), pp. 254–257.

12. Roger Hahn, *The Anatomy of a Scientific Institution: The Paris Academy of Sciences, 1666–1803* (Berkeley: California Univer-sity Press, 1971), p. 106; Paul Hazard, *European Thought in the Eighteenth Century* (Cleveland: Meridian Books, 1963), pp. 269–271; and Durand Echeverria, *Mirage in the West: A History of the French Image of American Society to 1815* (Princeton: Princeton University Press, 1957), pp. 57–59.

13. Nicholas Hans, "UNESCO of the Eighteenth Century: *La Loge des Neuf Soeurs* and Its Venerable Master, Benjamin Franklin," *Proceedings of the American Philosophical Society*, XCVII (October, 1953), pp. 513–524.

14. This lodge is known in German as *Zur Wahren Eintracht*, but in this study I shall refer to it as the True Harmony. I have not been able to find information to explain why the lodge was given this name.

15. Ludwig Abafi, *Geschichte der Freimaurerei* in *Oesterreich-Ungarn* (Budapest, 1890), IV, 278–290.

16. Abafi,*Freimaurerei*, IV, 278–281.

17. Paul Bernard, *Jesuits and Jacobins* (Urbana: Illinois Univer-sity Press, 1971), pp. 75–76; and Paul Nettl, *Mozart and Masonry* (New York: Da Capo Press, 1970), pp, 13–17.

18. J. M. Roberts, *The Mythology of the Secret Societies* (Lon-don: Secker and Warburg, 1972), pp. 57–64.

19. Enlightenment aims are discussed by Peter Gay, *The En-lightenment: An Interpretation, The Rise of Modern Paganism* (New York: Vintage Books, 1968), I, 4–9; by Ernst Cassirer, *The Philoso-phy of the Enlightenment* (Boston: Beacon Press, 1955), pp. 3–8; and

by Franco Venturi, *Utopia and Reform in the Enlightenment* (Cambridge: Cambridge University Press, 1971), pp. 2–5.

20. I. Bernard Cohen, *Franklin and Newton: An Inquiry into Speculative Newtonian Experimental Science* (Cambridge: Harvard University Press, 1966), pp. 113–118; and Robert E. Schofield, *Mechanism and Materialism: British Natural Philosophy in an Age of Reason* (Princeton: Princeton University Press, 1970), pp. 3–4.

21. Schofield, *Mechanism and Materialism*, pp. 19–39; Alexander Koyré, *From the Closed World to the Infinite Universe* (Baltimore: Johns Hopkins University Press, 1957), pp. 176–198, and pp. 273–276; and Margaret C. Jacob, *The Cultural Meaning of the Scientific Revolution* (New York: Knopf, 1988), pp. 141–142.

22. Cohen, *Franklin and Newton*, pp. 153–158; and Schofield, *Mechanism and Materialism*, pp. 9–10.

23. Schofield, *Mechanism and Materialism*, pp. 64–72.

24. Isaac Kramnick, *Bolingbroke and His Circle* (Cambridge: Harvard University Press, 1968), pp. 39–48 and pp. 115–127; and W. A. Speck, *Stability and Strife, England, 1714-1760* (Cambridge: Harvard University Press, 1977), pp. 11–30.

25. J. G. A. Pocock, *The Machiavellian Movement: Florentine Political Thought and the Atlantic Republican Tradition* (Princeton: Princeton University Press, 1975), pp. 349–351, pp. 354–355, p. 371, pp. 384-385, pp. 408-410, and pp. 446–461.

26. J. E. McGuire and P. M. Rattansi, "Newton and the 'Pipes of Pan,' " *Notes and Records of the Royal Society*, XXI (December, 1966), pp. 108–112 and pp. 115–116.

27. Roland Stromberg, *An Intellectual History of Modern Europe* (New York: Appleton, 1966), pp. 113–114; and Gay, *Enlightenment: Paganism*, I, 374–382.

28. Gay, *Enlightenment: Paganism*, I, 376–380; G. R. Cragg, *The Church and the Age of Reason (1648-1789)* (Baltimore: Pelican Books, 1960), pp. 157–162; and Margaret Jacob, *The Newtonians and the English Revolution* (Ithaca: Cornell University, 1976), pp. 217–220.

29. Jacob, *The Newtonians*, pp. 60–68.

30. A. R. Humphreys, *The Augustan World: Society, Thought, and Letters in Eighteenth Century England* (New York: Harper and Row, 1963), pp. 42–43 and p. 254.

31. Humphreys, *Augustan World*, pp. 223–233.

32. Marjorie Nicolson, *Science and Imagination* (Ithaca: Cornell University Press, 1956), pp. 218–219.

33. Charles Gillispie, *The Edge of Objectivity* (Princeton: University Press, 1967), pp. 112–115.

34. George Rudé, *Hanoverian London* (Berkeley: California University Press, 1971), pp. 64–67.

35. John Timbs, *Clubs and Club Life in London* (2nd ed.; Detroit: Gale Company, 1967), pp. 298–304 and pp. 504–505; and Rudé, *Hanoverian London*, pp. 70–79.

36. Aytoun Ellis, *The Penny Universities* (London: Secker and Warburg, 1956), p. 105 and p. 225; and Brian Harrison, *Drink and the Victorians: The Temperance Question in England 1815–1872* (Pittsburgh: University of Pittsburgh Press, 1971), p. 46, p. 50, and p. 52.

37. Peter Gay, *Voltaire's Politics: The Poet as Realist* (New York: Vintage Books, 1965), pp. 54–58.

38. Keith Baker, *Condorcet: From Natural Philosophy to Social Mathematics* (Chicago: Chicago University Press, 1975), p. 89; and Arnold Thackray, *Atoms and Powers* (Cambridge: Harvard University Press, 1970), pp. 92–97.

39. Roger Hahn, *The Paris Academy of Sciences*, p. 94.

40. Schofield, *Mechanism and Materialism*, pp. 226–231; and Thackray, *Atoms and Powers*, pp. 92–95.

41. Edward Lucie-Smith, *A Concise History of French Painting* (New York: Praeger, 1966), pp. 155–168; and Michael Levey, *Rococo to Revolution* (New York: Praeger, 1966), pp. 148–152.

42. John Lough, *An Introduction to Eighteenth Century France* (London: Longmans, 1960), pp. 283–286.

43. Peter Gay, *The Enlightenment: The Science of Freedom* (New York: Knopf, 1969), II, 249–260.

44. Frank Manuel, *The Eighteenth Century Confronts the Gods* (New York: Atheneum, 1967), pp. 6–10 and pp. 250–251.

45. Gay, *Enlightenment: Freedom*, II, 58.

46. Leo Gershoy, *From Despotism to Revolution* (New York: Harper and Row, 1944), pp. 265–270; and Baker, *Condorcet*, p. 118.

47. Harold T. Parker, *The Cult of Antiquity and the French Revolutionaries* (New York: Octagon Books, 1965), pp. 1–2, pp. 18–19, and pp. 26–27.

48. Alan Charles Kors, *D'Holbach's Coterie: An Enlightenment in Paris* (Princeton: Princeton University Press, 1976), ix–xi.

49. Franklin Ford, *Robe and Sword* (New York: Harper and Row, 1965), pp. 246–252; and Robert Shackleton, *Montesquieu* (London: Oxford University Press, 1961), pp. 266–283.

50. Lough, *Eighteenth Century France*, pp. 180–181; and Daniel Roche, *Le siècle des lumières en province: Académies et académiciens provinciaux, 1680–1789* (Paris: Mouton, 1978), I, 66–68. Roche explains that the *musées* of Gébelin and Rozier served as models for those in operation in Bordeaux and Toulouse.

51. Baker, *Condorcet*, pp. 11–12; and Hahn, *Paris Academy*, pp. 79–80.

52. Hahn, *Paris Academy*, pp. 122–129; Lough, *Eighteenth Century France*, pp. 284–287; and Roche, *Le siècle des lumières*, pp. 73–74 and pp. 257–280. Roche cogently demonstrates that learned societies in such provincial cities as Bordeaux, Lyon, and Toulouse assisted in the diffusion of scientific, medical, literary, and political ideas and operated much like their counterparts in Paris. He also shows that Masonic lodges in French provincial cities consisted of intellectuals and nobles, sponsored many social activities, staged a few cultural events, and thus functioned as Enlightenment agencies.

53. Hazard, *Eighteenth Century Thought*, pp. 199–206; and Robert Darnton, *The Business of Enlightenment: A Publishing History of the Encyclopédie, 1775–1800* (Cambridge: Harvard University Press, 1979), pp. 1–37. Darnton explains how the various folio volumes of the *Encyclopédie* were prepared, financed, and disseminated. However, Darnton says nothing about Parisian Masonry and its alleged financing of the *Encyclopédie*.

54. Dorothy Schlegel, "Freemasonry and the *Encyclopédie* Reconsidered," *Studies on Voltaire and the Eighteenth Century*, XC (1972), 1433–1460; and Hazard, *Eighteenth Century Thought*, pp. 214–215.

55. Gay, *Enlightenment: Freedom*, II, 483–496.

56. John C. Gagliardo, *Enlightened Despotism* (New York: Cromwell, 1967), pp. 60–85; and Roger Wines (ed.), *Enlightened Despotism* (Boston: Heath Company, 1967), pp. 57–77.

57. Ernst Wangermann, *The Austrian Achievement, 1700–1800* (London: Harcourt, 1973), pp. 18–19; and Robert A. Kann, *A History of the Habsburg Empire, 1526–1918* (Berkeley: California University Press, 1974), pp. 170–171 and p.176.

58. Alphons Lhotsky, *Osterreichische Historiographie* (Munich: Oldenbourg, 1962), pp. 124–128; and Fritz Valjavec, *Der Josephinis-*

mus (2nd ed.; Munich, 1945), pp. 9–10.

59. Bernard, *Jesuits and Jacobins*, pp. 171–172; and Gagliardo, *Despotism*, pp. 92–99.

60. Kann, *Habsburg Empire*, p. 67; and William McGill, *Maria Theresa* (New York: Twayne, 1972), p. 177.

61. Paul Bernard, *Joseph II* (New York: Twayne, 1972), pp. 96–97.

62. Kann, *Habsburg Empire*, pp. 68–69.

63. Robert A. Kann, *A Study in Austrian Intellectual History* (New York: Praeger, 1960), pp. 181–189; and Carlo Francovich, *Storia della Massoneria in Italia* (Florence: Nuova Italia, 1974), pp. 239–240.

64. Victor Tapié, *The Rise and Fall of the Habsburg Monarchy*, trans. Stephen Harman (New York: Praeger, 1971), p. 227; and Bernard, *Joseph II*, pp. 46–48.

65. Bernard, *Jesuits and Jacobins*, pp. 81–83; and Tapié, *Rise and Fall*, pp. 218–220.

66. Kann, *Habsburg Empire*, p. 193.

67. C. A. Macartney, *The Habsburg Empire: 1780–1918* (New York: Macmillan, 1969), pp. 120–121.

68. Wangermann, *Austrian Achievement*, p. 122.

69. Stanley Kimball, *The Austro-Slav Revival: A Study of Nineteenth-Century Literary Foundations* (Philadelphia: The American Philosophical Society, 1973), p. 22.

70. Bernard, *Jesuits and Jacobins*, p. 171 and p. 174.

71. Donald Grout, *A History of Western Music* (New York: Norton, 1973), pp. 302–309 and pp. 343–344; and Paul Lang, *Music in Western Civilization* (New York: Norton, 1941), pp. 598–603.

72. Grout, *History of Music*, pp. 313–316; and Lang, *Music in Civilization*, pp. 658–673.

73. Frank Brechka, *Gerard van Swieten and His World* (The Hague: Nijhoff, 1970), pp. 134–136.

74. Cecil J. Schneer, (ed.), *Towards A History of Geology* (Cambridge: M.I.T. Press, 1969), pp. 186–187; and Thackray, *Atoms and Powers*, pp. 218–219.

75. Kimball, *The Austro-Slav Revival*, p. 22.

76. Charles H. O'Brien, *Ideas of Religious Toleration at the Time of Joseph II* (Philadelphia: The American Philosophical Society, 1969), p. 59.

Notes to Chapter II

1. Bernard E. Jones, *Freemasons' Guide and Compendium* (London: Harrap, 1956), p. 76.

2. Douglas Knoop and G. P. Jones, *An Introduction to Freemasonry* (Manchester: Manchester University Press, 1937), pp. 13–15 and p. 58; and Jones, *Freemasons' Compendium*, pp. 69–73.

3. Knoop and Jones, *Introduction to Freemasonry*, pp. 16–17 and pp. 59–61; and Jones, *Freemasons' Compendium*, pp. 70–73.

4. David Stevenson, *The Origins of Freemasonry: Scotland's Century, 1590–1710* (Cambridge: Cambridge University Press, 1988), pp. 1–12 and pp. 105–116; and Knoop and Jones, *Introduction to Freemasonry*, pp. 54–55.

5. Knoop and Jones, *Introduction to Freemasonry*, pp. 62–63; and Jones, *Freemasons' Compendium*, pp. 97–104. It is interesting to note that during the seventeenth century, the antiquarians Elias Ashmole and Randle Holme, men who demonstrated great interest in the study of ancient architecture, were admitted to English Operative lodges.

6. Henry W. Coil, *Freemasonry Through Six Centuries* (Fulton: Bell Press, 1966), I, 125–128; Frances Yates, *The Rosicrucian Enlightenment* (Boston: Routledge and Kegan, 1972), pp. 213–217; and Mary Ann Clawson, *Constructing Brotherhood: Class, Gender, and Fraternalism* (Princeton: Princeton University Press, 1989), pp. 53–58 and pp. 65–73. Three works of Margaret Jacob also contain incisive accounts regarding the evolution of Modern Masonry in London. See *The Radical Enlightenment: Pantheists, Freemasons, and Republicans* (London: Allen and Unwin, 1981), pp. 122–130; *Living the Enlightenment: Freemasonry and Politics in Eighteenth Century Europe* (New York: Oxford University Press, 1991), pp. 31–35 and pp. 65–69; and *Newtonians*, pp. 219–224. I found that many members of Modern London Masonic elites tended to be either liberals or moderates.

7. Rudé, *Hanoverian London*, pp. 37–39.

8. Coil, *Freemasonry Through Six Centuries*, I, 132; and Alfred Robbins, *English-Speaking Freemasonry* (London: Benn, 1930), p. 36.

9. Jones, *Freemasons' Compendium*, pp. 168–169; and Findel, *History*, pp. 136–137.

10. W. Harry Rylands (ed.), *Records of the Lodge of Antiquity* (London: Private Publication, 1928), I, 17–18.

11. Coil, *Freemasonry Through Six Centuries*, I, 141–142.

12. Coil, *Freemasonry Through Six Centuries*, I, 141–142; and Jones, *Freemasons' Compendium*, p. 169. Payne, however, served during the early 1720s on the Grand Lodge Historical Committee.

13. John Stokes, "Life of John Theophilus Desaguliers," *Ars Quatuor Coronatorum*, XXXVIII (1925), 285. This journal is hereafter cited as *AQC*.

14. Stokes, "Life of Desaguliers," 286.

15. Schofield, *Mechanism and Materialism*, p. 80.

16. C. H. Collins Baker and Muriel I. Baker, *The Life and Circumstances of James Brydges: First Duke of Chandos* (Oxford: Clarendon Press, 1949), pp. 129–131.

17. Coil, *Freemasonry Through Six Centuries*, I, 133.

18. Findel, *History*, p. 143.

19. Coil, *Freemasonry Through Six Centuries*, I, 133.

20. W. G. Fisher, "John Montagu, The First Noble Grand Master," *AQC*, LXXIX (1966), 69–89.

21. Findel, *History*, pp. 144–146.

22. J. H. Thorp, "The Rev. James Anderson and the Earls of Buchan," *AQC*, XVIII (1905), 9–12; Robbins, *English Speaking Freemasonry*, pp. 51–52; and Coil, *Freemasonry Through Six Centuries*, I, 143–144.

23. Coil, *Freemasonry Through Six Centuries*, I, 145.

24. Lionel Vibert (ed.), *Anderson's Constitutions of 1723* (Washington: Masonic Service Association, 1924), pp. 32–35 and pp. 39–44.

25. Vibert (ed.), *Constitutions*, pp. 49–50.

26. Ibid., pp. 54–55.

27. Ibid., p. 69.

28. Ibid., pp. 70–73 and p. 77.

29. Ibid., pp. 91–92.

30. J. R. Clarke, "The Royal Society and Early Grand Lodge Freemasonry," *AQC*, LXXX (1967), 110–119. Clarke shows that between 1720 and 1740 twenty-five members of the Royal Society served as grand lodge administrators and that eighty fellows of the society during this period were affiliated with the lodges of Modern Masonry.

31. Vibert, (ed.), *Constitutions*, p. 93.

32. Ibid., pp. 93–94. Eight fellows of the Royal Society between 1720 and 1740 served as Grand Warden of Modern Masonry.

33. Jones, *Freemasons' Compendium*, p. 175.

34. Stokes, "Life of Desaguliers," 301.

35. Jones, *Freemasons' Compendium*, p. 171 and pp. 179–180; and Roberts, *Mythology*, pp. 26–28.

36. David Owen, *English Philanthropy, 1660–1960* (Cambridge: The Belknap Press, 1964), pp. 2–3 and p. 20.

37. Stokes, "Life of Desaguliers," 299.

38. Ibid., p. 299. See also R. William Weisberger, "John Theophilus Desaguliers: Huguenot, Freemason, and Newtonian Scientist," *Transactions of the Huguenot Society of South Carolina*, XC (1985), 63–67.

39. Ibid., p. 300.

40. Ibid., p. 302.

41. There is a controversy about the development of the Modern Masonic degrees; some Masonic scholars believe that there were only two degrees during the 1720s and that the third degree was added as an honorary degree during the early 1730s. However, most Masonic writers subscribe to the three degree theory, believing, as I do, that Modern Masonry by 1723 had three degrees. The primary advocate of the two degree system is Coil, *Freemasonry Through Six Centuries*, I, 163–165. The major proponent of the three degree theory is Jones, *Freemasons' Compendium*, pp. 242–243.

42. Masonic scholars have not written about the interesting topic relating to the language of Masonry.

43. Tiger, *Men in Groups*, pp. 180–185.

44. Albert Mackey, *Symbolism of Freemasonry* (Chicago: Powner, 1975), pp. 142–143; and Jones, *Freemasons' Compendium*, pp. 274–275.

45. Mackey, *Symbolism of Freemasonry*, pp. 100–101.

46. Ibid., pp. 92–93.

47. Ibid., pp. 94–95.

48. Jones, *Freemasons' Compendium*, p. 294.

49. Mackey, *Symbolism of Freemasonry*, pp. 223–224.

50. Ibid., p. 189, p. 209, and p. 219.

51. Oliver Street, *Symbolism of the Three Degrees* (Washington: Masonic Service Association, 1922), pp. 106–108.

52. Jones, *Freemasons' Compendium*, pp. 289–290 and pp. 305–306.

53. Mackey, *Symbolism of Freemasonry*, pp. 232–234 and pp. 251–254.

54. Ibid., pp. 194–197.

55. A. S. McBride, *Speculative Freemasonry* (Richmond: Macoy, 1924), pp. 36–44.

56. Jones, *Freemasons' Compendium*, p. 183. Charge refers to major regulations of the Craft.

57. The first three degrees of Modern Masonry are known as the Blue Degrees. Blue lodges refer to those institutions in which these degrees are conferred.

58. Jones, *Freemasons' Compendium*, pp. 259–262.

59. Vibert (ed.), *Constitutions*, pp. 80–81 and pp. 85–86.

60. Robbins, *English-Speaking Freemasonry*, pp. 344–348.

61. Jones, *Freemasons' Compendium*, pp. 474–477.

62. Ibid., p. 362.

63. Ibid., pp. 363–364.

64. Ibid., pp. 375–377.

65. Ibid., pp. 378–380.

66. Ibid., pp. 388–389.

67. Ibid., pp. 364–365. As Jones maintains, local lodge secretaries were not required, however, to record minutes. As a result of the lack of documents about local lodges, historians have encountered problems in investigating these bodies.

68. Ibid., pp. 360–361,

69. Ibid., p. 464 and p. 467.

70. Ibid., pp. 441–442 and p. 467.

71. Ibid., p. 389.

72. Ibid., pp. 471–472.

73. Robbins, *English-Speaking Freemasonry*, pp. 54–55.

74. Jones, *Freemasons' Compendium*, pp. 335–336.

75. Rudé, *Hanoverian London*, pp. 71–73; and Ellis, *The Penny Universities*, pp. 159–164.

76. Timbs, *Clubs and Club Life*, p. 56, p. 333, p. 354, pp. 417–419, and pp. 434–438.

77. Cohen, *Franklin and Newton*, p. 243; Schofield, *Mechanism and Materialism*, pp. 103–105; and Jacob, *Cultural Meaning of the Scientific Revolution*, pp. 143–144.

78. Cohen, *Franklin and Newton*, p. 247.

79. Clarke, "The Royal Society and Early Freemasonry," 118–119.

80. Most of the lectures of Desaguliers delivered in coffee-houses and taverns appeared in the *Transactions* of the Royal Society, in his *Lectures of Experimental Philosophy*, issued in 1719, and in his

A Course of Experimental Philosophy, published in 1734. When Desaguliers gave his demonstrations, Richard Bridges and William Vreen, about whom little is known, usually served as his assistants.

81. R. T. Gunther, *Early Science in Oxford* (London: Oxford University Press, 1937), IX, 296–297; and Larry Stewart, "The Selling of Newton: Science and Technology in Early Eighteenth Century England," *Journal of British Studies*, XXV (1986), 185–186.

82. J. T. Desaguliers, *A Course of Experimental Philosophy* (London: Senex, 1734), I, i. This work was dedicated to the Mason Frederick, Prince of Wales and was financed in part by the Masons John Senex, Martin Folkes, and the Duke of Chandos.

83. Desaguliers, *A Course of Experimental Philosophy* I, xi.

84. Desaguliers, *loc. cit.*

85. Ibid., I, xii.

86. J. T. Desaguliers, *Lectures of Experimental Philosophy* (London: Mears, 1719), p. 5.

87. Ibid., pp. 7–12.

88. Desaguliers, *A Course of Experimental Philosophy*, I, 4.

89. Desaguliers, *loc. cit.*

90. Desaguliers, *loc. cit.*

91. Desaguliers, *A Course of Experimental Philosophy*, I, 10.

92. Ibid., I, 42.

93. Ibid., I, 43.

94. Desaguliers, *loc. cit.*

95. Ibid., I, 49.

96. Ibid., I, 54.

97. Ibid., I, 284.

98. Desaguliers, *loc. cit.*

99. Ibid., I, 300.

100. Desaguliers, *loc. cit.*

101. Ibid., I, 305–306.

102. Ibid., I, 307.

103. Ibid., I, 308.

104. Ibid., I, 317.

105. Desaguliers, *loc. cit.*

106. Ibid., I, 324.

107. Ibid., I, 334,

108. Ibid., I, 335.

109. Ibid., I, 335–337.

110. Ibid., I, 348–349 and 353.

111. Ibid., I, 356.

112. Desaguliers, *loc. cit.*

113. Ibid., I, 359.

114. Ibid., I, 594.

115. Desaguliers, *A Course of Experimental Philosophy*, II, 16–18.

116. Ibid., II, 20–21.

117. J. T. Desaguliers, "Some Thoughts Concerning the Cause of Elasticity," *The Abridged Transactions of the Royal Society of London*, XLI (1739), 340–346.

118. J. T. Desaguliers, "An Account of an Experiment to Prove an Interspersed Vacuum," *Transactions Abridged*, XXX (1717), 321–322.

119. J. T. Desaguliers, "An Experiment before the Royal Society to Show that Bodies of the Same Bulk do not contain equal quantities of Matter in an Interspersed Vacuum," *Transactions Abridged*, XXXI (1720), 480–481.

120. Schofield and Jacob comment on the role of Desaguliers as a lecturer. Schofield views Desaguliers as the most successful private lecturer of his day, while Jacob believes this role to be overly stressed. See Schofield, *Mechanism and Materialism*, p. 80 and Jacob's review of *Isaac Newton im Zwielicht zwischen Mythos und Forschung: Studien zur Epoche der Aufklärung* by Fritz Wagner in *The American Historical Review*, LXXXII (December, 1977), 1234.

121. J. T. Desaguliers, *A Course of Experimental Philosophy*, II, 414.

122. Ibid., II, 414–417.

123. Martin Clare, *The Motion of Fluids, Natural and Artificial* (3rd ed.; London: Ward, 1747), p. 2.

124. Clare, *Motion of Fluids*, pp. 60–61 and pp. 72–73.

125. Desaguliers, *A Course of Experimental Philosophy*, II, 417–418.

126. J. T. Desaguliers, "A Description of an Engine to Raise Water by the Help of Quicksilver," *Transactions Abridged*, XXXII (1722), 550–555.

127. J. T. Desaguliers, "An Account of Experiments Concerning the Running of Water in Pipes," *Transactions Abridged*, XXXIV (1726), 137–140.

128. Desaguliers, *A Course of Experimental Philosophy*, II, 367–368; and David Landes, *The Unbound Prometheus: Technological*

Change and Industrial Development in Western Europe from 1750 to the Present (Cambridge: Cambridge University Press, 1969), pp. 101–104.

129. J. T. Desaguliers, "Observations on the Crane with Improvements," *Transactions Abridged*, XXXVI (1729), 369–370.

130. Desaguliers, "Observations on the Crane," 370–374.

131. J. T. Desaguliers, "How Damp or Foul Air may be Drawn from Mines," *Transactions Abridged*, XXXV (1727), 208–210.

132. J. T. Desaguliers, "An Account of a Machine for Changing the Air of Sick People," *Transactions Abridged*, XXXIX (1735), 12–13; and Stokes, "Life of Desaguliers," 286–287.

133. Stokes, "Life of Desaguliers," 287.

134. Cohen, *Franklin and Newton*, pp. 255–257.

135. J. T. Desaguliers, "Some Thoughts and Experiments concerning Electricity," *Transactions Abridged*, XLI (1739), 346.

136. Desaguliers, "Experiments concerning Electricity," 347.

137. Ibid., 349–351.

138. Ibid., 352–353.

139. J. T. Desaguliers, "Some Remarks and Experiments concerning Electricity," *Transactions Abridged*, XLI (1740), 472–480.

140. Schofield, *Mechanism and Materialism*, p. 86; and Stokes, "Life of Desaguliers," 306.

141. "George Parker," *The Dictionary of National Biography*, XV, 234–235. This journal is hereafter cited as *DNB*.

142. "John Machin," *DNB*, XII, 554.

143. "Brook Taylor," *DNB*, XIX, 404–405.

144. "James Bradley," *DNB*, II, 1074–1079.

145. James Bradley, "A New Apparent Motion Discovered in the Fixed Stars," *Transactions Abridged*, XXXIII (1723), 308–309.

146. James Bradley, "Observations on the Comet that Appeared in 1723," *Transactions Abridged*, XXXIII (1724), 13–15.

147. Martin Folkes, "An Account of the Aurora Borealis seen in London," *Transactions Abridged*, XXX (1717), 291–292; and Martin Folkes, "An Observation of Three Mock Suns seen in London on September 17, 1736," *Transactions Abridged*, XL (1737), 137–138.

148. J. R. Clarke, "The Medical Profession and Early Freemasonry," *AQC*, LXXXV (1972), 305–306. According to Clarke, thirty-four Masonic doctors were affiliated with the Royal College of Physicians and thirteen with the Royal Society.

149. "Thomas Pellett," *DNB*, XV, 710–711. Pellett also edited in 1728 *Chronology of Ancient Kingdoms* written by his friend Sir Isaac Newton.

150. "Sir Richard Manningham," *DNB*, XII, 959–960.

151. Clarke, "The Medical Profession and Freemasonry," 301.

152. Ibid., 302.

153. "Thomas Short," *DNB*, XVIII, 154.

154. "James Douglas," *DNB*, V, 1235–1236.

155. "Frank Nicholls," *DNB*, XIV, 437–438. Nicholls was affiliated with the Busy Body Lodge in Charing Cross.

156. "William Becket," *DNB*, II, 78.

157. "William Rutty," *DNB*, XVII, 521; and William Rutty, "A Tumor on the Loins of an Infant," *Transactions Abridged*, XXXI (1720), 487–489. Rutty belonged to the Bedford Head Tavern Lodge.

158. William Rutty, "An Account of a Prenatural Bony Substance Found in the Cavity of the Thorax," *Transactions Abridged*, XXXIV (1726), 156–160.

159. "John Radcliffe," *DNB*, XVI, 572; and "Meyer Schomberg," *DNB*, XVII, p. 925. Radcliffe belonged to the Ship without Temple Barr Lodge and Schomberg to the Swan and Rummer Lodge.

160. "Samuel Sharp," *DNB*, XVII, 1352–1353. Sharp appeared to belong to the Mitre Tavern Lodge.

161. W. J. Williams, "Alexander Pope and Freemasonry," *AQC*, XXXVIII (1925), 112. Williams doubts that Dr. John Arbuthnot and Jonathan Swift, two literary friends of Pope, were associated with Speculative Freemasonry. The question concerning the possible connections of Arbuthnot and Swift with Masonry still remains a moot one.

162. Marjorie Nicolson and G. S. Rousseau, "*This Long Disease, My Life,*" *Alexander Pope and the Sciences* (Princeton: Princeton University Press, 1968), p. 221 and pp. 229–233.

163. Nicolson and Rousseau, "*This Long Disease,*" p. 269.

164. Peter Dixon (ed.), *Alexander Pope* (Columbus: Ohio State University Press, 1972), p. 87.

165. Nicolson and Rousseau, "*This Long Disease,*" p. 209.

166. Ibid., pp. 209–211.

167. W. J. Williams, "Masonic Personalia, 1723–1739," *AQC*, XL (1927), 39 and 133. Williams claims that Mendes served as Grand Steward of Modern Masonry in 1738 and that his mother lodge cannot be determined.

168. "George Jeffreys," *DNB*, X, 721.

169. Williams, "Masonic Personalia," 32. Beckingham belonged to the Bedford Head Lodge.

170. Ibid., XL, 129.

171. Ibid., XL, 132, 136, and 160. Miller belonged to the Sun Tavern Lodge, Palmer to the Green Lettice Lodge, and Quinn to the Bear and Harrow Lodge.

172. James s'Gravesande, *Mathematical Elements of Natural Philosophy*, trans. J. T. Desaguliers (London: Senex, 1747), I, xxxviii-xl.

173. Vibert (ed.), *Constitutions*, p. 80.

174. Gay, *Enlightenment: Paganism*, I, 8-9.

175. Williams, "Masonic Personalia," 32 and 134. Ball belonged to the Sun Tavern Lodge and Newman to the Swan Lodge. In the *Pantheisticon* and in other works, Toland advances his deistic views; he believes that the principles of Christianity could be combined with those of deism. Toland headed a secret society and evidently looked to Masonry to recruit additional followers. See Margaret Jacob, *The Newtonians*, pp. 220-226.

176. Williams, "Masonic Personalia," 39. Evans belonged to the Freemason's Coffeehouse Lodge. For the brief confrontation between Masons and Christian deists, see Jacob, *The Newtonians*, pp. 220-221.

177. Joan Evans, *A History of the Society of Antiquaries* (London: Oxford University Press, 1956), p. 58.

178. Evans, *Society of Antiquaries*, p. 541; and "Henry Hare," *DNB*, VIII, 1251. The Earl of Coleraine was a member of the Swan Lodge and was elected in 1728 as Grand Master of Modern Masonry.

179. Clarke, "The Medical Profession and Freemasonry," 300. Stukeley also served as the Gulstonian Lecturer of the College in 1722.

180. Evans, *Society of Antiquaries*, p. 53; and R. F. Gould, "William Stukeley," *AQC*, VI (1898), 130. Gould was correct about the lodge into which Stukeley was inducted but was wrong to think that Christian principles prompted Stukeley to seek entry into Freemasonry.

181. Evans, *Society of Antiquaries*, p. 55.

182. Stuart Piggott, *William Stukeley: An Eighteenth Century Antiquary* (Oxford: Clarendon Press, 1950), pp. 37-40.

183. Evans, *Society of Antiquaries*, p. 80.

184. Piggott, *Stukeley*, pp. 100–101 and pp. 120–121.

185. Evans, *Society of Antiquaries*, p. 54; and "Samuel Gale," *DNB*, VII, 816–817. Gale was a Mason, but the lodge to which he belonged has not been determined.

186. "Peter Le Neve," *DNB*, XI, 915–916. Le Neve belonged to the Bedford Head Lodge.

187. "Richard Rawlinson," *DNB*, XVI, 774–776. Rawlinson belonged to the Three Kings Lodge.

188. "Philip Webb," *DNB*, XX, 1018–1019. Webb was a member of the Sun Lodge.

189. Evans, *Society of Antiquaries*, p. 96 and pp. 100–102.

190. "Thomas Hunt," *DNB*, X, 279. Hunt belonged to the Cock and Bottle Lodge.

191. "Ephraim Chambers," *DNB*, IV, 16-17. The scientific ideas found in the encyclopedia of Chambers have been examined by Philip Shorr, *Science and Superstition in the Eighteenth Century* (New York: Columbia University Press, 1932), pp. 8–33.

192. Vibert, (ed.), *Constitutions*, p. 73.

193. Mackey, *Symbolism of Freemasonry*, pp. 318–319; and John S. Ackerman, *Palladio* (Baltimore: Penguin Books, 1966), pp. 160–161 and p. 182.

194. Ackerman, *Palladio*, pp. 19–29.

195. Baker and Baker, *The Life of Chandos*, pp. 155–158; and Williams, "Masonic Personalia," 137 and 138. George Dance belonged to the Bell Tavern Lodge and John Price to the Old Devill Lodge.

196. Williams, "Masonic Personalia," 42. Hawkesmore was associated with the Oxford Arms Lodge.

197. Peter Quenell, *Hogarth's Progress* (New York: Viking Press, 1955), pp. 25–26, pp. 49–50, and pp. 124–125; and Williams, "Masonic Personalia," 36, 127, and 128. Richard Cooper belonged to the Blew Boar Lodge and Thomas Hudson to the Ship Lodge.

198. Ibid., XL, 128 and 167. Hogarth belonged to the Hand and Apple Tree Lodge.

199. Quenell, *Hogarth's Progress*, p. 42 and pp. 89–90.

200. Ibid., pp. 130–136.

201. Ibid., pp. 210–211.

202. Williams, "Masonic Personalia," 170. Tom Worlidge belonged to the Rummer Lodge.

203. R. F. Gould, "*Philo-Musicae et Architecturae Societas,*" *AQC,* XVI (1903), 112–118; and Williams, "Masonic Personalia," 165. Shuttleworth belonged to the Queen's Head Lodge.

204. Paul Lang, *George Frideric Handel* (New York: Norton, 1966), pp. 116–117. Heidegger was a Grand Steward of Modern Masonry in 1725.

205. Paul Nettl, *Mozart and Masonry* (New York: Da Capo Press, 1970), p. 31. Immyns belonged to the King's Arms Lodge.

206. Lang, *Handel,* pp. 140–141. Handel knew and interacted with many Masons, but definite evidence concerning his affiliation with the Craft has never been discovered.

207. Ibid., pp. 142–143 and pp. 258–265.

208. Vibert (ed.), *Constitutions,* p. 80.

209. Rudé, *Hanoverian London,* pp. 77–78; and Timbs, *Clubs and Club Life,* p. 153 and p. 333.

210. Williams, "Masonic Personalia," 36 and 138. Raphel Courteville was affiliated with the Crown and Anchor Lodge and Dr. Thomas Pyle with the Vine Tavern Lodge.

211. Speck, *Stability and Strife,* p. 102; and Williams, "Masonic Personalia," 31. Asgill belonged to the Three Tuns Lodge.

212. Pelham, Nugent, Hardinge, and other Whiggish supporters of the Jew Bill were not Masons. An extensive account of this bill is found in Thomas W. Perry, *Public Opinion, Propaganda, and Politics in Eighteenth-Century England: A Study of the Jew Bill of 1753* (Cambridge: Harvard University Press, 1962), pp. 49–71.

213. E. P. Thompson, *Whigs and Hunters: The Origins of the Black Act* (New York: Pantheon Books, 1975), pp. 199–200. On the reaction of Walpole to the patronage system, see Kramnick, *Bolingbroke and His Circle,* pp. 121–122.

214. Thompson, *Whigs and Hunters,* pp. 179–181.

215. Speck, *Stability and Strife,* pp. 28–29; and Williams, "Masonic Personalia," 33 and 165. Blackerby was inducted into the Horn Lodge and in 1729 served as Deputy Grand Master of Modern Masonry. Stanhope belonged to the Bear and Harrow Lodge.

216. Excellent accounts of the South Sea Bubble Crisis appear in P. G. M. Dickson, *The Financial Revolution in England: A Study in the Development of Public Credit 1688–1756* (New York: St. Martin's Press, 1967), pp. 91–156; and in Speck, *Stability and Strife,* pp. 196–201. John Clark was a member of the Blew Boar Lodge. Williams, "Masonic Personalia," 35.

217. Wilfred Fisher, "A Cavalcade of Freemasons in 1731," *AQC*, LXXV (1962), 34. Williams belonged to the Rummer Tavern Lodge.

218. Williams, "Masonic Personalia," 33. Bladen belonged to the Rummer Tavern Lodge.

219. Ibid., XL, 41. Gurney belonged to the Golden Lion Tavern Lodge.

220. Ibid., XL, 34. Richard Cantillon belonged to the Bedford Head Lodge. The maid of Cantillon learned about his dishonest business practices and in 1734 murdered him.

221. Ibid., XL, 40. Lord Hervey of Ickworth belonged to the Queen's Head Lodge.

222. Timbs, *Clubs and Club Life*, pp. 105–111.

223. Kramnick, *Bolingbroke and His Circle*, pp. 17–24. Despite his sympathy for deistic ideas and his involvement in London clubs and taverns, Bolingbroke was not affiliated with Modern Masonry,

224. Ibid., p. 6, p. 60, and pp. 70–76.

225. Williams, "Masonic Personalia," 35. The Viscount of Cobham belonged to the Bell Tavern Lodge.

226. Ibid., XL, 34. John Byram belonged to the Swan Lodge.

227. Ibid., XL, 168. Edwin Ward was a member of the Bell Tavern Lodge.

228. Ibid., XL, 42. John Lumley belonged to the Rummer Tavern Lodge.

229. Alfred Robbins, "Frederick, Prince of Wales as a Freemason," *AQC*, XXIX (1916), 9–12. Robbins has also noted that since the induction of George IV into the Craft, every English king has been a Mason.

230. J. H. Plumb, *The First Four Georges* (New York: Macmillan, 1957), p. 80 and p. 83.

231. Schofield, *Mechanism and Materialism*, pp. 87–90.

232. Rudé, *Hanoverian London*, p. 236. Rudé claims that aristocratic and bourgeois patrons of the arts and sciences during the last half of the eighteenth century spent more time at their country estates than in their London mansions.

233. Henry Coil, *Freemasonry Through Six Centuries* (Fulton: Ovid Bell Press, 1967), II, 5 and 18; and Jones, *Freemasons' Compendium*, pp. 193–194.

234. Jones, *Freemasons' Compendium*, p. 504.

235. George Steinmetz, *The Royal Arch: Its Hidden Meaning* (Richmond: Macoy, 1946), pp. 104–105; and Jones, *Freemasons'*

Compendium, pp. 514–519 and pp. 526–527.

236. Jones, *Freemasons' Compendium* p. 205; and Coil, *Freemasonry Through Six Centuries,* II, 20–21. Antient Masonry during the last half of the eighteenth century became well established in Scotland, in Ireland, and in America.

237. Jones, *Freemasons' Compendium,* pp. 221–223.

Chapter III

1. There are few primary and secondary sources regarding the formation and the operations of the Grand Lodge of France. Masonic scholars also do not agree about the origins and activities of this grand lodge. See Pierre Chevallier, *Histoire de la Franc-Maçonnerie Française: La Maçonnerie: École de L'Egalité, 1725–1799* (Paris: Fayard, 1974), pp. 3–7; W. E. Moss, "Freemasonry in France in 1725–1735," *AQC,* XLVII (1934), 87–114; Findel, *History,* pp. 200–203; and Coil, *Freemasonry Through Six Centuries,* I, 230–234.

2. Findel, *History,* p. 201; and Chevallier, *Histoire de la Franc-Maçonnerie Française,* pp. 40–41.

3. Martin, *Franc-Maçonnerie Française,* pp. 14–27.

4. Harold T. Parker, *The Cult of Antiquity,* pp. 1–2. Parker does not mention, however, the role of Freemasonry in circulating the ideas of the ancients in eighteenth century France.

5. Street, *Symbolism,* pp. 56–57 and pp. 121–122.

6. René Le Forestier, *La Franc-Maçonnerie Templière et Occultiste aux XVIIIe et XIXe Siècles* (Paris: Aubier-Montaigne, 1970), pp. 29–31; and D. Ligou, "Structures et Symbolisme Maçonniques," *Annales Historiques de la Révolution Française,* CXVII (July, 1969), pp. 520–521.

7. Street, *Symbolism,* pp. 106–107 and pp. 118–121; and Mackey, *Symbolism of Freemasonry,* pp. 222–223.

8. Ligou, "Structures et Symbolisme Maçonniques," 521–523. Bernard Fay and other advocates of the conspiracy theory believe that by espousing the doctrines of natural liberties, French Freemasons were major contributors to the French Revolution. In *Revolution and Freemasonry,* Fay claims that "18th Century Freemasonry fostered the revolutionary spirit" and that "the revolutionary spirit brought about the American and French Revolutions," See p. 305 and p. 314.

9. Pierre Chevallier, *Les Ducs Sous L'Acacia* (Paris: Vrin, 1964), p. 54.

10. Chevallier, *Les Ducs*, p. 55.

11. Ibid., pp. 56–57.

12. Ibid., p. 60.

13. Shackleton, *Montesquieu*, p. 140.

14. Ibid., pp. 264–281.

15. Ibid., pp. 298–301.

16. Shackleton, *Montesquieu*, pp. 39–45; and Pauline Kra, "Religion in Montesquieu's *Lettres persanes*," *Studies on Voltaire and the Eighteenth Century*, LXXII (1970), 35, 56–57, 90, and 110.

17. Chevallier, *Les Ducs*, p. 63. Despite being inactive in the affairs of the order, Montesquieu maintained his membership in Masonry.

18. Ibid., p. 69.

19. Ibid., p. 65 and p. 69.

20. Ibid., pp. 73–74.

21. Ibid., pp. 72–73.

22. Ibid., p. 74.

23. Ibid., pp. 76–78.

24. Chevallier, *Les Ducs*, pp. 17–18; and Roberts, *Mythology*, pp. 32–33.

25. Chevallier, *Les Ducs*, p. 183. Chevallier also claims that the *Bussi-Aumont* Lodge, which did not maintain close relations with the two other Parisian lodges, was not involved in the Jacobite controversy.

26. Chevallier, *Histoire de la Franc-Maçonnerie Française*, pp. 14–15.

27. Chevallier, *Les Ducs*, p. 101, p. 104, and p. 113,

28. However, Louis did not affiliate with Masonry.

29. Findel, *History*, p. 203; and Eugen Lennhoff, *The Freemasons*, trans. Einar Frame (London: Lewis, 1978), pp. 283–286.

30. C. N. Batham, "Chevalier Michael Ramsay: A New Appreciation," *AQC*, LXXXI (1968), 280–291; Coil, *Freemasonry Through Six Centuries*, I, 234–235; and Roberts, *Mythology*, p. 35.

31. Findel, *History*, p. 203. For alleged connections between French Freemasonry and Jacobitism, see Paul K. Monod, *Jacobitism and the English People, 1688–1788* (Cambridge: Cambridge University Press, 1989), pp. 302–304.

32. Chevallier, *Les Ducs*, pp. 143–144 and p. 149.

33. Chevallier, *Histoire de la Franc-Maçonnerie Française*, pp. 19–24; and Coil, *Freemasonry Through Six Centuries*, I, 237.

34. Le Forestier, *Franc-Maçonnerie Templière*, p. 5; and Roberts, *Mythology*, p. 96. Several early leaders of the Scottish Rite might have come from Scotland, but even this point has never been substantiated. Moreover, Scottish ideas and traditions have nothing to do with Scottish Rite Masonry. Why this new Masonic system was called the Scottish rather than the French Rite has never been explained.

35. Le Forestier, *Franc-Maçonnerie Templière*, pp. 64–65; and Chevallier, *Histoire de la Franc-Maçonnerie Française*, pp. 81–82.

36. Chevalvier, *Histoire de la Franc-Maçonnerie Française*, pp. 111–114.

37. Alain Bernheim, "Règlements Généraux de 1743 et Statuts de 1755," *AHRF*, CXCVII (1969), 379–384.

38. Bernheim, "Règlements Généraux," 387–390; and Alain Le Bihan, *Franc-Maçons et Ateliers Parisiens de la Grande Loge de France au XVIIIe Siècle (1760–1795)* (Paris, 1973), pp. 393–401.

39. Le Bihan, *Franc-Maçons et Ateliers Parisiens*, pp. 402–406 and pp. 429–434.

40. Ibid., pp. 481–485.

41. Ibid., pp. 473–477.

42. Albert Pike, *Morals and Dogma* (Charleston, 1871), pp. 106–113.

43. Pike, *Morals and Dogma*, pp. 114–118; and Bernard Groethuysen, *The Bourgeois: Catholicism vs. Capitalism in Eighteenth Century France*, trans. Mary Ilford (New York: Holt, 1968), pp. 39–45.

44. Pike, *Morals and Dogma*, pp. 219–239.

45. Ibid., pp. 248–264.

46. Ibid., pp. 241–245.

47. Ibid., pp. 276–311.

48. J. Servier, "Utopie et Franc-Maçonnerie au XVIIIe Siècle," *AHRF*, CXCVII (1969), 409–413.

49. Chevallier, *Histoire de la Franc-Maçonnerie Française*, pp. 151–155; Findel, *History*, pp. 218–219; and Le Bihan, *Franc-Maçons et Ateliers Parisiens*, pp. 74–79.

50. Chevallier, *Histoire de la Franc-Maçonnerie Française*, pp. 172–177; and Martin, *Franc-Maçonnerie Française*, pp. 17–28.

51. Claude Helvétius was a major contributor to the French Enlightenment. In his major work *De l'esprit*, published in 1758,

Helvétius endorses the sensationalistic concepts of Locke, maintaining that sense perceptions enabled humans to acquire knowledge and to understand the laws of Nature. In this work, he also claims that public education was essential for the amelioration of French society. Although not a contributor to the *Encyclopédie*, Helvétius participated in the circle of Diderot and d'Holbach, thus being provided with the opportunity to interact with many Parisian *philosophes*. Helvétius too was quite active in Masonry and perceived the Craft as a significant vehicle of the Enlightenment. He established in 1766 the Parisian Lodge of Science and served as Master of this lodge until his death in 1771. On his philosophical ideas and educational views, see Albert Keim, *Helvétius: Sa Vie et Son Oeuvre* (Geneva, 1970), pp. 42–46; Irving Horowitz, *Claude Helvétius: Philosopher of Democracy and Enlightenment* (New York: Paine-Whitman, 1954), pp. 12–17; and D. W. Smith, *Helvétius: A Study in Persecution* (Oxford: Clarendon Press, 1965), pp. 11–13. On the involvement of Helvétius in the cultural group of d'Holbach, consult Kors, *Coterie*, p. 31 and p. 90. A short but important account of the role of Helvétius in Parisian Masonry is presented by Louis Amiable, *Une Loge Maçonnique D'Avant 1789* (Paris: Alcan, 1897), p. 10.

52. Amiable, *Loge Maçonnique*, pp. 14–15.

53. Ibid., p. 16.

54. Ibid., p. 18.

55. Chevallier, *Histoire de la Franc-Maçonnerie Française*, p. 280. Chevallier claims that the opponents of Lalande, for the most part, objected to the proposed name of the lodge.

56. Amiable, *Loge Maçonnique*, pp. 19–20.

57. Ibid., p. 32.

58. Ibid., p. 31.

59. Ibid., pp. 31–32.

60. Ibid., p. 30.

61. Ibid., pp. 33–34.

62. Ibid., p. 35. Amiable has included in his work the 1778 lodge roster. Franklin sent to the American Philosophical Society a listing of members from a meeting in 1780.

63. Ibid., p. 28.

64. Ibid., pp. 22–23.

65. Ibid., p. 22 and p. 26.

66. Ibid., pp. 26–28.

67. Ibid., p. 23; and Echeverria, *Mirage*, p. 59.

68. Amiable, *Loge Maçonnique*, pp. 45–63. Amiable wrote a confusing account to explain why Voltaire made the decision to apply to the Nine Sisters. He even failed to mention Parisian Masons of the Nine Sisters who knew Voltaire.

69. Hazard, *European Thought*, p. 271.

70. Amiable, *Loge Maçonnique*, pp. 53–54.

71. Ibid., pp. 65–66.

72. Ibid., p. 69.

73. Ibid., pp. 68–69.

74. Ibid., pp. 82–89.

75. Ibid., p. 132.

76. Constance Salm-Salm-Dyck, *Eloge Historique de Monsieur Lalande* (Paris: Sajou, 1810), pp. 16–22; and Helene Monod-Cassidy, "Un astronome-philosophe, Jerome Lalande," *Studies on Voltaire and the Eighteenth Century*, LVI (1967), 907–914.

77. Amiable, *Loge Maçonnique*, p. 133.

78. Ibid., p. 121 and p. 134.

79. Ibid., p. 134.

80. Paul W. Conner, *Poor Richard's Politicks* (New York: Oxford Press, 1965), p. 174 and pp.205–206; and Carl Van Doren, *Benjamin Franklin* (New York: Viking Press, 1964), pp. 156–162 and pp. 423–428.

81. Amiable, *Loge Maçonnique*, p. 137; and Esmond Wright, *Franklin of Philadelphia* (Cambridge: Belknap Press, 1986), pp. 321–322.

82. Amiable, *Loge Maçonnique*, pp. 143–144. Amiable and other historians have devoted minimal attention to the participation of Franklin in the Salon of Madame Helvétius.

82. Ibid., pp. 148–149.

84. Ibid., pp. 146–147.

85. Ibid., p. 24.

86. Echeverria, *Mirage*, p. 73.

87. Bernard Fay, *The Revolutionary Spirit in France and America*, trans. Ramon Guthrie (New York: Cooper Square Publications, 1966), p. 159.

88. Hilliard d'Auberteuil, *Essais historiques et politiques sur les Anglo-Americains* (Brussels, 1781), xiii-xiv and pp. 2–5.

89. Ibid., pp. 150–155.

90. Amiable, *Loge Maçonnique*, pp. 150–151.

91. Ibid., p. 152.

92. Amiable, *Loge Maçonnique*, p. 172; and Echeverria, *Mirage*, p. 171.

93. Amiable, *Loge Maçonnique*, pp. 172–173 and p. 175.

94. Ibid., pp. 159–176. Amiable describes the reform views of Dupaty and Pastoret, but mentions nothing about the cultural operations of the lodge during their Masterships.

95. Fay, *Revolutionary Spirit*, pp. 89-91; and Echeverria, *Mirage*, pp. 55–56.

96. Fay, *Revolutionary Spirit*, pp. 240–241; and Echeverria, *Mirage*, p. 133.

97. Amiable, *Loge Maçonnique*, p. 152 and pp. 189–190. Amiable explains that the journal of the Apollonian Society has never been found.

98. Ibid., pp. 191–193.

99. W. A. Smeaton, *Fourcroy: Chemist and Revolutionary* (Cambridge: Heffer, 1962), pp. 15–16.

100. Pilâtre de Rozier, *Premier Musée* (Paris, 1782), pp. 1–4.

101. Amiable, *Loge Maçonnique*, pp. 201–203. Amiable maintains that while teaching in the *lycée*, Condorcet, Marmontel, and La Harpe did not belong to the Nine Sisters.

102. Schofield, *Mechanism and Materialism*, p. 235.

103. Amiable, *Loge Maçonnique*, pp. 288–289; and Richard Herr, *The Eighteenth Century Revolution in Spain* (Princeton: Princeton University Press, 1969), pp. 228–229. The Spanish diplomat Count Pena Florida was not an active participant in the Nine Sisters, but attempted to recruit several members of the lodge to the faculty of the University of Madrid. Herr maintains that Pena Florida wanted enlighteners to become members of an international fraternity devoted to the welfare of humanity.

104. Edwin Smith, *Jean Sylvain Bailly: Astronomer, Mystic, Revolutionary* (Philadelphia: American Philosophical Society, 1954), pp. 454–455.

105. Smith, *Bailly*, pp. 429–432.

106. Ibid., pp. 436–437.

107. Ibid., p. 457.

108. Ibid., pp. 466–467.

109. Richard H. Shryock, *The Development of Modern Medicine: An Interpretation of the Social and Scientific Factors Involved* (New York: Hafner, 1969), pp. 152–157.

110. Amiable, *Loge Maçonnique*, p. 282.

111. Ibid., pp. 282–283.

112. Claude Lehec and Jean Cazeneuve (eds.), *Oeuvres Philosophiques de Cabanis* (Paris, 1956), I, 6–9; and Amiable, *Loge Maçonnique*, p. 291.

113. Lehec and Cazeneuve (eds.), *Oeuvres*, I, 137–138.

114. P. J. G. Cabanis, *Sketch of the Revolutions of Medical Science*, trans. A. Henderson (London: Johnson, 1806), pp. 4–6.

115. Cabanis, *Sketch of Revolutions*, pp. 10–12.

116. Ibid., pp. 297–299 and pp. 302–305. An explanation of the role of Cabanis in the Lodge of the Nine Sisters is offered by Martin S. Staum, *Cabanis: Enlightenment and Medical Philosophy in the French Revolution* (Princeton: Princeton University Press, 1980), pp. 18–19.

117. Smeaton, *Fourcroy*, pp. 191–192.

118. Ibid., pp. 25–26 and pp. 94–95.

119. Ibid,, pp. 125–126.

120. Ibid., p. 36.

121. Amiable, *Loge Maçonnique*, p. 295.

122. Claude Berthollet, *Essay on the New Method of Bleaching* (Edinburgh: Creech, 1790), pp. 21–23.

123. John Forster, *An Easy Method of Assaying and Classing Mineral Substances* (London: Dilly, 1772), pp. 2–6.

124. Amiable, *Loge Maçonnique*, p. 295. For a fine explanation of the flights of the Montgolfiers, see Charles C. Gillispie, *The Montgolfier Brothers and the Invention of Aviation, 1783–1784* (Princeton: Princeton University Press, 1983), pp. 3–7, pp. 10–17, pp. 21–24, pp. 44–47, and pp. 118–120.

125. Ibid., pp. 92–93.

126. Ibid., pp. 329–331.

127. Anita Brookner, *Greuze* (Greenwich: New York Graphic Society, 1972), pp. 51–63.

128. Brookner, *Greuze*, p. 64.

129. Ibid., p. 80.

130. Levey, *Rococo to Revolution*, pp. 149–151.

131. Amiable, *Loge Maçonnique*, pp. 333–334.

132. Ibid., pp. 346–350.

133. Ibid., p. 344.

134. Ibid., p. 316 and pp. 326–327.

135. Ibid., p. 309.

136. Ibid., p. 310.

137. Louis Amiable, "Un Poeme Revolutionnaire en 1779: 'Les Mois' de Roucher," *La Révolution française*, XXIX (1895), 246.

138. Amiable, *Loge Maçonnique*, p. 316.

139. Ibid., p. 303.

140. Ibid., p. 304.

141. Jean Gaulmier, *Volney* (Paris: Hachette, 1959), pp. 21–23; and C. F. Volney, *The Ruins*, trans. Peter Eckler (New York: Truth Seeker, 1913), pp. 110–118 and pp. 184–202.

142. Court de Gébelin, *Histoire Naturelle De La Parole* (Paris: Boudet, 1776), p. 2.

143. Gébelin, *Parole*, pp. 15–18.

144. Ibid., pp. 19–23.

145. Court de Gébelin, *Monde Primitif* (Paris: Boudet, 1773), I, i.

146. Gébelin, *Monde Primitif*, I, ii–iii.

147. Ibid., I, 307–308.

148. Ibid., I, 306.

149. Ibid., I, 319–324.

150. Frank Manuel, *The Eighteenth Century Confronts the Gods*, pp. 250–254; and Count Albon, *Eloge de Court de Gébelin* (Paris: Moutard, 1785), pp. 4–9.

151. Echeverria, *Mirage*, pp. 106–108.

152. Abbé Robin, *Nouveau voyage dans l'Amérique Septentrionale* (Paris: 1782), pp. 13–17.

153. Echeverria, *Mirage*, pp. 114–115.

154. J. P. Brissot, *Nouveau Voyage* (Paris, 1788), pp. 312–313.

155. Amiable, *Loge Maçonnique*, pp. 310–311; and Echeverria, *Mirage*, p. 123.

156. Amiable, *Loge Maçonnique*, p. 311.

157. Echeverria, *Mirage*, pp. 19–20. For the views of members of the Nine Sisters about America, see R. William Weisberger, "Benjamin Franklin: A Masonic Enlightener in Paris," *Pennsylvania History*, LIII (1986), 165–180.

158. Amiable, *Loge Maçonnique*, pp. 300–301; and Henry Majewski, *The Preromantic Imagination of L. S. Mercier* (New York: Humanities Press, 1971), pp. 10–17.

159. Amiable, *Loge Maçonnique*, pp. 206–207.

160. Gay, *Enlightenment: Freedom*, II, 438–443.

161. Amiable, *Loge Maçonnique*, pp. 214–222.

162. Ibid., pp. 177–179.

163. Claude Pastoret, *Des Loix Pénales* (Paris, 1790), I, 1–4 and 21–23.

164. Pastoret, *Loix*, I, 60–63.

165. Ibid., I, 38–43.

166. Amiable, *Loge Maçonnique*, p. 181.

167. Some members of the Nine Sisters espoused moderate republican ideas, supported the Girondin, and participated in the affairs of the National Assembly.

168. Amiable, *Loge Maçonnique*, pp. 179–180.

169. Ibid., pp. 182–184. The Lodge of the Nine Sisters was reestablished in 1805, but its cultural operations were of minimal importance. Connections between Freemasonry and the French Revolution are explored by Lynn Hunt, *Politics, Culture, and Class in the French Revolution* (Berkeley: University of California Press, 1984), pp. 199–203; and by Gary Kates, *The Cercle Social, the Girondins, and the French Revolution* (Princeton: Princeton University Press, 1985), pp. 89–92.

Notes to Chapter IV

1. There probably are similarities between the tenets of Masonry and the ideas of the seventeenth century Bohemian philosopher Comenius. In *The Way of Light*, published in 1668, Comenius speaks of the teachings of the ancient Hermes Trismegistus, stresses the importance of classifying the knowledge of Nature, and proposes universal education. Comenius also favored the creation of a society in which philosophers and scientists would record knowledge in the *Book of Pansophia*. For the views of Comenius, see Frances Yates, *The Rosicrucian Enlightenment* (London: Rutledge and Kegan, 1972), pp. 179–180; and Matthew Spinka, *John Amos Comenius: That Incomparable Moravian* (Chicago: Chicago University Press, 1943), pp. 78–79.

2. Robert J. Kerner, *Bohemia in the Eighteenth Century* (New York: Ams Press, 1969), p. 315. Kerner claims that Masonic lodges in Prague helped to promote the doctrine of religious toleration and worked to create secular schools.

3. Abafi, *Freimaurerei*, I, 49.

4. Ibid., I, 50.

5. Abafi, *Freimaurerei*, I, 51; and Heinrich Benedikt, *Franz Anton Graf Sporck (1662–1738)* (Vienna, 1923), pp. 227–232. Sporck served as Master of the Three Stars Lodge until 1729.

6. Street, *Symbolism*, pp. 105–107.

7. Mackey, *Symbolism of Freemasonry*, p. 95 and p. 163.

8. Street, *Symbolism*, pp. 68–71.

9. Benedikt, *Sporck*, pp. 236–238.

10. Ibid., p. 238.

11. Ibid,, pp. 16–29 and pp. 239–240.

12. Abafi, *Freimaurerei*, I, 42-48.

13. Ibid., I, 49.

14. Ibid., I, 50–52.

15. Ibid,, I, 53–55.

16. Findel, *History*, pp. 274–275.

17. Abafi, *Freimaurerei*, I, 220-221.

18. Ibid., I, 222–225.

19. Pike, *Morals and Dogma*, pp. 219–239 and pp. 248–264.

20. Pike, *Morals and Dogma*, pp. 276–311. Delegates attending the Strict Observance Convention at Kohlo in 1772 agreed that their lodges should confer the Templar Degree of Stark rather than that of Hund. For a discussion of the Templar Degree of Stark, see Abafi, *Freimaurerei*, I, 226–227.

21. Ibid., II, 108–110.

22. Ibid., II, 111–112.

23. Ibid., I, 181.

24. Abafi, *Freimaurerei*, II, 108–109; and Constantin Wurzbach, *Biographisches Lexicon des Kaiserthums Oesterreich* (Vienna, 1856), II, 382–383.

25. Abafi, *Freimaurerei*, III, 6–10.

26. Ibid., III, 12–13.

27. Findel, *History*, pp. 281–283.

28. Abafi, *Freimaurerei*, I, 64–68.

29. Street, *Symbolism*, p. 62, p. 106, and p.144.

30. Ibid., p. 147.

31. Street, *Symbolism*, p. 87; and Mackey, *Symbolism of Freemasonry*, pp. 163–164.

32. Abafi, *Freimaurerei*, I, 71–73.

33. Ibid., I, 74.

34. Ibid., I, 78–79 and 82–83.

35. Ibid., I, 84–87.

36. Ibid., I, 95–99.

37. Ibid., I, 100–101.

38. Ibid., I, 102–103.

39. Ibid., I, 109–110.

40. Ibid., I, 113–119.

41. Ibid., I, 123–125.

42. Ibid., I, 127–131.

43. Ibid., III, 103–107.

44. Pike, *Morals and Dogma*, pp. 219–239 and pp. 248–264.

45. Abafi, *Freimaurerei*, I, 238–240.

46. Ibid., III, 89–92.

47. Ibid., III, 93–94.

48. Ibid., III, 146–148. Schmidburg was a lieutenant in the imperial army.

49. Ibid., II, 180–184.

50. Ibid., II, 185–187.

51. Ibid., II, 218–221.

52. Wurzbach, *Lexicon*, I, 143–144; Ibid., IV, 104; and Ibid., XII, 324–325.

53. Abafi, *Freimaurerei*, II, 224–229. Although there were no Viennese lodges by 1782 under its jurisdiction, Strict Observance Masonry until its gradual disappearance in the late 1780s continued to operate in other cities in Eastern Europe.

54. Abafi, *Freimaurerei*, IV, 65–66; and Findel, *History*, pp. 292–295.

55. Abafi, *Freimaurerei*, IV, 67; Bernard, *Jesuits and Jacobins*, p. 74.

56. Findel, *History*, pp. 298–300.

57. Heinrich Boos, *Geschichte der Freimaurerei* (Aarau, 1906), pp. 311–317; and Street, *Symbolism*, p. 62 and p. 87.

58. Heinrich Schneider, *Lessing: Zwolf Biographische Studien* (Berne: Francke, 1951), pp. 166–167; and Henry E. Allison, *Lessing and the Enlightenment* (Ann Arbor: Michigan University Press, 1966), pp. 135–136. Lessing, who belonged to the Hamburg Lodge of the Three Golden Roses, presented his views of Masonry in *Ernst und Falk*, a work first published in 1778.

59. G. E. Lessing, *Werke* (Berlin, 1962), II, 719–721.

60. Abafi, *Freimaurerei*, IV, 208–211 and 215; and Wurzbach, *Lexicon*, LVIII, 143–146.

61. Wurzbach, *Lexicon*, I, 171–173.

62. Abafi, *Freimaurerei*, IV, 205 and 213.

63. Paul Bernard, "The *Philosophe* as Public Servant: Tobias Gebler," *East European Quarterly*, VII (1973), 41–43.

64. Abafi, *Freimaurerei*, IV, 327–328.

65. Ibid., IV, 329.

66. Ibid., IV, 332–333.

67. Bernard, *Jesuits and Jacobins*, pp. 58–59 and pp. 68–69.

68. Ibid., pp. 110–113.

69. Abafi, *Freimaurerei*, IV, 239–240 and 263; and Erwin F. Ritter, *Johann Baptist von Alxinger and the Austrian Enlightenment* (Berne: Lang, 1970), p. 41.

70. Ritter, *Alxinger and the Austrian Enlightenment*, p. 18.

71. Abafi, *Freimaurerei*, IV, 228–229 and 239–240. There were approximately twenty-two military men and thirteen merchants associated with the St. Joseph Lodge.

72. Ibid., IV, 255.

73. Abafi, *Freimaurerei*, IV, 262–264; and Wurzbach, *Lexicon*, II, 118–119.

74. Ritter, *Alxinger and the Austrian Enlightenment*, p. 17 and p. 125.

75. Bernard, *Jesuits and Jacobins*, pp. 96–99 and pp. 131–132.

76. Bernard, *Jesuits and Jacobins*, pp. 84–85; and O'Brien, *Ideas of Religious Toleration*, pp. 67–68.

77. Bernard, *Jesuits and Jacobins*, p. 84; and Ritter, *Alxinger and the Austrian Enlightenment*, p. 38.

78. Ritter, *Alxinger and the Austrian Enlightenment*, pp. 125–126.

79. Johann Alxinger, "Prophezeihung," *Wiener Musenalmanach (1788)*, 31–36.

80. Abafi, *Freimaurerei*, IV, 278.

81. Ibid., IV, 279–280. For a study of this lodge, see R. William Weisberger, "The True Harmony Lodge: A Mecca of Masonry and the Enlightenment in Josephinian Vienna," *East European Quarterly*, XX (1986), 129–140.

82. Ibid., IV, 280–282.

83. Ibid., IV, 283–284.

84. Ibid., IV, 285.

85. Ibid., IV, 286.

86. Nettl, *Mozart and Masonry*, pp. 50–51.

87. Bernard, *Jesuits and Jacobins*, p. 76.

88. Robert Keil, *Wiener Freunde* (Vienna: Konegen, 1883), pp. 2–4.

89. Abafi, *Freimaurerei*, IV, 310.

90. Bernard, *Jesuits and Jacobins*, pp. 32–33 and pp. 36–39.

91. Kann, *Austrian Intellectual History*, pp. 181–190.

92. Abafi, *Freimaurerei*, IV, 311.

93. Ibid., IV, 287–289.

94. Barbel Becker-Cantarino, *Aloys Blumauer and the Literature of Austrian Enlightenment* (Berne: Lang, 1973), pp. 3–9.

95. Alois Blumauer, "Vorerinnerung," *Journal für Freymaurer*, I (1784), Part 1, 3–14. This journal hereafter is cited as *JFM*. Blumauer began in 1783 to collect materials for the first volume of the lodge literary journal, but this volume was not published until the following year.

96. "Antediluvian Masons" believed that the story of Noah and the Great Flood rather than that of Adam and Eve explained the origins of the Earth. See Jones, *Freemasons' Compendium*, pp. 314–316.

97. Schneer (ed.), *A History of Geology*, pp. 128–141.

98. Torbern Bergman, *Outlines of Mineralogy*, trans. William Withering (Birmingham: Piercy and Jones, 1783), pp. 9–10.

99. Bergman, *Mineralogy*, pp. 17–36.

100. Letter of July 29, 1778 from Born to Bergman appearing in Gote Carlid and Johan Nordstrom (eds.), *Torbern Bergman's Foreign Correspondence* (Stockholm: Almqvist and Wiskell, 1965), p. 7.

101. Letter of April 2, 1780 from Born to Bergman in *Bergman's Correspondence*, p. 9.

102. Peter Pallas, "Schreiben aus St. Petersburg," *Physikalische Arbeiten der Einträchtigen Freunde in Wien*, I (1783), 1–7. This journal hereafter is cited as *PAEF*.

103. Wurzbach, *Lexicon*, X, 266.

104. Joseph Raab, "Über die gallizischen Salzen," *PAEF*, II (1784), 62–67.

105. Karl Haidinger, "Verzeichnis in den Wielickaer Salzwerken," *PAEF*, III (1785), 9–18.

106. Andreas Stütz, "Die Mineralgeschichte von Oesterreich," *PAEF*, I (1783), 77–92.

107. Johann B. Ruprecht, "Schreiben ueber das rothliche Ganggestein," *PAEF*, I (1783), 68–73.

108. Johann B. Ruprecht, "Zergleiderung und Beschaffenheit der nächsten Bestandtheile eines zu Nagyág," *PAEF*, II (1784), 54–56.

109. Johann Muller, "Versuche ueber den Spiesglastonige," *PAEF*, I (1783), 63–68.

110. Johann Muller, "Der Versuche in dem Sebirge Faczebay," *PAEF*, III (1785), 36–39.

111. Wurzbach, *Lexicon*, IX, 159.

112. Johann Hunczovsky, *Medicinisch Chirurgische* (Vienna: Graffer, 1783), pp. 29–31 and pp. 41–42.

113. Wurzbach, *Lexicon*, XIV, 266–268.

114. Abbé Jacquet, *Précis De L'Electricité* (Vienna: Trattner, 1775), pp. 8–10 and pp. 217–224.

115. Joseph von Retzer, *Physikalische Abhandlung von den Eigenschasten des Donners* (Vienna: Trattner, 1772), pp. 3–7 and pp. 27–31.

116. Philip C. Ritterbush, *Overtures to Biology: The Speculations of Eighteenth-Century Biology* (New Haven: Yale University Press, 1964), pp. 58–59 and pp. 156–159 presented an illuminating account about the application of electricity to the study of biology and geology.

117. Alois Blumauer, "Gesundheit auf den Kaiser," *JFM*, II (1785), Part 1, 193–194.

118. Alois Blumauer, "Es leben unsre sehr ehrwürd Schwester Logen," *JFM*, I (1784), Part 3, 212.

119. Alois Blumauer, "Rede uber die Leiden und Freuden des menschlichen Lebens," *JFM*, I (1784), Part 2, 159–161.

120. O'Brien, *Ideas of Religious Toleration*, p. 62.

121. Ibid., pp. 63–64.

122. Robert Keil, *Aus Klassischer Zeit: Wieland und Reinhold* (Leipzig, 1890), pp. 5–8.

123. Karl Reinhold, *"Mönchthum und Maureren," JFM*, II (1785), Part 1, 166–169, 176–178, and 184–187.

124. Keil, *Aus Zeit*, pp. 17–19.

125. Ritter, *Alxinger and the Austrian Enlightenment*, pp. 17–18.

126. J. F. Ratschky, *Gedichte* (Vienna: Graffer, 1791), pp. 120–121.

127. Ignatz von Born, "Ueber die Mysterien der Aegyptier," *JFM*, I (1784), Part 1, 17–19.

128. Born, "Ueber die Mysterien," 22–46 and 86–97. Excellent chapters about the Osiris Cult appear in R. T. Clark, *Myth and Symbol in Ancient Egypt* (London: Thames and Hudson, 1978), pp. 97–180.

129. Ignatz von Born, "Ueber die Mysterien der alten hëbraet," *JFM*, III (1786), Part 1, 8 and 28–29.

130. Born, "Ueber die Mysterien der alten hëbraet," 30–33.

131. Ignatz von Born, "Geschichte des Pythägoraischen Bundes," *JFM*, II (1785), Part 1, 13–16.

132. Ignatz von Born, "Ueber die Magie der alten Perser," *JFM*, I (1784), Part 3, 30–34.

133. Count Schittelsberg, "Ueber das Zeremoniel," *JFM*, I (1784), Part 2, 105–107.

134. Schittelsberg, "Ueber das Zeremoniel," 105–107.

135. Andreas Stütz, "Ueber die Reisen des Maurers," *JFM*, I (1784), Part 3, 158–159.

136. Stütz, "Ueber die Reisen des Maurers," 158–159.

137. Joseph von Retzer, "Ueber die Wohlthätigkeit des Maurers," *JFM*, I (1784), Part 2, 171–178.

138. Alois Blumauer, "Zuge maurerischer Wohlthätigkeit," *JFM*, II (1785), Part 4, 201–207.

139. Joseph von Retzer, "Ueber die Harmonie," *JFM*, II (1785), Part 2, 175–181.

140. Alois Blumauer, "Ueber den Kosmopolitismus des Maurers," *JFM*, II (1785), Part 3, 114–117.

141. Nettl, *Mozart and Masonry*, pp. 42–43.

142. Karl Geiringer, *Haydn: A Creative Life in Music* (Berkeley: California University Press, 1968), p. 93.

143. Geiringer, *Haydn*, p. 93.

144. Nettl, *Mozart and Masonry*, p. 15.

145. Ibid., p. 17.

146. Ibid., pp. 46–47.

147. Ibid., pp. 47–48.

148. Ibid., p. 57.

149. Ibid., p. 68 and p. 73.

150. Jacques Chailley, *The Magic Flute, Masonic Opera*, trans. Herbert Weinstock (New York: Knopf, 1971), pp. 184–186 and pp. 226–232.

151. Chailley, *Magic Flute*, pp. 138–145.

152. Boos, *Geschichte der Freimaurerei*, pp. 354–356.

153. Ernst Wangermann, *From Joseph II to the Jacobin Trials: Government Policy and Public Opinion in the Habsburg Dominions in the Period of the French Revolution* (New York: Oxford University Press, 1969), pp. 36–43.

154. Roberts, *Mythology*, pp. 212–213.

155. Klaus Epstein, *The Genesis of German Conservatism* (Princeton: Princeton University Press, 1966), pp. 517–526; and Roberts, *Mythology*, pp. 214–216.

156. Epstein, *German Conservatism*, pp. 87–90.

157. Ibid., pp. 91–92.

158. Leopold Engel, *Geschichte des Illuminaten-Ordens* (Berlin, 1906), pp. 192–194 and pp. 201–204.

159. Saul K. Padover, *The Revolutionary Emperor: Joseph the Second* (New York: Ballou, 1933), p. 265.

160. Wangermann, *Joseph II to the Jacobin Trials*, p. 36.

161. Johann Alxinger, "Ueber Maurerintoleranz," *JFM*, II (1785), Part 4, 29–32.

162. Keil, *Wiener Freunde*, pp. 60–61.

163. Abafi, *Freimaurerei*, IV, 162–163.

164. Ibid., IV, 165–167.

165. Bernard, *Jesuits and Jacobins*, pp. 64–65; and Wangermann, *Joseph II to the Jacobin Trials*, pp. 137–149.

Notes to Chapter V

1. Robbins, *English-Speaking Freemasonry*, pp. 33-37.

2. Findel, *History*, pp. 200–203; and Roberts, *Mythology*, pp. 31–33.

3. Jones, *Freemasons' Compendium*, pp. 193–198.

4. Epstein, *German Conservatism*, pp. 90–94 and pp. 104–107.

5. McBride, *Speculative Freemasonry*, pp. 36–39.

6. Kramnick, *Bolingbroke and His Circle*, pp. 39–48 and pp. 56–62; and Thompson, *Whigs and Hunters*, pp. 197–198.

7. Ford, *Robe and Sword*, pp. 235–238.

8. Schofield, *Mechanism and Materialism*, pp. 7–13.

9. Shryock, *Development of Modern Medicine*, p. 68.

10. Brechka, *Gerard van Swieten*, pp. 78–92.

11. Thackray, *Atoms and Powers*, pp. 270–271.

12. Mornet, *French Thought in the Eighteenth Century*, pp. 60–62.

13. Wangermann, *Austrian Achievement*, pp. 136–147.

14. Nicolson, *Science and Imagination*, pp. 213–215.

15. Lough, *Eighteenth Century France*, pp. 283–286.

16. Grout, *History of Western Music*, pp. 302–305.

17. Mona Ozouf, *La Fête revolutionnaire* (Paris: Gallimard, 1976), pp. 333–335.

18. Clarke, "The Royal Society and Freemasonry," 110–117.

19. Clarke, "The Medical Profession and Freemasonry," 298–302.

BIBLIOGRAPHY

A. Masonic Bibliographies and Catalogues

Several Masonic library catalogues were consulted for the prepa-
ration of my work. These catalogues list very few primary materials
about eighteenth century Masonry, but refer to many histories published about the Craft. Sir Algernon Tudor-Craig published a *Catalogue of the United Grand Lodge of England* (London, 1938). This
work is indispensable for Masonic researchers, listing significant studies in the Grand Lodge of England Library about eighteenth century
British, French, and Habsburg Masonry. Most of the works found in
Tudor-Craig about eighteenth century Masonry are listed in the *Catalogues of the Library of the Grand Lodge of Iowa* (Iowa City, 1878–)
and in the *Masonic Catalogue of the Library of the Grand Lodge of
Pennsylvania* (Philadelphia, 1881). A survey of the *Catalogue de la
bibliothèque du Grand Orient de France* (Paris, 1879) indicates that
few primary sources have been published regarding eighteenth century
Parisian Masonry. This catalogue, however, refers to dated histories
of French Masonry during the eighteenth century. No comprehensive
catalogues or bibliographies have been published about eighteenth
century Viennese and Prague Masonry. What is needed are contemporary catalogues and bibliographies concerning English, French, and
Habsburg Masonry.

Several dated bibliographies list materials about secret societies
and Freemasonry. M. E. Jouin and V. Descreux published *Bibliographie Occultiste et Maçonnique* (Paris, 1930). This bibliography
refers to few works about eighteenth century Masonry, but emphasizes primary and secondary materials about the Rosicrucians. James
Hughan, *Masonic Bibliography* (London: Kenning, 1896) mentions
numerous nineteenth century works about Modern and Antient Masonry in eighteenth century England. Hughan only mentions several

studies about French and Habsburg Masonry. August Wolfsteig, *Bibliographie der freimaurerischen Literatur* (3 vols., Leipzig, 1911–1913) has published the most comprehensive reference tool concerning the Craft. This topically arranged work for the most part lists primary and secondary sources about Masonic lodges and rites during the eighteenth and nineteenth centuries. Some works mentioned by Wolfsteig were helpful for the writing of this work.

B. General Titles

Adams, Frank D. *The Birth and Development of the Geological Sciences.* New York: Dover Books, 1938.

Albanese, Catherine T. *Sons of the Fathers: The Civil Religion of the American Revolution.* Philadelphia: Temple University Press, 1976.

Anchor, Robert. *The Enlightenment Tradition.* New York: Harper and Row, 1967.

Anderson, M. S. *Historians and Eighteenth-Century Europe, 1715–1789.* Oxford: Clarendon Press, 1979.

Bellah, Robert N. *Beyond Belief: Essays on Religion in a Post-Traditional World.* New York: Harper and Row, 1970.

——. *The Broken Covenant: American Civil Religion in Time of Trial.* New York: Seabury Press, 1975.

Benimeli, José Antonio Ferrer. *Masoneria, Iglesia e Illustración. Inquisición: Procesos históricos (1739–1750).* Madrid: Fundación Universitaria Espanola, 1976.

——. *Masoneria, Iglesia e Illustración. Las bases de un conflicto (1700–1739).* Madrid: Fundación Universitaria Espanola, 1976.

Boas, Marie. *The Scientific Renaissance.* New York: Harper Torchbooks, 1962.

Boos, H. *Geschichte der Freimaurerei.* Aarau, 1906.

Burtt, Edwin. *The Metaphysical Foundations of Modern Science.* Garden City: Anchor Books, 1954.

Cajori, Florian. *A History of Physics.* New York: Dover Books, 1962.

Carnes, Mark C. *Secret Ritual and Manhood in Victorian America.* New Haven: Yale University Press, 1989.

Carter, James. *Masonry in Texas.* Waco: Masonic Education Service for the Grand Lodge of Texas, 1955.

Cassirer, Ernst. *The Philosophy of the Enlightenment.* Boston: Beacon Press, 1955.

____. *The Philosophy of Symbolic Forms.* Trans. Ralph Mannheim. 3 vols. New Haven: Yale University Press, 1953–1957.

Chalkin, C. W., and M. A. Havinden, eds. *Rural Change and Urban Growth, 1500–1800.* London, 1974.

Clark, R. T. *Myth and Symbol in Ancient Egypt.* London: Thames and Hudson, 1978.

Clawson, Mary Ann. *Constructing Brotherhood: Class, Gender, and Fraternalism.* Princeton: Princeton University Press, 1989.

Cobban, Alfred. *In Search of Humanity: the Role of the Enlightenment in Modern History.* London, 1960.

Cohen, I. Bernard. *The Birth of a New Physics.* Garden City: Anchor Books, 1960.

Coil, Henry W. *Freemasonry Through Six Centuries.* 2 vols. Fulton: Bell Press, 1966 and 1967.

Cragg, Gerald R. *The Church and the Age of Reason (1648–1789).* Baltimore: Pelican Books, 1960.

Dijksterhuis, E. J. *The Mechanisation of the World Picture.* Oxford: Clarendon Press, 1961.

Eisenstein, Elizabeth L. *The Printing Press as an Agent of Change: Communications and Cultural Transformation in Early Modern Europe.* 2 vols. New York: Cambridge University Press, 1979.

Findel, J. G. *History of Freemasonry.* Trans. Murray Lyon. London: Asher, 1869.

Forbes, R. J., and E. J. Dijksterhuis. *A History of Science and Technology.* 2 vols. Baltimore: Penguin Books, 1963.

Gay, Peter. *The Enlightenment: An Interpretation, The Rise of Modern Paganism.* New York: Random House, 1966.

____. *The Enlightenment: An Interpretation, The Science of Freedom.* New York: Knopf, 1969.

Geikie, Sir Archibald. *The Founders of Geology.* New York: Dover Books, 1962.

Gerbi, Antonello. *The Dispute of the New World: The History of a Polemic, 1750–1900.* Trans. Jeremy Moyle. Pittsburgh: University of Pittsburgh Press, 1973.

Gershoy, Leo. *From Despotism to Revolution.* New York: Harper Torchbooks, 1944.

Gillispie, Charles. *The Edge of Objectivity.* Princeton: Princeton University Press, 1967.

Goodwin, Albert, ed. *The European Nobility in the Eighteenth Century.* New York: Harper Torchbooks, 1967.

Gould, Robert. *The History of Freemasonry.* New York: Yorston, 1885.

Grout, Donald, *A History of Western Music.* New York: Norton, 1973.

Hausknecht, Murray. *The Joiners: A Sociological Description of Voluntary Association Membership in the United States.* New York: Bedminster Press, 1962.

Haywood, H. L. *Symbolical Masonry.* Washington: Masonic Service Association, 1923.

Herr, Richard. *The Eighteenth Century Revolution in Spain.* Princeton: Princeton University Press, 1969.

Hobsbawm, E. J. *Primitive Rebels: Studies of Archaic Forms of Social Movement in the 19th and 20th Centuries.* New York: Norton, 1959.

Jacob, Margaret C. *Living the Enlightenment: Freemasonry and Politics in Eighteenth Century Europe.* New York: Oxford University Press, 1991.

――――. *The Cultural Meaning of the Scientific Revolution.* New York: Knopf, 1988.

――――. *The Radical Enlightenment: Pantheists, Freemasons, and Republicans.* London: Allen and Unwin, 1981.

Jones, Richard F. *Ancients and Moderns.* St. Louis: Washington University Press, 1961.

Katz, Jacob. *Jews and Freemasons in Europe.* Trans. Leonard Oschry. Cambridge: Harvard University Press, 1970.

Kearney, Hugh. *Science and Change.* New York: McGraw-Hill Company, 1971.

Koyré, Alexander. *From the Closed World to the Infinite Universe.* Baltimore: The Johns Hopkins University Press, 1957.

Landes, David. *The Unbound Prometheus: Technological Change and Industrial Development in Western Europe from 1750 to the Present.* Cambridge: Cambridge University Press, 1969.

Lang, Paul H. *Music in Western Civilization.* New York: Norton, 1941.

Lennhoff, Eugen. *The Freemasons.* Trans. Einar Frame. London: Lewis, 1978.

Lipson, Dorothy. *Freemasonry in Federalist Connecticut.* Princeton: Princeton University Press, 1977.

Mackey, Albert. *The History of Freemasonry.* Vol. IV. New York: Masonic History Company, 1898.

_____. *Symbolism of Freemasonry*. Chicago: Powner, 1975.

Mason, Stephen. *A History of the Sciences*. New York: Collier Books, 1962.

McBride, A. S. *Speculative Freemasonry*. Richmond: Macoy, 1924.

McLoughlin, William G., and Robert N. Bellah, eds. *Religion in America*. New York: Houghton and Mifflin, 1968.

Muraskin, William. *Middle-Class Blacks in a White-Society*. Berkeley: California University Press, 1975.

Newton, Joseph F. *The Three Degrees and Great Symbols of Masonry*. Washington: Masonic Service Association, 1924.

Nordenskiöld, Erik. *The History of Biology*. Trans. Leonard Eyre. New York: Tudor, 1936.

Nussbaum, Frederick. *The Triumph of Science and Reason*. New York: Harper Torchbooks, 1953.

Ornstein, Martha. *The Role of Scientific Societies in the Seventeenth Century*. Chicago: Chicago University Press, 1913.

Owen, John B. *The Eighteenth Century: 1714–1815*. New York: Norton, 1976.

Pike, Albert. *Morals and Dogma*. Charleston, 1871.

Ritterbush, Philip C. *Overtures to Biology: The Speculations of Eighteenth Century Naturalists*. New Haven: Yale University Press, 1964.

Roberts, J. M. *The Mythology of the Secret Societies*. London: Secker and Warburg, 1972.

Roberts, Penfield. *The Quest for Security*. New York: Harper Torchbooks, 1947.

Schneer, Cecil J., ed. *Toward a History of Geology*. Cambridge: M.I.T. Press, 1969.

Schofield, Robert E. *Mechanism and Materialism: British Natural Philosophy in an Age of Reason*. Princeton: Princeton University Press, 1970.

Shorr, Philip. *Science and Superstition in the Eighteenth Century*. New York: Columbia University Press, 1932.

Shryock, Richard H. *The Development of Modern Medicine: An Interpretation of the Social and Scientific Factors Involved*. New York: Hafner, 1969.

Singer, Charles. *A Short History of Scientific Ideas*. Oxford: Clarendon Press, 1959.

Smith, Preserved. *The Enlightenment, 1687–1776*. New York: Holt, 1934.

Steinmetz, George. *The Lost Word: Its Hidden Meaning.* Richmond: Macoy, 1953.

———. *The Royal Arch: Its Hidden Meaning.* Richmond: Macoy, 1946.

Street, Oliver. *Symbolism of the Three Degrees.* Washington: Masonic Service Association, 1922.

Stromberg, Roland. *An Intellectual History of Modern Europe.* New York: Meredith, 1966.

Tiger, Lionel. *Men in Groups.* New York: Vintage Books, 1969.

Tiryakian, Edward, ed. *On the Margin of the Visible: Sociology, the Visible, and the Occult.* New York: Wiley and Sons, 1974.

Venturi, Franco. *Italy and the Enlightenment.* New York: Longman, 1972.

———. *Utopia and Reform in the Enlightenment.* Cambridge: Cambridge University Press, 1971.

Webster, Nesta. *Secret Societies and Subversive Movements.* London, 1924.

Weisberger, Richard William. "The Cultural and Organizational Functions of Speculative Freemasonry During the Enlightenment: A Study of the Craft in London, Paris, Prague, and Vienna." Ph.D. dissertation, University of Pittsburgh, 1980.

Wilson, John F. *Public Religion in American Culture.* Philadelphia: Temple University Press, 1979.

Wolf, Abraham. *A History of Science, Technology, and Philosophy in the Eighteenth Century.* London: Unwin Brothers, 1939.

Yates, Frances. *The Rosicrucian Enlightenment.* London: Routledge and Kegan, 1972.

C. Works Concerning Eighteenth Century English History and Masonry

1. Primary Sources

Bradley, James. "A New Apparent Motion Discovered in the Fixed Stars." *The Abridged Transactions of the Royal Society of London,* XXXIII (1723), 308–309.

———. "Observations on the Comet that Appeared in 1723." *The Abridged Transactions of the Royal Society of London,* XXXIII (1724), 13–15.

Clare, Martin. *The Motion of Fluids, Natural and Artificial.* 3rd ed. London: Ward, 1747.

Cohen, I. Bernard, ed. *Isaac Newton: Papers and Letters on Natural Philosophy and Related Documents.* Cambridge: Harvard University Press, 1958.

Desaguliers, J. T. "An Account of a Book entitled Vegetable Statistics." *The Abridged Transactions of the Royal Society of London,* XXXIV (1727), 188–191.

____. "An Account of An Experiment to Prove an Interspersed Vacuum." *The Abridged Transactions of the Royal Society of London,* XXX (1717), 321–322.

____. "An Account of Experiments Concerning the Running of Water in Pipes." *The Abridged Transactions of the Royal Society of London,* XXXIV (1726), 137–140.

____. "An Account of A Machine for Changing the Air of Sick People." *The Abridged Transactions of the Royal Society of London,* XXXIX (1735), 12–13.

____. "An Account of Some Experiments on Lights and Colors." *The Abridged Transactions of the Royal Society of London,* XXIX (1716), 229–239.

____. "An Account of Some Experiments to find how much the resistance of the Air retards falling Bodies." *The Abridged Transactions of the Royal Society of London,* XXX (1719), 428–431.

____. "An Attempt to Account for the Rising and Falling of the Water on Some Ponds Near the Sea." *The Abridged Transactions of the Royal Society of London,* XXXIII, (1724), 39–41.

____. *A Course of Experimental Philosophy.* 2 vols. London: Senex, 1734–1744.

____. "A Description of An Engine to Raise Water by the Help of Quicksilver." *The Abridged Transactions of the Royal Society of London,* XXXII (1722), 550–555.

____. "A Dissertation Concerning the Figure of the Earth." *The Abridged Transactions of the Royal Society of London,* XXXIII (1724), 61–69.

____. "An examination of Perault's Axis in Peritrochio." *The Abridged Transactions of the Royal Society of London,* XXXVI (1730), 377–381.

____. "An Experiment before the Royal Society to show that Bodies of the Same Bulk do not contain equal quantities of Matter in an Interspersed Vacuum." *The Abridged Transactions of the Royal Society of London,* XXXI (1720), 480–481.

____. "An Experiment explaining a Mechanical Paradox." *The*

Abridged Transactions of the Royal Society of London, XXXVII (1731), 482–484.

———. "Experiments to Prove that the Force of Moving Bodies is Proportionable to their Velocities." *The Abridged Transactions of the Royal Society of London*, XXXII (1723), 632–637.

———. "How damp or Foul Air may be drawn from Mines." *The Abridged Transactions of the Royal Society of London*, XXXV (1727), 208–210.

———. *Lectures of Experimental Philosophy.* London: Mears, 1719.

———. "A New Contrivance For Taking Levels." *The Abridged Transactions of the Royal Society of London*, XXXIII (1724), 49–53.

———. "Observations on the Crane with Improvements." *The Abridged Transactions of the Royal Society of London*, XXXVI (1729), 369–374.

———. "Remarks on Perpetual Motion." *The Abridged Transactions of the Royal Society of London*, XXXI (1721), 542–544.

———. "The Rise of Vapours, the Formation of Clouds, and the Descent of Rain." *The Abridged Transactions of the Royal Society of London*, XXXVI (1729), 323–331.

———. "Sir Isaac Newton's Doctrine of the Refrangibility of the Rays of Light." *The Abridged Transactions of the Royal Society of London*, XXIX (1716), 239–241.

———. "Some Remarks and Experiments Concerning Electricity." *The Abridged Transactions of the Royal Society of London*, XLI (1740), 470–473.

———. "Some Thoughts and Experiments concerning Electricity," *The Abridged Transactions of the Royal Society of London*, XLI (1739), 346–358.

———. "Some Thoughts Concerning the Cause of Elasticity." *The Abridged Transactions of the Royal Society of London*, XLI (1739), 340–346.

Folkes, Martin. "An Account of the Aurora Borealis seen at London." *The Abridged Transactions of the Royal Society of London*, XXX (1717), 291–292.

———. "An Observation of Three Mock Suns seen in London on September 17, 1736." *The Abridged Transactions of the Royal Society of London*, XL (1737), 137–138.

Geikie, Sir Archibald. *Annals of the Royal Society Club: The Record of a London Dining Club in the 18th and 19th Centuries.* London: Macmillan, 1917.

s'Gravesande, William J. *Mathematical Elements of Natural Philosophy.* Trans. J. T. Desaguliers. 2 vols. London: Senex, 1747.

Hall, A. Rupert, and Laura Tilling, eds. *The Correspondence of Isaac Newton, 1718–1727.* Vol. 7. New York: Cambridge University Press, 1977.

Newton, Isaac. *Opticks: or, A Treatise of the Reflexions, Refractions, Inflexions and Colours of Light.* London: Smith and Walford, 1704.

——. *The Principia.* Trans. Florian Cajori. 2 vols. Los Angeles: California University Press, 1966.

Rutty, William. "An Account of a Prenatural Bony Substance found in the Cavity of the Thorax." *The Abridged Transactions of the Royal Society of London,* XXXIV (1726), 156–160.

——. "A Tumor on the Loins of an Infant." *The Abridged Transactions of the Royal Society of London,* XXXI (1720), 487–489.

Rylands, Harry W., ed. *Records of the Lodge of Antiquity.* London, 1928.

Stukeley, William. *Memoirs.* London: Surtees Society, 1882.

Vibert, Lionel, ed. *Anderson's Constitutions of 1723.* Washington: Masonic Service Association, 1924.

2. Secondary Works

Ackerman, James S. *Palladio.* Baltimore: Penguin Books, 1966.

Allen, Robert J. *The Clubs of Augustan London.* Cambridge: Harvard University Press, 1933.

Allibone, T. E. *The Royal Society and its Dining Clubs.* New York: Pergamon Press, 1976.

Andrade, Edward N. *A Brief History of the Royal Society.* London: Royal Society, 1960.

——. *Isaac Newton.* New York, 1954.

Ashton, T. S. *The Industrial Revolution.* London: Oxford Press, 1968.

Baker, C. H., and Muriel I. Baker. *The Life and Circumstances of James Brydges: The First Duke of Chandos.* Oxford: Clarendon University Press, 1949.

Beattie, J. M. *The English Court in the Reign of George I.* Cambridge, 1967.

Calvert, Albert. *The Grand Lodge of England.* London: Jenkins Limited, 1917.

Carswell, John. *The South Sea Bubble*. Stanford: Stanford University Press, 1960.

Chenevix Trench, Charles. *George II*. London: Allen Lane, 1973.

Clark-Kennedy, A. E. *Stephen Hales, D.D. and F.R.S*. Cambridge: Cambridge University Press, 1929.

Cohen, I. Bernard. *Franklin and Newton: An Inquiry into Speculative Newtonian Experimental Science*. Cambridge: Harvard University Press, 1966.

Cook, Richard I. *Jonathan Swift As a Tory Pamphleteer*. Seattle: University of Washington Press, 1967.

Dickinson, H. T. *Liberty and Property: Political Ideology in Eighteenth Century England*. New York: Holmes and Meir Publishers, 1978.

————. *Politics and Literature in the Eighteenth Century*. London, 1974.

————. *Walpole and the Whig Supremacy*. London: English Universities Press, 1973.

Dickson, P. G. M. *The Financial Revolution in England: A Study in the Development of Public Credit, 1688–1756*. New York: Macmillan, 1967.

Dixon, Peter, ed. *Alexander Pope*. Athens: Ohio University Press, 1972.

Dobbs, Betty. *The Foundations of Newton's Alchemy, or, "The Hunting of the Greene Lyon."* London: Cambridge University Press, 1975.

Dobrée, Bonamy. *English Literature in the Early Eighteenth Century, 1700–1740*. Oxford: Clarendon Press, 1959.

Ellis, Aytoun. *The Penny Universities*. London: Secker and Warburg, 1956.

Evans, Joan. *A History of the Society of Antiquaries*. London: Oxford University Press, 1956.

Ford, Boris ed., *From Dryden to Johnson*. Baltimore: Penguin Books, 1960.

Fritz, Paul. *The English Ministers and Jacobitism, 1714–1745*. Toronto, 1975.

————, and David Williams, eds. *City and Society in the 18th Century*. Toronto: Hakkert, 1973.

————, eds. *The Triumph of Culture: 18th Century Perspectives*. Toronto: Hakkert, 1972.

Gilbert, Alan D. *Religion and Society in Industrial England: Church,*

Chapel, and Social Change, 1740-1914. London: Longman, 1976.

Gunther, R. T. *Early Science in Oxford.* Vols. I and IX. Oxford: Oxford University Press, 1923 and 1937.

Harrison, Brian. *Drink and the Victorians. The Temperance Question in England 1815-1872.* Pittsburgh: University of Pittsburgh Press, 1971.

Hatton, Ragnhild. *George I: Elector and King.* Cambridge: Harvard University Press, 1978.

Hellmuth, Eckhart, ed. *The Transformation of Political Culture. England and Germany in the Late Eighteenth Century.* London: Oxford University Press, 1990.

Humphreys, A. R. *The Augustan World: Society, Thought, and Letters in Eighteenth Century England.* New York: Harper and Row, 1963.

Jacob, Margaret. *The Newtonians and the English Revolution.* Ithaca: Cornell University Press, 1976.

Jones, Bernard. *Freemasons' Guide and Compendium.* London: Harrap, 1956.

Kenyon, John P. *Revolution Principles: The Politics of Party, 1689-1720.* Cambridge: Cambridge University Press, 1977.

Knoop, Douglas, and G. P. Jones. *The Genesis of Freemasonry.* Manchester: Manchester University Press, 1947.

____. *An Introduction to Freemasonry.* Manchester: Manchester University Press, 1937.

____. *A Short History of Freemasonry to 1730.* Manchester: Manchester University Press, 1940.

Kramnick, Isaac. *Bolingbroke and His Circle.* Cambridge: Harvard University Press, 1968.

Lang, Paul. *George F. Handel.* New York: Norton Books, 1966.

Lindeboom, G. A. *Herman Boerhaave: The Man and His Work.* London: Methuen, 1968.

Lyon, Sir Henry. *The Royal Society, 1660-1940.* New York: Greenwood, 1968.

Mantoux, Paul. *The Industrial Revolution in the 18th Century.* New York: Harper Torchbooks, 1965.

Manuel, Frank, *A Portrait of Sir Isaac Newton.* Cambridge: Harvard University Press, 1968.

____. *The Religion of Isaac Newton.* New York: Oxford University Press, 1971.

Mingay, G. E. *English Landed Society in the Eighteenth Century.* London: Routledge and Kegan, 1963.

Mitchell, R. J., and M. D. R. Leys. *A History of London Life*. Baltimore: Penguin Books, 1963.

Monod, Paul K. *Jacobitism and the English People, 1688–1788*. Cambridge: Cambridge University Press, 1989.

More, L. T. *Sir Isaac Newton*. New York: Scribner Sons, 1934.

Nicolson, Marjorie. *Newton Demands the Muse*. Princeton: Princeton University Press, 1946.

———. *Science and Imagination*. Ithaca: Cornell University Press, 1956.

———, and G. S. Rousseau. *"This Long Disease, My Life." Alexander Pope and The Sciences*. Princeton: Princeton University Press, 1968.

Owen, David. *English Philanthropy, 1660–1960*. Cambridge: Belknap Press, 1964.

Oxford, Arnold. *An Introduction to the History of the Royal Somerset House and Inverness Lodge Acting by Immemorial Constitution*. London: Quatritch, 1928.

Perry, Thomas W. *Public Opinion, Propaganda, and Politics in Eighteenth-Century England: A Study of the Jew Bill of 1753*. Cambridge: Harvard University Press, 1962.

Piggott, Stuart. *William Stukeley: An Eighteenth Century Antiquary*. Oxford: Clarendon Press, 1950.

Plumb, J. H. *The First Four Georges*. New York: Macmillan, 1957.

———. *The Growth of Political Stability in England, 1675–1725*. Baltimore: Penguin Books, 1969.

———. *Sir Robert Walpole: The King's Minister*. Boston: Houghton Mifflin, 1961.

Pocock, J. G. A. *The Machiavellian Movement: Florentine Political Thought and the Atlantic Republican Tradition*. Princeton: Princeton University Press, 1975.

Purver, Margery. *The Royal Society: Concept and Creation*. Cambridge: The M.I.T. Press, 1967.

Quennell, Peter. *Hogarth's Progress*. New York: Viking Press, 1955.

Robbins, Alfred. *English-Speaking Freemasonry*. London: Benn, 1930.

Robbins, Caroline. *The Eighteenth Century Commonwealthmen*. Cambridge: Harvard University Press, 1959.

Rogers, Nicholas. *Whigs and Cities, Popular Politics in the Age of Walpole and Pitt*. Oxford: Clarendon Press, 1989.

Rudé, George. *Hanoverian London: 1714–1808.* Berkeley: California University Press, 1971.

Sherburn, George. *The Early Career of Alexander Pope.* Oxford: Clarendon Press, 1934.

Speck, W. A. *Stability and Strife: England, 1714–1760.* Cambridge: Harvard University Press, 1977.

Sprat, Thomas. *History of the Royal Society.* St. Louis: Washington University Press, 1958.

Stephen, Sir Leslie. *English Thought in the Eighteenth Century.* 2 vols. New York: Harbinger Books, 1962.

Stevenson, David. *The Origins of Freemasonry: Scotland's Century, 1590–1710.* Cambridge: Cambridge University Press, 1988.

Stimson, Dorothy. *Scientists and Amateurs: A History of the Royal Society.* New York, 1948.

Summerson, John. *Ingio Jones.* Baltimore: Penguin Books, 1966.

Sykes, Norman. *Church and State in England in the 18th Century.* Hamden: Archon Books, 1962.

Thackray, Arnold. *Atoms and Powers.* Cambridge: Harvard University Press, 1970.

Thompson, E. P. *Whigs and Hunters: The Origins of the Black Act.* New York: Pantheon Books, 1975.

Timbs, John. *Clubs and Club Life in London.* 2nd ed. Detroit: Gale Research, 1967.

Torlais, Jean. *Un Rochelais grand-maître de la Franc-Maçonnerie et physicien au XVIIIe Siècle: Le Révérend J. T. Desaguliers.* La Rochelle: Pijollet, 1937.

Wagner, Fritz. *Isaac Newton im Zwielicht zwischen Mythos und Forschung: Studien zur Epoche der Aufklärung.* Freiburg: Alber, 1976.

Weld, Charles. *History of the Royal Society.* 8 vols. London: Parker, 1848.

Westfall, Richard S. *Never at Rest: A Biography of Isaac Newton.* Cambridge: Cambridge University Press, 1980.

Williams, Basil. *The Whig Supremacy.* Oxford: Clarendon Press, 1962.

Wright, Dudley. *England's Masonic Pioneers.* London: Kenning, 1925.

3. Periodical Literature

Clarke, J. R. "The Establishment of the Premier Grand Lodge." *Ars Quatuor Coronatorum*, LXXXI (1968), 1–8.

——. "The Medical Profession and Early Freemasonry." *Ars Quatuor Coronatorum*, LXXXV (1972), 298–311.

——. "The Royal Society and Early Grand Lodge Freemasonry." *Ars Quatuor Coronatorum*, LXXX (1967), 110–119.

Fisher, W. G. "A Cavalcade of Freemasons in 1731." *Ars Quatuor Coronatorum*, LXXV (1962), 34–48.

——. "John Montagu, The First Noble Grand Master." *Ars Quatuor Coronatorum*, LXXIX (1966), 69–89.

Gould, R. F. "*Philo-Musicae et Architecturae Societas.*" *Ars Quatuor Coronatorum*, XVI (1903), 112–128.

Jacob, Margaret C. "Newtonianism and the Origins of the Enlightenment: A Reassessment." *Eighteenth Century Studies*, II (Fall, 1977), 1–25.

McGuire, J. E., and P. M. Rattansi. "Newton and the 'Pipes of Pan.' " *Notes and Records of the Royal Society of London*, XXI, No. 2 (December, 1966), 108–143.

Newton, Edward. "Brethren Who Made Masonic History." *Ars Quatuor Coronatorum*, LXXVIII (1965), 130–145.

Robbins, Alfred. "Frederick, Prince of Wales as a Freemason." *Ars Quatuor Coronatorum*, XXIX (1916), 9–14.

Scott, John C. "Membership and Participation in Voluntary Associations." *American Sociological Review*, XXII, No. 3 (June, 1957), 315–326.

Stewart, Larry. "The Selling of Newton: Science and Technology in Early Eighteenth Century England." *Journal of British Studies*, XXV (1986), 178–192.

Stokes, John. "Life of John Theophilus Desaguliers." *Ars Quatuor Coronatorum* XXXVIII (1925), 285–306.

Thorp, J. H. "The Rev. James Anderson and the Earls of Buchan." *Ars Quatuor Coronatorum*, XVIII (1905), 9–12.

Tunbridge, Paul. "The Climate of European Freemasonry." *Ars Quatuor Coronatorum*, LXXXI (1968), 88–128.

Weisberger, R. William. "John Theophilus Desaguliers: Huguenot, Freemason, and Newtonian Scientist." *Transactions of the Huguenot Society of South Carolina*, XC (1985), 63–67.

Williams, W. J. "Alexander Pope and Freemasonry." *Ars Quatuor*

Coronatorum, XXXVIII (1925), 112–128.

_____. "Masonic Personalia, 1723–39." *Ars Quatuor Coronatorum*, XL (1927), 30–42, 126–138, and 160–170.

Worts, F. R. "The Development of the Content of Masonry during the 18th Century." *Ars Quatuor Coronatorum*, LXXVIII (1965), 1–15.

D. Works Regarding Eighteenth Century French History and Masonry

1. Primary Sources

Albon, Count. *Eloge de Court Gébelin*. Paris: Moutard, 1785.

Bachaumont, Louis Petit de. *Mémoires Secrets pour Servir á l'Histoire de la République des Lettres en France*. 36 vols. London: Adamson, 1780–1789.

Beaumont, Elie. *Question sur la Légitimité du Mariage des Protestants François*. Paris: Cellot, 1764.

Berthollet, Claude. *Elements of the Art of Dyeing*. 2 vols. London, 1791.

_____. *Essay on the New Method of Bleaching*. Edinburgh: Creech, 1790.

Bingley, William. *Travels in North America*. London: Harvey and Darton, 1821.

Brissot, J. P. *New Travels in the United States of America Performed in 1788*. London: Jordan, 1792.

Cabanis, P. J. G. *An Essay on the Certainty of Medicine*. Paris, 1803.

_____. *Notice sur Benjamin Franklin*. Paris: Didot, n.d.

_____. *Rapports du Physique et du Moral de l'homme*. 2 vols. Paris: Crapart, 1805.

_____. *Sketch of the Revolutions of Medical Science*. Trans. A. Henderson. London: Johnson, 1806.

D'Auberteuil, Hilliard. *Essais Historiques et Politiques sur Les Anglo-Americains*. Vol. I. Brussels, 1781.

Fallet, M. *Tibére et Sérénus*. Toulouse: Broulhiet, 1783.

Forster, John R. *An Easy Method of Assaying and Classing Mineral Substances*. London: Dilly, 1772.

Fourcroy, Antoine F. *Elements of Natural History and of Chemistry*. London: Robinson, 1788.

_____. *General System of Chemical Knowledge and Its Application to the Phenomena of Nature and Art*. Trans. William Nicholson.

London: Cadell and Davies, 1804.

Gébelin, Court de. *Histoire Naturelle de la Parole*. Paris: Boudet, 1776.

———. *Monde Primitif.* Vols. I, IV, and V. Paris, 1773, 1776, and 1778.

Ginguené, P. L. *Notice sur La Vie et les Ouvrages de Nicolas Piccinni.* Paris: The Year IX.

Hale, Edward E. *Franklin in France*. 2 vols. Boston: Roberts, 1887–1888.

Lalande, Jerome. *Art du cartonnier*. Paris, 1762.

———. *Art du tanneur*. Paris, 1764.

———. *Astronomie des dames.* 6th ed. Paris: Menard, 1820.

———. *Mémoire sur le passage de Venus; observé le 3 juin 1769.* Paris, 1772.

———. *Voyage d'un François en Italie, fait dans les années 1765 et 1766.* 8 vols. Paris: Desaint, 1769.

Mercier, Louis S. *Memoirs of the Year Two Thousand Five Hundred.* Trans. W. Hooper. 2 vols. London: Robinson, 1772.

Montgolfier, Joseph. *Note sur Le Bélier Hydraulique.* Paris: Gillé, 1806.

Pastoret, Claude E. *Des Loix Pénales.* 2 vols. Paris: Buisson, 1790.

———. *Zoroastre, Confucius, et Mahomet.* Paris: Buisson, 1787.

Robin, Abbé. *Nouveau voyage dans l'Amérique Septentrionale.* Paris, 1782.

Rozier, Pilâtre. *Premier Musée.* Paris, 1782.

Salm-Salm-Dyck, Constance. *Eloge Historique de M. De La Lande.* Paris: Sajou, 1810.

Volney, C. F. *The Ruins.* Trans. Peter Eckler. New York: Truth Seeker, 1913.

2. Secondary Literature

Aldridge, Alfred Owen. *Benjamin Franklin: Philosopher and Man.* Philadelphia: Lippincott, 1965.

———. *Franklin and his French Contemporaries.* New York: New York University Press, 1957.

———. *Voltaire and the Century of Light.* Princeton: Princeton University Press, 1975.

Baker, Keith Michael. *Condorcet: From Natural Philosophy to Social Mathematics.* Chicago: Chicago University Press, 1975.

_____. *Inventing the French Revolution. Essays on French Political Culture in the Eighteenth Century.* Cambridge: Cambridge University Press, 1990.

Barber, Elinor G. *The Bourgeoisie in 18th Century France.* Princeton: Princeton University Press, 1955.

Béclard, Leon. *Sébastien Mercier.* Paris: Champion, 1903.

Behrens, C. B. A. *The Ancien Régime.* London: Harcourt, 1967.

Besterman, Theodore. *Voltaire.* New York: Harcourt, 1969.

Bien, David. *The Calas Affair.* Princeton: Princeton University Press, 1960.

Brookner, Anita. *Greuze.* Greenwich: New York Graphic Society, 1972.

Chevallier, Pierre. *Les ducs sous l'acacia ou les premiers pas de la Franc-Maçonnerie française 1725-1743.* Paris, 1964.

_____. *Histoire de la Franc-Maçonnerie Française: La Maçonnerie: Ecole de l'Egalité, 1725-1799.* Paris: Fayard, 1974.

_____. *La Première Profanation du Temple Maçonnique.* Paris: Vrin, 1968.

Conner, Paul W. *Poor Richard's Politicks.* New York: Oxford Press, 1965.

Crocker, Lester. *Nature and Culture: Ethical Thought in the French Enlightenment.* Baltimore: Johns Hopkins Press, 1963.

Crosland, Maurice. *The Society of Arcueil.* Cambridge: Harvard University Press, 1967.

Dakin, Douglas. *Turgot and the Ancien Régime in France.* London: Methuen, 1939.

Darnton, Robert. *The Business of Enlightenment: A Publishing History of the Encyclopédie, 1775-1800.* Cambridge: Harvard University Press, 1979.

_____. *Mesmerism and the End of the Enlightenment in France.* New York: Schocken Books, 1970.

Echeverria, Durand. *Mirage in the West: A History of the French Image of American Society to 1815.* Princeton: Princeton University Press, 1957.

Ehrard, Jean, and Albert Soboul, eds. *Gilbert Romme et Son Temps.* Paris, 1966.

Ellery, E. *Brissot de Warville.* New York, 1915.

Fay, Bernard. *Revolution and Freemasonry.* Boston: Little Brown, 1935.

_____. *The Revolutionary Spirit in France and America.* Trans.

Ramon Guthrie. New York: Cooper Square Publishers, 1966.

Ford, Franklin. *Robe and Sword.* New York: Harper and Row, 1965.

Gaulmier, Jean. *Volney.* Paris: Hachette, 1959.

Gaxotte, Pierre. *Le Siècle de Louis XV.* Paris: Hachette, 1979.

Gay, Peter. *The Party of Humanity.* New York: Norton, 1954.

———. *Voltaire's Politics: The Poet as Realist.* New York: Vintage Books, 1965.

Gillispie, Charles C. *The Montgolfier Brothers and the Invention of Aviation, 1783-1784.* Princeton: Princeton University Press, 1983.

Groethuysen, Bernard. *The Bourgeois: Catholicism vs. Capitalism in Eighteenth Century France.* Trans. Mary Ilford. New York: Holt, 1968.

Guillois, Antoine. *Le Salon de Madame Helvétius.* Paris, 1894.

Hahn, Roger. *The Anatomy of a Scientific Institution: The Paris Academy of Sciences, 1660-1803.* Los Angeles: California University Press, 1971.

Havens, George R. *The Age of Ideas.* New York: Collier Books, 1955.

Hazard, Paul. *European Thought in the 18th Century.* Cleveland: Meridian Books, 1963.

Headings, Mildred J. *French Freemasonry under the Third Republic.* Baltimore: Johns Hopkins Press, 1949.

Higonnet, Patrice. *Sister Republics: The Origins of French and American Republicanism.* Cambridge: Harvard University Press, 1988.

Horowitz, Irving Louis. *Claude Helvétius: Philosopher of Democracy and Enlightenment.* New York: Paine-Whitman, 1954.

Hunt, Lynn. *Politics, Culture, and Class in the French Revolution.* Berkeley: University of California Press, 1984.

Kates, Gary. *The Cercle Social, the Girondins, and the French Revolution.* Princeton: Princeton University Press, 1985.

Keim, Albert, *Helvétius: Sa Vie et Son Oeuvre.* Geneva, 1970.

Kors, Alan Charles. *D'Holbach's Coterie: An Enlightenment in Paris.* Princeton: Princeton University Press, 1976.

Ladret, Albert. *Le Grand Siècle de la Franc-Maçonnerie.* Paris: Dervy-Livres, 1976.

Lantoine, Albert. *Histoire de la Franc-Maçonnerie Française.* Paris: Nourry, 1925.

Le Bihan, Alain. *Franc-Maçons et Ateliers Parisiens de la Grande Loge de France Au XVIIIe Siècle (1760-1795).* Paris: Bibliotheque Nationale, 1973.

_____. *Franc-Maçons parisiens du Grand Orient de France.* Paris, 1966.

_____. *Loges et Chapitres de la Grande Loge et du Grand Orient de France.* Paris, 1967.

Le Forestier, René. *La Franc-Maçonnerie Templière et Occultiste Aux XVIIIe et XIXe Siècles.* Paris: Aubier-Montaigne, 1970.

Levey, Michael. *Rococo to Revolution.* New York: Praeger, 1966.

Lopez, Claude-Anne. *Mon Cher Papa: Franklin and the Ladies of Paris.* New Haven: Yale University Press, 1966.

Lough, John. *An Introduction to Eighteenth Century France.* London: Longmans, 1960.

Lucie-Smith, Edward. *A Concise History of French Painting.* New York: Praeger, 1966.

Majewski, Henry F. *The Preromantic Imagination of L. S. Mercier.* New York: Humanities Press, 1971.

Manuel, Frank E. *The Eighteenth Century Confronts the Gods.* New York: Atheneum, 1967.

Martin, Gaston. *La Franc-Maçonnerie française et la Préparation de la Révolution.* Paris: Paris University Press, 1926.

McCloy, Shelby T. *The Humanitarian Movement in Eighteenth Century France.* Lexington: Kentucky Press, 1957.

Mornet, Daniel. *French Thought in the Eighteenth Century.* Trans. Lawrence Levin. New York: Prentice Hall, 1929.

Niklaus, Robert. *A Literary History of France: The Eighteenth Century, 1715-1789.* London: Benn, 1970.

Ozouf, Mona. *La Fête revolutionnaire.* Paris: Gallimard, 1976.

Parker, Harold T. *The Cult of Antiquity and the French Revolutionaries.* New York: Octagon Books, 1965.

Petrie, Charles. *The Jacobite Movement.* London: Eyre and Spottiswoode, 1959.

Poland, Burdette. *French Protestantism and the French Revolution.* Princeton: Princeton University Press, 1957.

Roche, Daniel. *Le siècle des lumières en province: Académies et académiciens provinciaux, 1680-1789.* 2 vols. Paris: Mouton, 1978.

Schama, Simon. *Citizens: A Chronicle of the French Revolution.* New York: Knopf, 1989.

Schmidt, Paul. *Court de Gébelin á Paris.* Paris: Fischbacher, 1908.

Shackleton, Robert. *Montesquieu.* London: Oxford Press, 1961.

Shennan, J. H. *The Parlement of Paris.* Ithaca: Cornell University Press, 1968.

Smeaton, W. A. *Fourcroy: Chemist and Revolutionary.* Cambridge: Heffer, 1962.

Smith, D. W. *Helvétius: A Study in Persecution.* Oxford: Clarendon Press, 1965.

Smith, Edwin B. *Jean-Sylvain Bailly: Astronomer, Mystic, Revolutionary, 1736–1793.* Philadelphia: American Philosophical Society, 1954.

Staum, Martin S. *Cabanis: Enlightenment and Medical Philosophy in the French Revolution.* Princeton: Princeton University Press, 1980.

Teppe, Julien. *Chamfort.* Paris: Clairac, 1950.

Van Doren, Carl. *Benjamin Franklin.* New York: Viking Press, 1964.

Van Duzer, Charles H. *Contributions of the Ideologues to French Revolutionary Thought.* Baltimore: Johns Hopkins Press, 1935.

Van Kley, Dale. *The Jansenists and the Expulsion of the Jesuits from France, 1757–1765.* New Haven: Yale University Press, 1975.

Viatte, Auguste. *Les Sources Occultes du Romantisme.* 2 vols. Paris: Champion, 1965.

Wade, Ira O. *The Structure and Form of the French Enlightenment: Esprit Philosophique.* Vol. I. Princeton: Princeton University Press, 1977.

Wilson, Arthur M. *Diderot.* New York: Oxford Press, 1972.

Wright, Esmond. *Franklin of Philadelphia.* Cambridge: Belknap Press, 1986.

3. Periodical Literature

Amiable, Louis, "Un Poème révolutionnaire en 1779: Les Mois de Roucher." *La Révolution française,* XXIX (1895), 132–149 and 233–254.

Baker, Keith M. "French Political Thought at the Accession of Louis XVI." *Journal of Modern History,* L (March, 1978), 279–303.

––––––. "Scientism, Elitism and Liberalism: the Case of Condorcet." *Studies on Voltaire and the Eighteenth Century,* LV (1967), 129–165.

Batham, C. N. "Chevalier Michael Ramsay: A New Appreciation." *Ars Quatuor Coronatorum,* LXXXI (1968), 280–291.

Bernheim, Alain. "Les Règlements Généraux de 1743 et Les Statuts de 1755." *Annales Historiques de la Révolution Française*, CLXXXVII (July, 1969), 380–391.

Britsch, A. "L'Anglomanie de Philippe Egalité, d'après sa correspondance autographe, 1778–1785." *Le Correspondant*, CCCIII (1926), 280–295.

Chapin, Seymour. "The Academy of Sciences during the 18th Century: An Astronomical Appraisal." *French Historical Studies*, V (1968), 371–404.

Chevalier, C. H. "Maçons Ecossais au XVIIIe Siècle." *Annales Historiques de la Révolution Française*, CLXXXXVII (July, 1969), 393–408.

Hans, Nicholas. "UNESCO of the Eighteenth Century: La Loge des Neuf Soeurs and its Venerable Master, Benjamin Franklin." *Proceedings of the American Philosophical Society*, XCVII (October, 1953), 513–524.

Kra, Pauline. "Religion in Montesquieu's *Lettres persanes*." *Studies on Voltaire and the Eighteenth Century*, LXXII (1970), 211–224.

Le Bihan, Alain. "Maçons du XVIIIe Siècle." *Annales Historiques de la Révolution Française*, CLXXXXVII (July, 1969), 415–423.

Leith, James A. "Le Culte de Franklin." *Annales Historiques de la Révolution Française*, CCXXVI (October, 1976), 541–571.

_____. "Les Trois Apotheoses de Voltaire." *Annales Historiques de la Révolution Française*, CCXXXVI (April, 1979), 161–209.

Ligou, D. "Structures et Symbolisme Maçonniques sous La Révolution," *Annales Historiques de la Révolution Française*, CLXXXXVII (July, 1969), 511–523.

Monod-Cassidy, Hélène. "Un Astronome-Philosophe, Jerome Lalande." *Studies on Voltaire and the Eighteenth Century*, LVI (1967), 907–930.

Schlegel, Dorothy. "Freemasonry and the *Encyclopédie* reconsidered." *Studies on Voltaire and the Eighteenth Century*, XC (1972), 1433–1460.

Servier, J. "Utopie et Franc-Maçonnerie au XVIIIe Siècle." *Annales Historiques de la Révolution Française*, CLXXXXVII (July, 1969), 409–413.

Smeaton, W. A. "The Early Years of the *Lycée* and the *Lycée des Arts*." *Annals of Science*, XI (1955), 257–267.

Weisberger, R. William. "Benjamin Franklin: A Masonic Enlightener in Paris." *Pennsylvania History*, LIII (1986), 165–180.

E. Works Concerning Eighteenth Century Habsburg History and Masonry

1. Primary Sources

a. Primary Printed Materials

Alxinger, Johann. "Prophezeihung." *Wiener Musenalmanach* (1788), 31–36.

_____. "Ueber die Bildung des innern Menschen." *Journal für Freymaurer*, II (1785), Part 4, 45–53.

_____. "Ueber Maurerintoleranz." *Journal für Freymaurer*, II (1785), Part 4, 29–42.

Bergman, Torbern. *Outlines of Mineralogy.* Trans. William Withering. Birmingham: Piercy and Jones, 1783.

Blumauer, Alois. "Es leben unsre sehr ehrwürd Schwester Logen." *Journal für Freymaurer*, I (1784), Part 3, 212.

_____. "Gesundheit auf den Kaiser." *Journal für Freymaurer*, II (1785), Part 1, 193–194.

_____. "Rede über die Leiden und Freuden des menschlichen Lebens." *Journal für Freymaurer*, I (1784), Part 2, 157–162.

_____. "Ueber den Kosmopolitismus des Maurers." *Journal für Freymaurer*, II (1785), Part 3, 114–120.

_____. "Vorerinnerung." *Journal für Freymaurer*, I (1784), Part 1, 3–14.

_____. "Zuge maurerischer Wohlthätigkeit." *Journal für Freymaurer*, II (1785), Part 4, 201–209.

_____, and Franz Ratschky, eds. *Wiener Musenalmanach auf das Jahr 1786–1792.* 7 vols. Vienna: Graffer, 1786–1792.

_____. *Wienerischer Musenalmanach auf das Jahr 1781–1785.* 5 vols. Vienna: Graffer, 1781–1785.

Bolla, Anthony. "Ueber den Maurerischen Tempelbau." *Journal für Freymaurer*, I (1784), Part 3, 139–147.

Born, Ignatz von. "Geschichte des Pythägoraischen Bundes." *Journal für Freymaurer*, II (1785), Part 1, 3–28.

_____. *Process of Amalgamation.* London, 1787.

_____. *Specimen of the Natural History of the Various Orders of Monks.* London: Johnson, 1783.

_____. *Travels through the Bannat of Temesvar, Transylvania, and Hungary in the Year 1770.* Trans. R. E. Raspe. London, 1777.

_____. "Ueber die Magie der alten Perser." *Journal für Freymaurer*, I (1784), Part 3, 9–63.

_____. "Ueber die Mysterien der Aegyptier." *Journal für Freymaurer*, I (1784), Part 1, 17–84.

_____. "Ueber die Mysterien der alten hëbraet." *Journal für Freymaurer*, III (1786), Part 1, 3–65.

_____. "Ueber die Mysterien der Indier." *Journal für Freymaurer*, I (1784), Part 4, 5–27,

Carlid, Göte, and Johan Nordström, eds. *Torbern Bergman's Foreign Correspondence*. Stockholm: Almqvist and Wiksell, 1965.

Grëzmuller. "Ueber den Freymaurereid." *Journal für Freymaurer*, I (1784), Part 2, 138–154.

Gruber, Tobias. "Anhang zu den Briefen hydrographischen und physikalischen Inhalts aus Krain." *Physikalische Arbeiten der Einträchtigen Freunde in Wien*, II (1784), 1–24.

_____. *Versuche über die ausdüngstung des wassers in leeren raume des barometers*. Dresden, 1789.

Haidinger, Karl. "Verzeichnis in den Wielickaer Salzwerken." *Physikalische Arbeiten der Einträchtigen Freunde in Wien*, III (1785), 9–18.

Hermann, Johann. *Naturgeschichte des Kupfers*. St. Petersburg, 1790.

Hunczovsky, Johann. *Medicinisch Chirurgische*. Vienna: Graffer, 1783.

Jacquet, Abbé. *Précis De L'Electricité*. Vienna: Trattner, 1775.

Keil, Robert. *Aus Klassischer Zeit: Wieland und Reinhold*. Leipzig, 1890.

_____. *Wiener Freunde, 1784–1808*. Wien: Konegen, 1883.

Leber, Ferdinand. *Vorlesungen über die Zergliederungskunst*. Vienna: Graffer, 1782.

Lessing, Gotthold Ephraim. *Werke*. Vol. II. Berlin, 1962.

Märter, Franz J. "Mineralogische Bemerlungen." *Physikalische Arbeiten der Einträchtigen Freunde in Wien*, III (1785), 82–87.

_____. "Professor Märters Nachrichten uber die naturaliche Geschichte Pennsylvaniens." *Physikalische Arbeiten der Einträchtigen Freunde in Wien*, III (1785), 20–39.

Mayer, Johann. "Abbildung und Beschreibung der Poa Bohemica." *Physikalische Arbeiten der Einträchtigen Freunde in Wien*, I (1783), 22–26.

Müller, Johann. "Der Versuche in dem Sebirge Faczebay." *Physikalische Arbeiten der Einträchtigen Freunde in Wien*, III (1785), 34–52.

———. "Versuche ueber den Spiesglastonige." *Physikalische Arbeiten der Einträchtigen Freunde in Wien*, I (1783), 63–68.

Pallas, Peter. "Schreiben aus St. Petersburg." *Physikalische Arbeiten der Einträchtigen Freunde in Wien*, I (1783), 1–22.

Raab, Joseph von. "Ueber die gallizischen Salzen." *Physikalische Arbeiten der Einträchtigen Freunde in Wien*, II (1784), 62–68.

Ratschky, Franz. *Auf die dem Freymaurerorden von Kaiser Joseph dem Zweyten offentlich bewilligte Duldung*. Vienna, 1785.

———. *Gedichte*. Wien: Graffer, 1791.

Reinhold, Karl. "Mönchthum und Maureren." *Journal für Freymaurer*, II (1785), Part 1, 166–187.

———. "Ueber die fabirischen Mysterien." *Journal für Freymaurer*, II (1785), Part 3, 3–10.

———. "Ueber die Freundschaft." *Journal für Freymaurer*, III (1786), Part 1, 119–134.

Retzer, Joseph von. *Physikalische Abhandlung von den Eigenschasten des Donners*. Vienna: Trattner, 1772.

———. "Ueber die Harmonie." *Journal für Freymaurer*, II (1785), Part 2, 175–181.

———. "Ueber die Wohlthätigkeit des Maurers." *Journal für Freymaurer*, I (1784), Part 2, 171–186.

Ruprecht, Johann. "Schreiben ueber das rothliche Ganggestein." *Physikalische Arbeiten der Einträchtigen Freunde in Wien*, I (1783), 68–73.

———. "Zergleiderung und Beschaffenheit der nächsten Bestandtheile eines zu Nagyág." *Physikalische Arbeiten der Einträchtigen Freunde in Wien*, II (1784), 54–56.

Schittelsberg, Count. "Ueber das Zeremoniel." *Journal für Freymaurer*, I (1784), Part 2, 105–118.

———. "Ueber die Beobachtung der maurerischen Gleichheit." *Journal für Freymaurer*, II (1785), Part 1, 77–82.

Sonnenfels, Joseph von. *Gesammelte Schriften*. 10 vols. Vienna, 1783–1787.

Stütz, Andreas. "Die Mineralgeschichte von Oesterreich." *Physikalische Arbeiten der Einträchtigen Freunde in Wien*, I (1783), 77–107.

———. "Ueber die Reisen des Maurers." *Journal für Freymaurer*, I (1784), Part 3, 157–166.

Werner, R. M., ed. *Aus dem Josephinischen Wien: Geblers und Nicolais Briefwechsel, 1771–1786*. Berlin, 1888.

b. Letters

Born, Ignatz von. Letter of introduction for Professor Märter. 21 November 1783.

Franklin, Benjamin. Letter of introduction for Professor Märter. 22 April 1783.

2. Secondary Sources

Abafi, Ludwig. *Geschichte der Freimaurerei in Oesterreich-Ungarn.* 5 vols. Budapest, 1890–1897.

Allgemeines Handbuch der Freimaurerei. 2 vols. Leipzig: Hesse, 1900–1901.

Allison, Henry E. *Lessing and the Enlightenment.* Ann Arbor: Michigan University Press, 1966.

Beales, Derek. *Joseph II: In the Shadow of Maria Theresa, 1741–1780.* Cambridge: Cambridge University Press, 1987.

Becker-Cantarino, Bärbel. *Aloys Blumauer and the Literature of Austrian Enlightenment.* Bern: Herbert Lang, 1973.

Benedikt, Heinrich. *Franz Anton Graf Sporck (1662–1738).* Vienna, 1923.

Bernard, Paul. *Joseph II.* New York, 1968.

_____. *Jesuits and Jacobins.* Urbana: Illinois University Press, 1971.

Brechka, Frank T. *Gerard Van Swieten and His World.* The Hague: Nijhoff, 1970.

Bruford, Walter H. *Germany in the 18th Century.* Cambridge, 1965.

Brunschwig, Henri. *Enlightenment and Romanticism in Eighteenth Century Prussia.* Trans. Frank Jellinek. Chicago: Chicago University Press, 1974.

Bulling, Karl. *Johann Baptist von Alxinger.* Leipzig, 1914.

Chailley, Jacques. *The Magic Flute, Masonic Opera.* Trans. Herbert Weinstock. New York: Knopf, 1971.

Clark, Robert T. *Herder: His Life and Thought.* Berkeley: California Press, 1955.

Crankshaw, Edward. *Maria Theresa.* New York, 1969.

Deutsch, Otto. *Mozart und die Wiener Logen.* Vienna, 1932.

Einstein, Alfred. *Mozart.* New York: Oxford Press, 1945.

Endres, Franz C. *Goethe und die Freimaurer.* Basel, 1949.

Engel, Leopold. *Geschichte des Illuminaten-Ordens.* Berlin, 1906.

Epstein, Klaus. *The Genesis of German Conservatism.* Princeton, 1966.

Fischer-Colbrie, A. *Michael Denis: Im schweigendem Tale des Mondes.* Vienna, 1958.

Francovich, Carlo. *Storia della Massoneria In Italia.* Firenze: Nuova Italia, 1974.

Gagliardo, John C. *Enlightened Despotism.* New York: Crowell, 1967.

Garland, H. B. *Lessing.* London: Macmillan, 1962.

Geiringer, Karl. *Haydn: A Creative Life in Music.* Berkeley: California Press, 1968.

Hatfield, Henry. *Goethe: A Critical Introduction.* New York: New Directions Paperback, 1963.

Hennings, Fred. *Und sitzet zur linken Hand: Franz Stephan von Lothringen.* Wien: Neff, 1961.

Hofmann-Wellenhof, Paul. *Alois Blumauer.* Vienna, 1885.

――――. *Michael Denis.* Vienna, 1881.

Kann, Robert A. *A History of the Habsburg Empire 1526–1918.* Berkeley: California Press, 1974.

――――. *A Study in Austrian Intellectual History. Late Baroque to Romanticism.* New York, 1960.

Kerner, Robert J. *Bohemia in the Eighteenth Century.* New York: Ams Press, 1969.

Kimball, Stanley. *The Austro-Slav Revival: A Study of Nineteenth-Century Literary Foundations.* Philadelphia: The American Philosophical Society, 1973.

Király, Béla. *Hungary in the Late Eighteenth Century: The Decline of Enlightened Despotism.* New York: Columbia University Press, 1969.

――――, and George Barany, eds. *East Central European Perceptions of Early America.* Lisse: The Peter De Ridder Press, 1977.

Krieger, Leonard. *An Essay on the Theory of Enlightened Despotism.* Chicago: Chicago University Press, 1975.

Kuess, G., and B. Scheichelbauer. *200 Jahre Freimaurerei in Osterreich.* Vienna, 1959.

Lewis, Ludwig. *Geschichte der Freimaurerei in Osterreich im Allgemeinen und der Wiener Loge zu St. Joseph inbesondere.* Vienna, 1861.

Lhotsky, Alphons. *Osterreichische Historiographie.* Munich: Oldenbourg, 1962.

Lindroth, Sten, ed. *Swedish Men of Science, 1650–1950.* Stockholm:

Swedish Institute, 1952.

Macartney, C. A. *The Habsburg Empire: 1790–1918.* New York: Macmillan, 1969.

_____. *Maria Theresa and the House of Austria.* London, 1969.

McGill, William J. *Maria Theresa.* New York: Twayne Publishers, 1972.

Mikoletzky, Hanns Leo. *Kaiser Franz I. Stephan und der Ursprung des Habsburgisch-Lothringischen Familienvermögens.* Munich: Oldenbourg, 1967.

Morris, C. L. *Maria Theresa: The Last Conservative.* New York, 1937.

Nadler, Josef. *Literaturgeschichte Osterreichs.* 2nd ed. Linz, 1951.

Nettl, Paul. *Mozart and Masonry.* New York: Da Capo Press, 1970.

O'Brien, Charles H. *Ideas of Religious Toleration at the Time of Joseph II,* Philadelphia: American Philosophical Society, 1969.

Osterloh, K. H. *Joseph von Sonnenfels und die österreichische Reformbewegung im Zeitalter des aufgëklarten Absolutismus.* Hamburg, 1970.

Padover, Saul. *The Revolutionary Emperor: Joseph II of Austria.* New York: Ballou, 1933.

Pascal, Roy. *The German Sturm und Drang.* Manchester: Manchester University Press, 1953.

Ritter, Erwin Frank. *Johann Baptist von Alxinger and the Austrian Enlightenment.* Bern: Herbert Lang, 1970.

Rommel, Otto. *Der Wiener Musenalmanach. Eine litterarhistorische Untersuchung.* Vienna, 1906.

Rose, Ernst. *A History of German Literature.* New York, 1960.

Rosen, Charles. *The Classical Style: Haydn, Mozart, Beethoven.* New York: Viking Press, 1971.

Rosenberg, Alfons. *Die Zauberflöte.* Munich, 1972.

Runkel, Ferdinand. *Geschichte der Freimaurerei in Deutschland.* 3 vols. Berlin, 1932.

Schneider, F. J. *Die Freimaurerei und ihr Einfluss auf die geistige Kultur in Deutschland am Ende des 18 Jahrhunderts.* Prague, 1909.

Schneider, Heinrich. *Lessing Zwolf Biographische Studien.* Bern: Francke, 1951.

_____. *Quest for Mysteries: The Masonic Background for Literature in 18th Century Germany.* Ithaca: Cornell University Press, 1947.

Seton-Watson, R. W. *A History of the Czechs and Slovaks.* Hamden: Archon Books, 1965.

Silagi, Denis. *Jakobiner in der Habsburger-Monarchie.* Vienna, 1962.

Spinka, Matthew. *John Amos Comenius: That Incomparable Moravian.* Chicago: Chicago University Press, 1943.

Tapié, Victor L. *The Rise and Fall of the Habsburg Monarchy.* Trans. Stephen Hardman. New York: Praeger, 1971.

Valjavec, Fritz. *Der Josephinismus.* 2nd ed. Munich, 1945.

Walker, D. P. *The Ancient Theology.* Ithaca: Cornell University Press, 1972.

Wangermann, Ernst. *The Austrian Achievement: 1700–1800.* London: Harcourt Brace and Jovanovich, 1973.

———. *From Joseph II to the Jacobin Trials.* London: Oxford University Press, 1969.

Wines, Roger, ed. *Enlightened Despotism.* Boston: Heath, 1967.

Winter, E. *Der Josefinismus.* 2nd ed. Berlin, 1962.

Winters, Stanley B., and Joseph Held, eds. *Intellectual and Social Developments in the Habsburg Empire from Maria Theresa to World War I.* New York: Columbia University Press, 1975.

Wurzbach, Constantin von. *Biographisches Lexicon des Kaisertums Osterreich 1750–1850.* 60 vols. Vienna, 1856–1891.

3. Periodical Literature

Bernard, Paul. "The Limits of Absolutism: Joseph II and the Allgemeines Krankenhaus." *Eighteenth Century Studies,* IX (Winter, 1975), 193–215.

———. "The *Philosophe* as Public Servant: Tobias Gebler." *East European Quarterly,* VII (1973), 41–47.

Gugitz, Gustav. "Alois Blumauer." *Jahrbuch der Grillparzer-Gesellschaft,* XVIII (1908), 27–135.

———. "Franz Kratter. Ein Beitrag zur Geschichte der Tagesschreiberei in der josephinischen Zeit." *Jahrbuch der Grillparzer-Gesellschaft,* XXIV (1913), 242–277.

———. "Johann Pezzl." *Jahrbuch der Grillparzer-Gesellschaft,* XVI (1906), 164–217.

———. "Lorenz Leopold Haschka." *Jahrbuch der Grillparzer-Gesellschaft,* XVII (1907), 32–127.

Kann, Robert A. "The Aristocracy of the Habsburg Empire in the 18th Century." *East European Quarterly,* VII (1973), 1–13.

Karter, Raymond L. "Gotthold Lessing – The Masonic Dramatist." *Ars Quatuor Coronatorum*, LXXXVIII (1975), 98–104.

Probst, Eugen. "Johann Baptist von Alxinger." *Jahrbuch der Grillparzer-Gesellschaft*, VII (1897), 171–202.

Spaethling, Robert. "Folklore and Enlightenment in the Libretto of Mozart's *Magic Flute.*" *Eighteenth Century Studies*, IX (Fall, 1975), 45–68.

Stanescu, Heinz. "Ignatz von Born." *Osterreich in Geschichte und Literatur*, XIV (1970), 369–371.

Weisberger, R. William. "The True Harmony Lodge: A Mecca of Masonry and the Enlightenment in Josephinian Vienna." *East European Quarterly*, XX (1986), 129–140.

INDEX